IMPRISONED RELIGION

The subject of religious life in prison in all of its varied manifestations is an acutely under-researched area. This volume makes a significant contribution to our understanding through both theoretically and empirically informed chapters.
Stephen J. Hunt, University of the West of England, UK

This book combines theoretical sophistication with subtle analysis of vibrant interviews conducted with inmates and former inmates of prisons in Eastern Germany. The fascinating light that it throws on the place of religion in prisons challenges many assumptions about religion, the state, modernity and prisons. The contribution that it makes towards our understanding of recent changes in inmates' experiences of religion and incarceration will be invaluable to a wide range of social scientists and policy makers.
James A. Beckford, University of Warwick, UK

This book explores the profound transformations that prisons and offender rehabilitation programmes in Eastern Germany have undergone with respect to religion. Drawing on participant observation and interviews of inmates, ex-prisoners, chaplains and prison visitors, this book connects the institutional to individual: focusing on the religious changes individuals experience when they are imprisoned and released. Including comparative studies from Italy and Switzerland, Becci reveals that despite diverse local, historical, denominational, political and social contexts the transformation patterns of individuals' relationship to religion, and their use of religious resources, are strongly shaped by the total character of prisons. Becci also explores the difficulties faced by released people in keeping their religious life alive under the harsh conditions of social stigma in a highly secular outside society.

Imprisoned Religion
Transformations of Religion during and after Imprisonment in Eastern Germany

IRENE BECCI
University of Lausanne, Switzerland

ASHGATE

Published by
Ashgate Publishing Limited
Wey Court East
Union Road
Farnham
Surrey, GU9 7PT
England

Ashgate Publishing Company
110 Cherry Street
Suite 3-1
Burlington, VT 05401-3818
USA

www.ashgate.com

British Library Cataloguing in Publication Data
Becci, Irene.
    Imprisoned Religion: Transformations of Religion during and after Imprisonment in Eastern Germany.
    1. Prisoners – Religious life – Germany (East) 2. Ex-convicts – Religious life – Germany (East) 3. Imprisonment – Religious aspects. I. Title
    204.2'086927'09431–dc23

Library of Congress Cataloging-in-Publication Data
Becci, Irene.
    Imprisoned Religion: Transformations of Religion during and after Imprisonment in Eastern Germany / Irene Becci.
      p. cm.
    Includes bibliographical references (p.) and index.
    1. Prisoners – Religious life – Germany. 2. Imprisonment – Religious aspects – Christianity. 3. Imprisonment – Religious aspects. 4. Psychology, Religious.
    5. Imprisonment – Germany. I. Title.
    BV4595.B43 2012
    274.30086'927–dc23   2012013759

ISBN   9781409411611 (hbk)
ISBN   9781409411628 (ebk-PDF)
ISBN   9781409472346 (ebk-ePUB)

Printed and bound in Great Britain by the
MPG Books Group, UK

Contents

List of Figures and Table   *vii*
Acknowledgements   *xi*

Introduction: Conceptual and Methodological Clarifications   1

1   Modern Prisons in Eastern Germany: Between Secular
     and Christian Projects   33

2   Religion in Post-Socialist Prisons and Release Programmes   57

3   Transformations of Religion during and after Imprisonment   79

4   Inmates and Ex-Inmates' Relations to Religion   123

5   New Religious Belongings: Inside, Outside and in Liminality   149

Conclusion in a Comparative Perspective   167

References   *179*
Index   *195*

List of Figures and Table

Figures

2.1 The painting, made by a prisoner, that won the Magedeburg
prison exhibition competition © Irene Becci, August 2006   72

3.1 'Cross on a hill with sunshine', tattoo drawn by Thilo
© Irene Becci, August 2004   90

3.2 An ex-convict at the halfway house © Irene Becci, March 2007   92

3.3 A drawing by an inmate in Brandenburg; the Caritas programme
put it on the cover of its invitation for the celebration of their tenth
anniversary © Irene Becci, March 2007   93

5.1 The altar and the seats for the religious service to be held in the
hall of the railway station in Halle/S. © Irene Becci, July 2006   161

Table

2.1 Religious affiliations (by percentage)   58

Acknowledgements

While carrying out this study I benefited from the valuable support of a number of colleagues and institutions. I first wish to thank the European University Institute in Florence, where I completed my dissertation under the joint supervision of Professor Peter Wagner and Professor James Beckford. I am also deeply indebted and grateful to Professor Beckford for his inspiration beyond my doctoral work as I carried out post-doctoral research and then engaged in further comparative studies. My post-doctoral fellowship at the Max Planck Institute for Social Anthropology in Halle/ Saale in Germany provided both perfect conditions and creative encouragement for my fieldwork, in addition to the necessary financial support to publish the results of my sustained studies. I am particularly grateful to Professor Chris Hann, whose advice and intellectual stimulation have been invaluable. My more recent work in Switzerland was made possible thanks to the constructive support of Claude Bovay and the financial help of the University of Applied Sciences of Western Switzerland and the Swiss National Science Foundation.

A number of other people assisted and supported my enterprise in various ways, starting with Jean Terrier's initial encouragement and ending with Elisabeth Arweck's patient editorial work on my manuscript. I am deeply grateful to every one of them, including all the participants in my research who gave their time to speak to me and who were willing to discuss – in such an open, honest and modest way – issues that were emotionally charged, given the challenging environment in which many of them had found themselves. However, I am, of course, solely responsible for the present work and for any misrepresentations that may have inadvertently found their way into it.

Introduction:
Conceptual and Methodological
Clarifications

When I started to design the project for the present study, the twin towers in downtown Manhattan were still part of its skyline and the clash of civilizations was an idea with which only some academic circles were concerned. Religion was not often used in connection with the word 'prison'. In Europe, only a few sociological studies had been carried out on religion and prison in the then current conditions. The public debate was preoccupied with issues of migration and increasing religious diversity. The latter, however, was not the object of systematic study as it presented itself in the context of the prison. Indeed, the only study I knew of was that conducted by James Beckford and Sophie Gilliat on religion in the prisons of the United Kingdom. This work, and the various research projects it inspired around Europe, assumed that religion was of great importance to prisoners, although the latter's perspective was not analysed. The study by Beckford and Gilliat focused on questions of equality and inequality in a situation of great religious diversity. The results demonstrated – among other things – that the establishment of the Anglican Church necessarily caused an imbalance. One example is the brokerage[1] in which the Anglican chaplains engaged: although they had the honourable aim of facilitating access to religion for members of other faiths, the unintended consequence of their brokering was to reinforce the perception that chaplains of other faiths were not part of the prison establishment. As I have mentioned, what this study did not entail was the prisoners' perspective.[2] My point

---

[1]   In using the term 'brokerage' I refer to the multiple ways in which chaplains facilitate the activities of visiting ministers in prison. After Beckford and Gilliat's study was published, the Anglican chaplains ceased to be responsible for 'brokering' on behalf of 'other faiths'. There is now a full-time Muslim advisor to the Prison Service who takes responsibility for Muslim prisoners. Inmates of other faiths have their own 'religious service providers': cf. James Beckford and Sophie Gilliat, *Religion in Prison: Equal Rites in a Multi-faith Society* (Cambridge: Cambridge University Press, 1998); Inger Furseth, *Muslims in Norwegian Prisons and the Defence* (Trondheim: Tapir Akademisk Forlag, 2001).

[2]   This has now been addressed: cf. in particular Fahrad Khosrokhavar, *L'islam dans les prisons* (Paris: Balland, 2004); James. A. Beckford, Danièle Joly and Farhad Khosrokhavar, *Muslims in Prison: Challenge and Change in Britain and France* (New York: Palgrave Macmillan, 2005); Mohammed Khalid Rhazzali, *L'Islam in carcere. L'esperienza religiosa dei giovani musulmani nelle prigioni italiane* (Milan: Franco Angeli, 2010); Irene Becci, 'Religion's Multiple Locations in Prison: Germany, Italy, Switzerland',

of departure was thus the aim to contribute to the understanding of religion and prison by including in my analysis knowledge from the standpoint of inmates and ex-inmates in the form of empirically collected data.

While the present work tackles questions that are central to the sociology of religion, it attempts to answer them by borrowing arguments and methodological insights that are peripheral to the field, such as those of critical sociology, anthropology, ethnomethodology or symbolic interactionism.[3] However, this work is not located – either methodologically or in terms of the questions it raises – within criminology. Imprisonment and release are studied here exclusively from the point of view of their relation to religion. It is important to note that neither the prison as an institution nor religion in prison is at the centre of this work: the main emphasis lies in the changing relationship to religion for the various actors and institutions concerned with imprisonment and release. My starting point is that both the way religion is present in prison and the way religious practices come or cease to make sense after prison release must be understood as bound, at least partly, to that relationship. Many of the questions that will accompany the reader throughout the book are linked to the controversy about the total and secular character of prisons. Is prison a mirror of society? If so, what does analysis of the relationship between the experience and the structure of prison and religion tell us about the dynamics at work in general society? Is prison an encapsulated place that has no relation at all to the outside world? As Philippe Combessie suggests,[4] sociological studies of prison have oscillated between two approaches: some authors have studied prison from a so-called 'diffusionist' perspective, which implies that social life inside and outside prison is considered to be linked and that understanding the prison system helps to comprehend society itself; other authors have rejected any generalization and stress the particularity of total institutions. I shall argue that, in many regards, prison is a distinct environment. However, many elements that make it different actually depend on the way crime is managed outside prison. A similar reasoning may be exercised as far as religion is concerned. The fact that prisons are now overcrowded and that certain social and religious groups, such as foreigners and the poor, are over-represented in the prison population does point to ongoing processes that concern both prison and society in general. In prison, individuals are confronted with existential questions in a particularly intensive way. The conditions of detention and everyday struggles for freedom in relation to space, time and body create a situation in which religion gains particular meaning.

Archives de sciences sociales des religions, 153/1 (2011), 65–84; Stephen Hunt, 'Testing Chaplaincy Reforms in England and Wales', *Archives de sciences sociales des religions*, 153/1 (2011), 43–64.

[3]   For common and unusual methodological approaches in the scientific study of religion, see James A. Beckford, '"Start Together and Finish Together": Shifts in the Premises and Paradigms Underlying the Scientific Study of Religion', *Journal for the Scientific Study of Religion*, 39/4 (2000), 481–95.

[4]   *Sociologie de la prison* (Paris: La Découverte, 2001).

Prisons are also spaces of socialization, which becomes very clear when looking at how religion is transformed at release, when conditions change drastically.

So, the present study addresses social interactions and discourses related to religion in and around institutional settings from different points of view. A first necessary step is to define the key notions that are used, religion and the state[5] being central to the investigation.

Religion in Modernity

Periodically, social scientists have provided (new) definitions of religion. And periodically, various authors have warned against getting trapped by the temptation to reify religion when defining it. James Beckford points out that religion should not be regarded 'as an object or a subject that could exist independently of human actors or social institutions. Religion does not "do" anything by itself. It does not have agency.'[6]

Linda Woodhead has recently identified five major ways within the social sciences in which religion has been defined.[7] These ways are not mutually exclusive but offer different views on religion, and their combination allows for a 'full and rounded study of religion'.[8] The mere fact that the community of sociologists of religion still has still not reached a convincing consensus on a definition of religion gives credit to the hypothesis that an *a priori* and universal definition is impossible. The link between the attempt at defining religion and the potential trap of reification is well expressed by Wilfred Cantwell Smith:

---

[5]   As Dario Melossi recommends, I shall be careful not to treat the state as an 'acting persona ... but as one of the discursive resources the actors themselves rely upon in order to give an account of what it is they do when, for instance, they punish ... Students of social control cannot treat "the state" as an independent variable. The social analyst is interested, however, in describing that particular effect of social control which consists in a state-orientation of society's members, and a legally described state-attribution of definite powers and effects' – Dario Melossi, *The State of Social Control: A Sociological Study of Concepts of State and Social Control in the Making of Democracy* (Cambridge: Polity Press, 1990), 153. Michel Foucault, as I shall discuss in the next chapter, reinforces the point about not approaching the state as an 'acting *persona*'.

[6]   James Beckford, *Social Theory and Religion* (Cambridge: Cambridge University Press, 2003), 4.

[7]   Accordingly, religion may be seen as a system within culture (focusing on beliefs, meaning, values, discourses or memory and tradition), as identity, as a social relationship connecting people, as a power relation, and, especially in the anthropology of religion, first and foremost as practice, ritual practice in particular. See Linda Woodhead, 'Five Concepts of Religion', *International Review of Sociology*, 21/1 (2011), 121–43,

[8]   Ibid., 138.

Many were the books that set out in search of the nature of religion, or of Buddhism or whatever; full of confidence that nature is somehow there. This is to carry the process of reification to its logical extreme: endowing the concepts that an earlier generation has constructed (rather haphazardly, and dubiously, in this case) with a final and inherent validity, a cosmic legitimacy.[9]

Since religion is the object of this study, I shall try to identify an operational definition of it and clarify how the shifts in the attempts to define religion are linked to shifts in attempts to understand secularization and thereby modernity. As Talal Asad points out, 'religion' is a modern concept as it participates, together with its conjoined twin, 'secularism', in the modern processes of

restructuration of practical times and spaces, a rearticulation of practical knowledges and powers, of subjective behaviors, sensibilities, needs, and expectations.[10]

On the other hand, modernity is, conceptually speaking, what Peter Wagner calls

a situation in which a certain double imaginary signification prevails. The two components of this signification, ambivalent on their own and also tension-ridden between them, are the idea of the *autonomy* of the human being as the knowing and acting subject, on the one hand, and the idea of the *rationality* of the world, i.e. its principled intelligibility, on the other.[11]

According to the discourse about the human capacity of self-determination (regarding one's identity and life) through science and the discovery of truth, we end up in a situation where we are emancipated from religion and tradition. In contrast to this modernist account, it might be argued that the capacity of self-determination can, in the modern context itself, often be dangerous, if it is not accompanied by some disciplining orientation. The tensions within modernity arise from these two points of view and also have broad implications for religion. As far as government is concerned, government necessarily exerts power and provides freedom. As a consequence, we need to analyse public institutions of

---

[9]   Wilfred Cantwell Smith, *The Meaning and End of Religion* (San Francisco, CA: Harper & Row, 1978 [1962]), 47–8.

[10]   Talal Asad, 'Reading a Modern Classic: W. C. Smith's "The Meaning and End of Religion"', in Hent de Vries and Samuel Weber (eds), *Religion and Media* (Stanford, CA: Stanford University Press, 2001), 131–47, at 146.

[11]   Peter Wagner, *Theorising Modernity: Inescapability and Attainability in Social Theory* (London: Sage, 2001), 4.

power as mechanisms that can individualize and standardize at the same time. State institutions are privileged places where such a dual process may be observed.[12]

The definition of religion in modernity is as tension ridden as the concept of modernity itself. In fact, if one dimension of religion – that of personal beliefs – has become independent of institutional determinacy, another remains linked to institutions and directed towards control. I would like to show in my work that both dimensions, the independent/individual and the institutional, have to be considered and that it is only by looking at the relations between them that we may provide a coherent account of the social location of religion in the contemporary world. Although Asad was right in arguing, almost twenty years ago, that 'there cannot be a universal definition of religion, not only because its constituent elements and relationships are historically specific, but because that definition is itself the historical product of discursive processes',[13] the historicity of numerous currently used definitions still needs to be made explicit. The concept of religion is the result of the constitution of a scholarly body in Europe that wanted to study 'other' people in comparison to their own and therefore started, at the end of the nineteenth century, to identify 'systems' around 'religious leaders'.[14] Hence there is not in reality a religion, or religions, but only practices, beliefs and institutions dealing with transcendent issues. For Smith, two different elements compose what is generally meant by 'religion': on the one hand, there are cumulative religious traditions that are empirically intelligible; on the other hand, there is faith that is strictly personal. There is no essence of religion, because religion is a concept with a history, but, as Smith writes,

> essences do not have a history. Essences do not change. Yet it is an observable fact that what have been called religions do, in history, change … One has radically misunderstood our world if one imagines that things can be defined; and especially living things, and especially human involvements.[15]

Therefore, an abstract notion of religion exists primarily for scholars and this is why we need to understand what different scholars mean when they refer to religion. What I see as a general difficulty is that religion has been theorized as a

---

[12]   Cf. in my view a remarkably insightful book: Nikolas Rose, *Governing the Soul: The Shaping of the Private Self* (London: Routledge, 1989).

[13]   Talal Asad, *Genealogies of Religion: Discipline and Reasons of Power in Christianity and Islam* (Baltimore, MD, and London: The John Hopkins University Press, 1993), 29–30. I also base my argument here on Russell McCutcheon, 'The Category "Religion" in Recent Publications: A Critical Survey', *Numen*, 42/3 (October 1995), 284–309.

[14]   For the importance of religious plurality in the birth of religious studies as an independent discipline from theology and the search for a universal definition of religion, cf. the very illuminating study by Tomoko Masuzawa, *The Invention of World Religions, or, How European Universalism was Preserved in the Language of Pluralism* (Chicago, IL: University of Chicago Press, 2005).

[15]   Smith, *Meaning*, 143–4.

phenomenon that concerns different dimensions of social life and thus involves multiple levels of social analysis. Religion as an object of scientific study can be approached from a variety of perspectives, for example from the point of view of the *person* or from the point of view of the *institution*. The institutional approach corresponds with an emphasis of the irreducibly collective nature of religion and hence, for instance, a consideration of the relationship between state and church as central objects of study, as opposed to an individual approach, whose focus is no longer the state or the church but personal beliefs and religious experience. In both cases, religion implies the individuals' 'connectivity' in relation to others, as the etymology of the word 'religion' indicates: *re-ligere*, 'binding together'.

The modernist perspective of religion considers contemporary societies as religiously unstructured and thus places religion at the level of the individual. The work of Danièle Hervieu-Léger presents an elaborate and challenging theory that develops some of the radical aspects of the modernist perspective without dissolving the individual in subjectivity.[16] It presents a plausible alternative to modernist theories and cannot simply be placed into the category of individualistic approaches.[17] Both dimensions are present in Danièle Hervieu-Léger's definition of religion[18] as an ideological, practical and symbolic system through which an individual and collective sense of belonging to a line of believers is produced, developed and controlled.

Another type of definition draws on function, in the multiple meanings entailed by this notion, rather than on substance. The social constructionist approach excludes substantial elements from the definition of religion and considers religion 'a social construct that varies in meaning across time and place'.[19] From this point of view, religion can be studied as 'an interpretative category that human beings apply to a wide variety of phenomena, most of which have to do with notions of ultimate meaning or value.'[20] In this book I refer to this definition in an operational way and pinpoint that the actors involved in religious systems of symbols[21] claim to represent a level of reality that is ultimately true and irreducible to any other meaning system. However, it is also crucial for me to recall that 'politics, the

---

[16]   In Hervieu-Léger's view, religion remains an active element in modern societies. She suggests that secularization be defined as the process of permanent reorganization of religion. See *Vers un nouveau Christianisme?* (Paris: Cerf, 1986), 227.

[17]   For the differences between modernist and individualist approaches, see recently Gert Pickel, 'Ostdeutschland im europäischen Vergleich – Immer noch ein Sonderfall oder ein Sonderweg?', in Pickel and Kornelia Sammet, *Religion und Religiosität im vereinigten Deutschland. Zwanzig Jahre nach dem Umbruch* (Wiesbaden: VS Verlag), 165–90, table at 167.

[18]   Danièle Hervieu-Léger, *Le pèlerin et le converti. La religion en mouvement* (Paris: Flammarion, 1987), 24.

[19]   Beckford, *Social Theory and Religion*, 7.

[20]   Ibid., 4.

[21]   This notion is taken from Fritz Stolz, *Grundzüge der Religionswissenschaft* (Göttingen: Vandenhoeck & Ruprecht, 1988).

state and the nation are symbolic entities which have – similarly to religion – transcendent functions'.[22]

Religion and Secularization

The current debate on secularization necessarily also questions the definition of religion. As soon as one aspect of religion is threatened by disappearance through the secularization process, sociologists find new *loci* of the sacred – ranging from the institution to the individual, from the political to the personal, from social function to individual utility or personal preference –, thereby extending the definition of religion and adding objects to their agenda. Other scholars make distinctions between different religions by categorizing them in terms of their secularizing potential. Detlef Pollack[23] writes that the wider the meaning given to the notion of religion, the most probable the rejection of the concept of secularization, and vice versa. However, there is probably more at stake than simply knowing how inclusive the notion of religion is. It is not easy to identify whether it is the definition of religion that determines the perspective from which secularization is viewed, or vice versa.

In brief, if we look through the orthodox lens of secularization,[24] we shall most certainly overemphasize the importance of the autonomy of personal beliefs and underestimate institutional influence. The emphasis will be placed on the disconnection between institutions and personal beliefs. Conversely, if we take a functional–institutional approach to religion – for instance, a Parsonian approach –, institutions will be presented as the main actors.[25] According to Robert Bellah,[26] functionalist approaches tend to see religion as being in decline. Thomas Luckmann's theory is also, as the German sociologist Hubert Knoblauch writes, 'well known as one of the most general functional theories of religion'.[27] However, if religion no longer fulfils social functions, how can it be approached from a functional point of view? The apparent contradiction is solved when we distinguish functions with regard to institutions or individuals. Religion may fulfil

---

[22]   Hubert Knoblauch, *Populäre Religion. Auf dem Weg in eine spirituelle Gesellschaft* (Frankfurt am Main: Campus Verlag, 2009), 35, my translation at 228–55.

[23]   In *Säkularisierung – ein moderner Mythos?* (Tübingen: Mohr Siebeck, 2003).

[24]   To simplify, according to the 'orthodox' thesis of secularization, there is a loss of religion both at the individual and at the institutional level. The first generation of sociologists of religion took for granted that with the differentiation process the 'old historical religions' would not 'survive the onslaught of the modern world' – José Casanova, *Public Religions in the Modern World* (Chicago, IL: University of Chicago Press, 1994), 18.

[25]   Cf. Talcott Parsons and Neil Smelser, *Economy and Society: A Study in the Integration of Economic and Social Theory* (Glencoe, IL: Free Press, 1956).

[26]   Robert Neelly Bellah, *Beyond Belief: Essays on Religion in a Post-traditional World* (New York: Harper & Row, 1970).

[27]   'Europe and Invisible Religion', *Social Compass*, 50/3 (2003), 267–74, at 268.

a function for an individual (providing answers to existential questions, and so on) or for society (enabling integration, for instance). While the former understanding is often characteristic of a modernist approach, the latter meaning was the object of earlier studies, as Beckford argues:

> as recently as the 1950s many social theorists ... found good reasons for analysing the 'functions' fulfilled by religious institutions for the social system, the role of religion as a mechanism for transmitting values and integrating individuals into society, and the affinities between religious values and democracy, work ethics and the stability of nuclear families ... Sectarian and cultic groups such as Jehovah's Witnesses or Christian Science could be explained in terms of the social system's internal re-adjustments to anomie, tension and conflict.[28]

Only in more recent years did the focus shift to the individual level, with an analysis of

> the mechanisms and processes whereby religious world-views were said to supply meaning and stave off despair. The scope of this more phenomenologically oriented approach included at one extreme claims about the anthropologically rooted necessity for religion or spirituality and, at the other, arguments about the marginal differentiation of religious world-views in an increasingly marketised world.[29]

On an institutional level religion may have lost its social functions, but on an individual level it still provides meaning, hopes, aspirations and motivations or, on the contrary, exclusion, submission and fear. However, such attributions cannot be studied merely from an individual standpoint since they are essentially interactive. Thus religion is an object whose analysis depends – like other cultural and social phenomena – on the way we circumscribe it or, as Asad puts it, on the fact that we 'leave out some things and ... include others'.[30] Religion, he argues, is constructed through definitional discourses, which interpret true meanings and exclude or include utterances and practices. It is the process of inclusion and exclusion that needs to be scrutinized. To differentiate and historicize what is considered to be secularization, as I propose to do in the next step, is a way to explore this reasoning.[31]

---

[28] Beckford, *Social Theory and Religion*, 156.

[29] Ibid. Concerning the shift from function to substance, see, among others, Armando Salvatore, 'The Euro-Islamic Roots of Secularity: A Difficult Equation', *Asian Journal of Social Science*, 33/3 (2005), 412–37, and Fritz Stolz, *Grundzüge*.

[30] 'Reading', 145.

[31] See Philip S. Gorski's article for a brilliant review of this thesis: 'Historicizing the Secularization Debate: Church, State, and Society in Late Medieval and Early Modern Europe, ca. 1300 to 1700', *American Sociological Review* 65/1 (February 2000), 138–67.

The Theological Roots of Secularization in Eastern Germany

My focus is Eastern Germany, the cradle of the Reformation and a European country that experienced Socialism at first hand. In the Eastern German context, the Protestant Reformation is considered the starting point of the displacement of social functions from the religious- to the secular sphere. Martin Luther lived in the very region on which the present study focuses.[32] The Reformers, with Luther at the forefront, attacked the church's legitimacy as a mediator between human beings and God, or God's Word. During the Reformation, the state lost its natural legitimacy and was newly conceived as a human necessity one had to accept because some kind of power was preferable to anarchy, as long as the divine order – the only order worth fighting for – could not dominate.[33] Luther developed a doctrinal separation between the spiritual community and the secular order. His doctrine of the two kingdoms contrasted a spiritual, invisible, eternal kingdom – a kingdom of freedom and belief – with a worldly, visible kingdom, the kingdom of constraints and violence, occupied by evil forces.[34] In his pamphlet *The Freedom of a Christian* (1520), Luther assigned the kingdom of freedom to the 'inner man', to the 'inner sphere' of the person, while the 'outer person' was subject irremediably to the system of worldly powers and was not free. By differentiating these two spheres, Luther's doctrine also drew a distinction between the inner person and the person's deeds. The outer person is constituted by his/her acts, which do not completely define the inner person. This doctrine offered a powerful theology for the conception of prison chaplaincy: when confronting prisoners, the chaplain was able to see them not solely in terms of the crimes they had committed.

Another aspect of Protestant theology, which is often mentioned in relation to this variation of secularization,[35] is the centrality of individual autonomy in religious life. Religious authority derives, Luther wrote, from *sola scriptura*: Scripture alone was acknowledged as the authentic and valid source of Christian truth so that the church's authority, as expressed by church councils or the pope, was cancelled. Luther provided additionally a translation of the New Testament in the vernacular. The vernacular was actually the language of all the tracts used to disseminate reformational ideas. All this implied that every individual could read for him/herself the Reformers' writings and would thereby be responsible for his/

---

[32] Luther was a professor in Wittenberg, and the disputation between him and Eck took place in Leipzig. He translated the Bible while staying in Eisenach, having taken refuge in the Wartburg.

[33] Jean Calvin and Ulrich Zwingli developed their doctrines in a different way from Luther: see, among others, Richard Henry Tawney, *Religion and the Rise of Capitalism: A Historical Study* (Harmondsworth: Penguin, 1938 [1969]).

[34] Cf. Hermann Jordan, *Luthers Staatsauffassung. Ein Beitrag zu der Frage des Verhältnisses von Religion und Politik* (Darmstadt: Wissenschaftliche Buchgesellschaft, 1968).

[35] For the idea of varieties of secularization, see recently Philip S. Gorski and Ates Altinordu, 'After Secularization?', *Annual Review of Sociology*, 34 (August 2008), 55–77.

her own religion. As a consequence, the Reformation lessened the pervasiveness of the ecclesiastical hold on people, but it strengthened the political hold.[36]

In this context, the term 'modern' does not entail the negation of Christianity but rather its full realization. Secular institutions, such as the state, are 'post-theological' in the sense of being established not as a replacement of religion but as products that have actually emerged out of or against religion. In 1817, the Protestant Church became an institution of public law. The Prussian kings were the 'supreme bishops' of the Prussian Church. The German Constitution of 1848 did not recognize that the state had any religious character, but this did not occasion a loss of the churches' influence on social life: Christian festivals were official days of celebration, for instance, and medical care followed a Christian ethic. The Conservatives in the German government upheld in principle the Protestant character of the State of Prussia, whereas the Liberal movement carried, within Protestantism, a strong idea of the separation between church and state. In 1919, the constitution of the Weimar Republic recognized the freedom of conscience and of religion (Art. 136) and affirmed the absence of a state religion (Art. 137). Individual religious freedom was stated as being independent of all other civic rights and obligations. Religious convictions were affirmed to be private, with everyone having the right to keep them private. Civic authorities needed to know them only for the positive interpretation of the freedom of religion. The right to form religious associations and to manage them autonomously was guaranteed. The result was a separation but also a definitional imbrication of religion and politics, of religion and the state.

Religion and the State

One of the core functions of the modern nation-state is, as Winnifred Sullivan writes, punishment: 'it is what distinguishes the modern state from premodern societies, where punishment was a private prerogative for settling scores or obtaining compensation.'[37] As a legal scholar, she also – rightly – points out that 'prisons are, perhaps ironically, places where one cannot get away from the state's relationship to religion'[38] and where, I would add, the relationship between state and religion may be observed with precision. Like Alison Liebling I indeed consider prison 'not simplistically as an instrument for social exclusion, but as a

---

[36]   One example often cited to illustrate this is the reduction of the number of sacraments that Protestantism brought about: these decreased from seven to two, communion and baptism. Cf. Sape A. Zylstra, 'Protestantism: Theology and Politics', in Sabrina Petra Ramet (ed.), *Protestantism and Politics in Eastern Europe and Russia: The Communist and Postcommunist Eras* (Durham, NC, and London: Duke University Press, 1992), 11–39.

[37]   Winnifred Fallers Sullivan, *Prison Religion: Faith-based Reform and the Constitution* (Princeton, NJ: Princeton University Press, 2009), 6.

[38]   Ibid.

state-run institution where symbolic and significant constructions of the state's relationship with the individual continue to be forged'.[39]

It is therefore useful to clarify our understanding of the entanglement of religion with politics – here understood as state politics – and vice versa. Carl Schmitt demonstrates that the concepts now used in Western political thinking actually have theological origins, referring in particular to the Bible and the history of the Hebrew people.[40] By contrast, Jan Assman argues that he observes the opposite – that is, that the most important theological notions are actually 'theologisierte politische Begriffe',[41] theologized political notions. To illustrate what he means by 'theologization', he reveals that the Bible, in particular the Mosaic Law, has political sources. A similar study had previously been carried out by Jean Bottéro.[42] According to this approach, religion has emerged out of the spirit of the political, 'dem Geist des Politischen'.[43] Bottéro's and Assmann's work may be linked to the anthropological discoveries made by Mary Douglas, who presents the cognitive background that forms the basis on which religious ideas are expressed.[44] Very recently, Winnifred Sullivan's studies also show clearly how intricate the relationship is between juridical argumentation and religious discourses in a situation of religious pluralism.[45] Of course, what is at the heart of all these authors' legacy is the very definition of politics, which cannot be discussed here. I shall limit myself to commenting on the provocative and challenging point these authors make about the relationship between religion and politics, to see whether it may be of help in the present study. It actually allows us to recognize that the relationship between religious and political discourses and institutions is dynamic. Therefore, religion is certainly not just the 'expression' of political ideas, but both religion and politics are concerned with similar issues: how to give meaning to one's life and govern it according to this meaning, how to deal with existential and ontological difficulties, and so on. Religion and politics necessarily contradict but also compete with and complement each other.

Hence the relationship between religion and state is very complex. The emergence of the modern state was a key moment in the changes that religion has undergone in institutional terms, changes that have also been interpreted in

---

[39]   In Alison Liebling and Helen Arnold, *Prisons and their Moral Performance: A Study of Values, Quality, and Prison Life* (Oxford: Oxford University Press, 2004), 165.

[40]   Carl Schmitt, *Politische Theologie. Vier Kapitel zur Lehre von der Souveränität* (Berlin: Duncker & Humblot, 2004), 43. An interesting historical analysis of these implications can be found in David Nicholls, *Deity and Domination* (London and New York: Routledge, 1989).

[41]   Jan Assmann, *Herrschaft und Heil. Politische Theologie in Altägypten, Israel und Europa* (Frankfurt am Main: Fischer, 2002), 29.

[42]   Jean Bottéro, *Naissance de Dieu. La Bible et l'historien* (Paris: Gallimard, 1992).

[43]   Assmann, *Herrschaft*, 29.

[44]   Mary Douglas, *Leviticus as Literature* (Oxford and New York: Oxford University Press, 1999).

[45]   See *Prison Religion*.

terms of secularization. In fact, nation-states presupposed a conception of society as composed of autonomous individuals, who are able to be secular in the public sphere and able to participate freely, as individuals, in political life. Modern states – or just 'states', as Gianfranco Poggi points out – offer or guarantee citizenship to individuals who 'possess (among others) specifically political capacities, interests and preferences, the exercise of which allows them to affect to a greater or lesser extent the content of state activity'.[46]

The role that state institutions and thus political power played in reducing the influence of religion is highly relevant; to neglect it in any discussion of secularization would create misleading accounts. Since this study focuses on a total institution of the state – the prison – and on institutional support for (ex-)prisoners, I shall offer, in the first chapter, a closer examination of the religious changes that affect these institutions.

In order to take both secularization and establishment into consideration, I shall elaborate two approaches in the following section: the first comprises a comparative enterprise, with a set of propositions relating to the 'new model of secularization' that theorizes religious interactions in terms of the market; the second presents a set of theories that may be described as 'state-centred'.[47]

Religious Establishment and the Market Model

José Casanova has given establishment a very important role, not least by contrasting Europe with the United States of America, where religious practice has intensified. Casanova's explanation of this difference points to the role of the state in the US. In fact, church–state relations in the past and present differ significantly in the US and Europe. In the former, there has never been an absolutist state or a caesaropapist state church. Although it is well known that civil religion is very strong in the US, it is true that, from the very beginning of its existence, the US has instituted the separation between state and church. For Casanova, the most important feature in church–state relations is that religious practice flourishes when the state does not establish any church or religious community. This is true not only for the US but also for large parts of Europe where non-established churches and sects have been able to survive the secularizing trends better than established churches. Casanova shows that the weakening of Christianity was not inevitable – rather, it was the result of particular social and political processes – and the principal reason for this weakening was that 'the main churches clung to political power for too

---

[46]   Gianfranco Poggi, *The State: Its Nature, Development and Prospects* (Cambridge: Basil Blackwell, 1990), 28.

[47]   In my article on the relationship between state and religion, I refer to them as 'state domination' theories: see Irene Becci, 'Les limites de la pluralisation et les limites de la régulation. Premiers pas vers une approche en termes de médiations pour la Suisse', *Social Compass* 48/1 (2001), 29–36.

long, thereby precipitating an avoidable clash with emerging secular nation states and churches resisting structural change'.[48] He thereby points to an important aspect that state recognition implies: it empowers but also limits autonomy. Once established, churches 'are allegedly unable to exercise independent leverage on political power or state authorities'.[49] Similarly, we shall see – when I discuss the analysis of the empirical data – that the prison chaplains, like the churches to which they are affiliated, find themselves in an equally ambivalent position: they are established actors but negotiate their independence. In short, in Casanova's opinion, the presence or absence of establishment is a factor that is more relevant than others for explaining the secularization process.

Establishment is also a key factor in the rational choice theory that considers the situation in terms of supply and demand. Developed by Rodney Stark, William Sims Bainbridge, Laurence Iannacone and Roger Finke,[50] this theory borrows its interpretative framework from economics. The authors criticize the assumption contained in the secularization theory about the decline of religious practice, by demonstrating that the variable of religious participation does not say anything about religious demand at the individual level but points instead to the persistence of a religious 'supply'. They seek to explain the variations in religious participation by looking at the varying degrees of regulation of and competition in the spiritual market. Based on statistical data from several Western countries, these authors have sought to identify the sociological principles at work. For example, they refer to the *pluralism proposition*, which opposes Berger's argument that pluralism diminishes the strength of religious commitment and the social legitimacy of religion: the greater the number of religions on offer, the greater the variety of religions and hence the greater the chance that anyone will find something to his/her taste and needs. In other words, the less a religious market is regulated, the more pluralistic it is; regulation here means the juridical and political intervention of the state. Seen from this perspective, measuring religious participation does not necessarily give any indication of individuals' religious 'pre-disposition' – it actually gives an

---

48   Cited in Beckford, *Social Theory and Religion*, 61.

49   Ibid.

50   See, for example, Rodney Stark, 'Research Note: Europe's Receptivity to New Religious Movements: Round Two', *Journal for the Scientific Study of Religion*, 32/4 (1993), 389–97; Rodney Stark and William Sims Bainbridge, *The Future of Religion: Secularization, Revival and Cult Formation* (Berkeley, CA: University of California Press, 1985); Laurence R. Iannacone, 'Voodoo Economics? Reviewing the Rational Choice Approach to Religion', *Journal for the Scientific Study of Religion*, 34/1 (1995), 76–89; Rodney Stark and Laurence R. Iannacone, 'Response to Lechner: Recent Religious Declines in Quebec, Poland, and the Netherlands: A Theory Vindicated?', *Journal for the Scientific Study of Religion*, 35/3 (1996), 265–71; Rodney Stark and Laurence R. Iannacone, 'A Supply-side Reinterpretation of the "Secularization" of Europe', *Journal for the Scientific Study of Religion*, 33/3 (1994), 230–52; Rodney Stark and Roger Finke, *Acts of Faith: Explaining the Human Side of Religion* (Berkeley, CA: University of California Press, 2000).

indication of how attractive religious 'firms' are. In spite of all the limitations that any study using methodological individualism entails, the merit of rational choice theory is that it has redirected attention towards the state.[51] By establishing one religious organization the state creates a situation of monopoly, hence a situation of little competition. As soon as the religious market is free from the intervention of the state, plurality develops and supply multiplies. Rational choice theory has developed a list of criteria that identify the extent to which a religion is established, such as received funding or legal dispositions. I shall come back to these criteria later and use an adapted version of the list in order to evaluate the extent to which religions are established in prison.

State-centred Theories

The distinctive feature of state-centred theories is the view that the control of beliefs and religious practices has not disappeared but has passed from the religious organizations to the state. The disciplining action of the state with regard to religion is actually more important than religion's drift towards autonomy: the state is central in structuring access to religious experience and even to beliefs. Pauline Côté and Jacques Zylberberg, the principal proponents of this approach, place the emphasis on the logic of power that configures the religious field. The privatization of religion means that religious institutions have been deprived progressively of their functions, resources and organizational autonomy. The power of the state is so encompassing that believing is seen primarily as a political activity, not as a personal activity that has no relevance in the public sphere.[52] Zylberberg, who defines the state as a 'construct of collective action'[53] with an organized set of targets, capacities, legitimacy and relationships to order, ventures that the action the state engages in is authoritarian, homogeneous and self-legitimizing; the state also has an organizational monopoly. As a consequence, religious institutions – a notion that refers broadly to 'domination groups that pursue sacred intentions' – are included in this 'state-dominated social space'.[54] According to Zylberberg and Côté, the state needs to be considered as a political

---

[51]   It should be noted that an approach to religion that borrows vocabulary from economics does not imply a person-centred approach. For instance, Pierre Bourdieu also uses the metaphor of the market to look at the religious field. In his model, however, the focus is on the way the boundaries and the dynamics of a field are created and kept alive (reproduced). Cf. Pierre Bourdieu, 'Genèse et structure du champ religieux', *Revue française de Sociologie*, XII (1971), 295–334.

[52]   For further details, see Liliane Voyé, *Figures des Dieux. Rites et mouvements religieux* (Paris and Brussels: De Boeck & Lercier, 1996).

[53]   Jacques Zylberberg, 'La régulation étatique de la religion: monisme et pluralisme', *Social Compass*, 37/1 (1990), 87–96, at 87. My translation.

[54]   Jacques Zylberberg and Pauline Côté, 'Les balises étatiques de la religion au Canada', *Social Compass*, 40/4 (1993), 529–53.

dimension involved when analysing religion. In other words, the state plays a fundamental role as a mediator of all sorts of human actions in modern societies.[55] In sum, this approach describes the development of religion in modernity in terms of an increase in and a widening of the state's domination of society.

As far as the conception of the state is concerned, the authors who are arguing this approach refer expressly to the work by Michel Crozier and Erhard Friedberg[56] and Mancur Olson.[57] However, the vocabulary they use and the type of *problématique* they present resonate with Foucauldian themes. Like Foucault, they stress the relevance of power in any relationship and, most importantly, they identify the state as a central form of power of our time, which is 'à la fois globalisante et totalisatrice'[58] – at the same time globalizing and totalizing. Yet it seems to me that these considerations would gain force in following further Foucault's reasoning of the link between church and state. In fact, Foucault saw very clearly the structural homology of the two institutions. In the Western world, he asserts, the state has integrated, in a new way, an old power technique that emerged from Christian institutions. Not only does Foucault advance the hypothesis of such a homology, but he also goes as far as pointing out which precise form of power the state has directly taken from the Christian churches – pastoral power.[59] The French philosopher argues that the pastorate first developed in the East, 'in a pre-Christian East … Mediterranean East',[60] where pastors guided a 'flock' to watch over it 'and avoid the misfortune that may threaten the least of its members'.[61] Pastors used to protect and feed the whole community and were ready to sacrifice themselves in order to ensure individuals' salvation. They promoted harmony among the members and gained their allegiance not by threatening, scaring, terrorizing or forcing tactics but by dedicating care and attention to every single one of them.[62] Pastors therefore knew all the

---

[55]   Voyé, *Figures*, 118.

[56]   *L'acteur et le système. Les contraintes de l'action collective* (Paris: Éditions du Seuil, 1977).

[57]   *The Logic of Collective Action: Public Goods and Theory of Groups* (Cambridge, MA: Harvard University Press, 1971).

[58]   Michel Foucault, 'Pourquoi étudier le pouvoir: la question du sujet', in Hubert L. Dreyfuss and Paul Rabinow, *Michel Foucault. Un parcours philosophique au-delà de l'objectivité et de la subjectivité* (Paris: Gallimard, 1992 [1988]), 298–308, at 304.

[59]   For my first discussion of Foucault's standpoint on pastoral power, see Irene Becci, 'Penser le pouvoir pastoral dans les prisons actuelles', in M. Cicchini and M. Porret (eds), *Les sphères du pénal avec Michel Foucault* (Lausanne: Antipodes, 2007), 237–50.

[60]   Michel Foucault, *Security, Territory, Population: Lectures at the Collège de France, 1977–1978*, ed. Michel Senellart (London: Palgrave Macmillan, 2007), 123.

[61]   Ibid., 127.

[62]   Michel Foucault, '"Omnes et singulatim": Towards a Critique of Political Reason', in James D. Faubion (ed.), *Power. Vol. 3 Essential Works of Foucault, 1954–1984* (New York: New Press, 2000), 298–325, at 303.

members well and became more closely acquainted by 'exploring their souls'.[63] According to Foucault, this form of power is individualizing, unlike forms of power addressing masses – which were typical in ancient Greece – because the pastor convinces every member of the flock individually, with personalized arguments.[64] He follows every single individual throughout his/her life. The relationship the pastor constructs with every individual is therefore moral and complex, because it aims to persuade him/her and thus to find a consensus.[65] For the pastor, harmony must prevail within the flock, not antagonism or competition. Foucault writes that this form of power 'was introduced into the Western world by way of the Christian Church'.[66] For centuries it was confined to the ecclesiastical organization, but with the emergence of 'the state in the modern sense of the word'[67] this form of power was extended to non-religious institutions. With the rise of the welfare system, it became common practice in state structures, such as prisons. Therefore, the chaplain's role as a mediator, his constant presence and discretion, clearly put him in a position of pastoral power. This means, Foucault argues, that in order to exercise its political power the state needs to enter the intimate sphere of the individuals' very existence; one of the strategies to obtain this is to institutionalize spiritual care. The Canadian authors cited above make the same assertion: the state rules over the religious presence in the social sphere. They suggest that 'fiscal, school, health, civic and criminal legislations as well as work, trade, migration, culture and communication regulations shape the modes, the diffusion and the content of religious socialisation'.[68] Thus religious socialization is dependent on all the state's regulations. The state's domination goes so far that the clergy no longer have any influence on the basic common human experiences such as birth, death and love. They are now the products of individual choice, but individual choices are in turn 'structurés, sinon signifiés, par le complexe organisationnel étatique'[69] – that is, organized as significant by the state.

Foucault has a very clear idea of how the form of power that he calls 'pastoral' is transformed when it passes to the state. First, the state aims to guarantee 'salvation' in this world, which means that the state is expected to ensure decent living conditions. Secondly, through the state and its diffused presence in society, this form of power widens. This process is the main difference in approaches

---

[63]   Michel Foucault, 'The Subject and Power', in Hubert L. Dreyfuss and Paul Rabinow (eds), *Michel Foucault: Beyond Structuralism and Hermeneutics* (Chicago, IL: Chicago University Press, 1983), 208–28, at 214.

[64]   Foucault, *Security*, 128.

[65]   Ibid.

[66]   Ibid., 129.

[67]   Foucault, '"Omnes"', 313.

[68]   Pauline Côté, 'Culture séculière, culture religieuse, ethos civique et administration publique du symbole', *Social Compass*, 46/1 (1999), 57–74, at 60.

[69]   Zylberberg and Côté, 'Balises', 533.

that stress conflict between the two powers, state and religion.[70] In opposition to this perspective, Foucault observes that it is not rivalry that exists between the two powers, but that an individualizing tactic develops in all social institutions, including the family, medicine, psychiatry, education, the workplace, and so on.[71] Similarly, Talal Asad traces the genealogy of the way in which socio-religious representations developed in relation to power configurations. The following statement shows his proximity to Foucault's approach:

> Given that the modern nation-state seeks to regulate all aspects of individual life … no one, religious or otherwise, can avoid encountering its ambitious powers.[72]

Therefore, the question is whether the loss of autonomy of religious organizations really means that they disappear, as Foucault argues. Zylberberg and Côté probably see the passing of some functions to the state as too definite a process, leaving the churches in complete submission. In reality, what emerges is a power complex in which both institutions need each other, as we shall see in the specific case of prisons and state-supported reintegration programmes for former prisoners.

Some reflections on the terms of pastoral and spiritual care illustrate this point. Pastoral care is a concept that was coined by the Christian churches to describe one aspect of their action, as institutions, towards salvation. The concept refers to the activity through which the churches reach out to the secular world and to its suffering and less privileged parts in particular, to provide moral, ethical and spiritual guidance. Through the action of 'comforting those in need', the boundary between the religious and the secular becomes blurred: pastoral care is a moral action that aims to keep the individual integrated in a particular context. For the established religions, pastoral care is thus in line with the aims that state and church pursue jointly, while the notion of 'spiritual care' refers primarily to the individual's needs in the spiritual realm, not to the institution. Spiritual care is an ethical action that addresses the individual's values and worldviews.[73] According to Max Weber, the idea of spiritual care exists in a variety of religions. It is, however, in the revealed prophetic religions that we find it systematically

---

[70]   Cf. Françoise Champion, 'Les rapports Eglise–Etat dans les pays européens de tradition protestante et de tradition catholique. Essai d'analyse', *Social Compass*, 40/4 (1993), 589–609; Françoise Champion, 'Des rapports Eglise(s)–Etat dans l'Europe communautaire', *Le Débat* (nov.–déc. 1993), 46–72; and Jean Baubérot, *La morale laïque contre l'ordre moral* (Paris: Seuil, 1997).

[71]   Foucault, 'Pourquoi étudier', 307.

[72]   Asad, Talal, 'Religion, Nation-State, Secularism', in Peter Van der Veer and Hartmut Lehmann (eds), *Nation and Religion: Perspectives on Europe and Asia* (Princeton, NJ: Princeton University Press, 1999), 178–96.

[73]   For the distinction between moral (as proposed by Emile Durkheim's social scientific approach) and ethical action (in line with Max Weber's theory), see Isacco Turina, 'Éthique et engagement dans un groupe antispéciste', *L'Année sociologique*, 60/1 (2010), 63–91.

rationalized.[74] Weber stresses that spiritual care or *Seelsorge* refers to an individual action: as he writes, it is 'die religiöse Pflege der Individuen' – the religious care of individuals – or the action of 'Spendung von individuellem religiösem Trost in innerer oder äusserer Not' – offering 'individual religious consolation' when someone is in 'internal' (emotional) or 'external' (material) need.[75] The prison chaplaincies and the religious support that is available for ex-inmates provide a good opportunity to observe the intermingling of the religious and the secular precisely because both are based on the notions of pastoral and spiritual care. It can be argued that the two notions characterize different types of action within the Christian churches in Europe: individualized spiritual care that focuses on ethical issues, and pastoral care that is concerned with moral action to maintain social cohesion. While one can argue with Michel Foucault that pastoral care includes spiritual care, the distinction provides an interesting indicator of how religious institutions perceive the way they relate to secular institutions.

As Dario Melossi argues, Foucault's critique of a state-centred power, in mid-1970s Europe, 'contributed to shift attention from the governmental level of political discourse to "diffuse" societal power and to the "microphysics of power"'.[76] As a consequence, it is important to consider that, in this approach, the notion of the state is in fact

> an abstraction for the state-orientation of individual politicians, teachers, prison-wardens, and all those involved in the business of reproducing ideologies. The problem of how the individual teacher, prison warden ... conceives of this homology and helps constructing it through the institutional channels of what she calls the state, is still an open problem.[77]

Maybe the present work is a step towards finding a solution to this problem. My reflections suggest that, as soon as the state establishes some religions and not others, the relationship between it and the established religions influences the experience and location of religion more generally. The state distributes privileges and channels the presence of religion in its institutions.

However, how can establishment be measured more accurately? In my previous work[78] I have suggested the following criteria, which I shall elaborate later: the political recognition of religious organizations, their juridical status, the amount of state funding they receive, and their demographic situation in terms of religious

[74]   Max Weber, *Wirtschaft und Gesellschaft. Grundriss der verstehenden Soziologie. 1. Vol.* (Köln and Berlin: Kiepenheuer und Witsch, 1964), 365.

[75]   Ibid.

[76]   Melossi, *The State*, 172.

[77]   Ibid., 173.

[78]   Irene Becci, 'Entre pluralisation et régulation du champ religieux. Premiers pas vers une approche en termes de médiations pour la Suisse', *Social Compass, 48 (2001), 21–36. This article contains a first categorization of theories on state–church relations.*

belonging.[79] In other words, the level of recognition is a key issue in the organization of the religious field. This implies an analysis of the discourses and practices emerging from, or happening at, the intersection of the two institutions (state and established religion) and the way they present themselves, the way their relationship is configured, and the way their place in society is presented. In addition, it is necessary to grasp the meaning of this relationship for different social actors. What impact does the configuration of state and religion have on the actors' worldviews and actions? Worldviews organize actions by giving the acting subject a context in which his/her action is meaningful; in turn, worldviews are structured by the social situations (interactions in particular – or frames, to use a Goffmanian term[80]) in which the subject takes part. This double logic is due to the fact that worldviews are not merely the products of individual idiosyncrasy: they are shared and shaped by social groups as well as mediated by institutions. Mary Douglas's study *How Institutions Think* provides probably the best indication of how to conceptualize the relationship between the individual and institutions. As she writes,

> The whole approach to individual cognition can only benefit from recognizing the individual person's involvement with institution-building from the very start of the cognitive enterprise. Even the simple acts of classifying and remembering are institutionalized.[81]

For Douglas, looking in a systematic and continuous way at the changes institutions undergo allows insight into the transformations of individuals' experiences. This is not due primarily to individuals' minds being influenced by the way institutions function, but to the fact that the functioning of institutions is itself a product of individuals' thinking in an institutional situation. Words, classifications, analogies, practices and so on are given meaning by the fact that they are embedded in an institution, and an institution only exists through words, classifications, analogies, practices and so on. Mary Douglas takes processes of naturalization as objects and interprets them as socially constructed. This is why she draws our attention to analogies and calls for our suspicion towards them: 'if it seems that an analogy does match nature, it is because the analogy is already in use for grounding dominant political assumptions. It is not nature that makes the match, but society.'[82]

Opposing the point of view that presents values as naturally inherent in an institution or a social group, Mary Douglas claims that they are the product of structural processes. I think this insight can be very useful in understanding and interpreting the way religious groups claim exclusivity in matters of tolerance or

---

[79]   Ibid., 30.

[80]   Erving Goffman, *Frame Analysis: An Essay on the Organization of Experience* (New York: Harper and Row, 1974).

[81]   Mary Douglas, *How Institutions Think* (Syracuse, NY: Syracuse University Press, 1986), 67.

[82]   Ibid., 90.

kindness – qualities that, as Douglas notes, are universal. Whoever appropriates them in claiming them to be natural and exclusive attributes initiates an arbitrary process. In order to show the link between structure (here *establishment*) and social categories (here the distinction between more or less legitimate or rehabilitative religious practices), we need to describe the two elements separately. Hence, in the first chapter, my focus will be establishment as a structural historical process. It is the result of particular configurations of power between secular and spiritual institutions. As I elaborate in the second chapter, *establishment* has a significant impact on the institutional framing of individuals' personal religious practice. Second, I shall explore this impact anthropologically in the context of prisons. This is not an easy task, for reasons ranging from access denial to time issues, personal security and emotions.

Referring mainly to the United States, Lorna Rhodes rightly regrets that

> Today a large and growing body of work alludes to, but does not explore, the prison as a central site for the exercise of disciplinary power ... Little work in anthropology concerns prisons.[83]

The consequence of this situation is that empirical sociologists or socio-anthropologists who approach this field do not have many role models to follow. As I conducted my fieldwork, I was inspired by multi-sited approaches[84] and by constructionism. This meant being receptive to the concerns of ethnomethodology[85] and, as Beckford writes, 'to scrutinise the interaction between the meanings attributed to religion by individuals and groups *within* the confines of institutions and organizations'.[86] In order to gain an understanding of the chaplaincy's role, I have approached it from an empirical point of view, following two steps. First, seen from a general point of view, what does the presence of a religious figure mean in prison and what is the narrative surrounding it today? What criteria are used to justify the presence of that particular religious figure? These questions

---

[83]   Lorna A. Rhodes, 'Towards an Anthropology of Prisons', *Annual Revue of Anthropology*, 30 (2001), 65–83, at 66.

[84]   In particular by Eva Nadai and Christoph Maeder, 'Contours of the Field(s): Multi-sited Ethnography as a Theory-driven Research Strategy for Sociology', in Mark-Anthony Falzon (ed.), *Multi-Sited Ethnography: Theory, Practice and Locality in Contemporary Research* (Farnham and Burlington, VT: Ashgate, 2009), 233–50.

[85]   In particular to the ethnosemantic approach in prison – cf. Christoph Maeder, 'Alltagsroutine, Sozialstruktur und soziologische Theorie. Gefängnisforschung mit ethnographischer Semantik', *Forum Qualitative Sozialforschung*, 3/1 (2002), at http://www.ssoar.info/ssoar/View?resid=9596&lang=en, accessed 31 May 2012 – and to conversational analysis as a method used to study institutions: cf. among others John Heritage, 'Conversation Analysis and Institutional Talk: Analyzing Data', in David Silverman (ed.), *Qualitative Research: Theory, Method and Practice* (London: Sage, 1997), 161–82.

[86]   Beckford, *Social Theory and Religion*, 17.

are answered with reference to discourse analysis and anthropological methods in the third chapter. The status of prison chaplains and the institutional support of ex-offenders are now clearly regulated and need to be considered so that we may picture the link between religion and imprisonment. Description of these arrangements allows me to present exactly the impact of religious *establishment* on prison. In a second step, I analyse the actual practices, discourses and uses of religion by the prison administration, the chaplains and the inmates and evaluate their meaning with regard to the broader question of the establishment of religion and the understanding of religion in the social sphere.

Following my assumption that the wider structures of establishment have an impact on individual action, I identify their possible impact on the realm of spirituality in prison. In the fourth chapter, I discuss some of the concepts that are central to current theories of modern spirituality, such as religious *bricolage* and conversion. Religious *bricolage* is the personalized result of individual processes that seek meaning in religion. The individual is now no longer constrained by social norms in adopting any religious behaviour, but is free to convert, search and live out spirituality as much as s/he wishes and wherever s/he wants. However, as Danièle Hervieu-Léger suggests, even the most autonomous individual needs to validate his/her beliefs in order to find meaning in them.[87] The chapters add complexity progressively to my exposition of the way religion is transformed in prison and at release. The way I have chosen to illustrate this complexity is certainly not the only possible method, but it allows me to point out the contours and overlapping areas of some of the most urgent questions contemporary societies are facing, such as the relationship with others in our midst, be they criminal, religious, or both.

Levels of Analysis and Methodological Standpoint

The aim of the present work is to show that religion needs to be seen as a dynamic force in power configurations. The method that enables me to identify the power relations at work in the religious field is situated on two levels: the contextual–structural and the discursive.

The focus on the contextual–structural level seeks to provide insight into the configuration of religion in prison as related to the state–church relationship. The arrangements between the two institutions of state and church have wide-ranging implications for the various ways in which individuals relate to religion in prison. This first level of analysis is institutional and aims to provide insight into the configuration of the state–church relationship on the one hand and the religion–prison relationship on the other. The second level addresses the question of the actual practices, uses, meanings and discourses of different actors – the prison chaplains, ministers, social workers, inmates and ex-inmates – and examines

---

[87] See *Le pèlerin.*

how these relate to the broader question of the establishment of religion and the understanding of religion in the social secular sphere. This part draws mainly on empirical data and focuses on the prison structure and the precise urban context respectively. As far as 'discourse analysis' is concerned, I reference 'a specific ensemble of ideas, concepts and categorization that are produced, reproduced and transformed in a particular set of practices and through which meaning is given to physical and social realities'.[88] Discourses about religion operate in the context of the institutional support and practices upon which they rely. This is why I shall first provide the background necessary to understand how the institutional support for discourses on religion presently appears; only following this may we analyse the discourses of the actors. We shall see how such discourses are expressed, in both written form – for example, in internal newspapers – and spoken form. The primary data I collected in three fieldwork sites[89] comprise three kinds:

- fifty in-depth, structured interviews with inmates, chaplains and prison governors, conducted in the field,
- observation notes,
- written responses to a questionnaire distributed to ex-inmates in Christian and secular relief programmes.

The secondary data I collected include the following:

- newspapers and newsletters (for example, flyers, brochures, parish newsletters, prison newspapers),
- statistical data about the general prison population and religious diversity in prisons,
- legal texts on church–state relations and religious freedom in prison.

The triangulation of the different discourses on religion and religious plurality will reveal the characteristics of particular positions that go beyond those of the individuals who are connected with establishment.[90] In the social sciences, triangulation is an important process of validating data by combining different research strategies and multiple sources. Within my fieldwork, the aim of triangulating discourses was not validation but identification of disparities in the configuration of the discourses. Whenever dissonance arose in the discourses

---

[88]   Marteen Hajer, *The Politics of Environmental Discourse* (Oxford: Oxford University Press, 1995), 44.

[89]   More details on fieldwork follow.

[90]   Concerning triangulation, cf. Norman K. Denzin, 'Strategies of Multiple Tri-angulation', in Denzin (ed.), *The Research Act in Sociology: A Theoretical Introduction to Sociological Method* (New York: McGraw-Hill, 1970), 297–313, and Uwe Flick, *Triangulation. Methodologie und Anwendung. Qualitative Sozialforschung*, Bd. 12 (Opladen: Leske+Budrich, 2002).

of different actors on a particular topic, I cross-checked the discourses against the structural settings. This method proved useful in organizing the chaplains' discourses with regard to their respective status or the inmates' and ex-inmates' discourses with regard to their religious involvement.

As a doctoral student I visited prisons repeatedly between 2002 and 2004 (in particular the chaplaincy, the library and the cells) in Brandenburg, Berlin and Saxony, collecting field notes, documents and first-hand impressions. Additionally, I participated in group meetings organized by the chaplaincy. I chose to interview and observe inmates and providers of religious, spiritual or moral support because my intentions were to grasp the meanings and interpretations they attach to what they see and do with regard to religion and to understand what they experience in a clearly defined context. I asked different people similar questions in different sites in order to triangulate them. These questions were related to the meaning of religion in everyday life, religious practice, the chaplaincy, the representation of the relationship between chaplaincy and prison administration, religious freedom and freedom of conscience, and the differential treatment of inmates belonging to different religions.[91] In the second phase of my work (2006–2007), I carried out fieldwork as a postdoctoral fellow in different rehabilitation programmes for ex-offenders in Saxony-Anhalt, Brandenburg and East Berlin. All the interviews were transcribed verbatim and coded in conjunction with the observation notes, partly *in vivo* and partly according to codes defined in advance by the questionnaire; overall, I followed the ideas of the grounded theory approach.[92] All the material was then used in my critical discourse analysis, which was in turn influenced by conversational analysis. On the one hand, my approach was therefore inductive; on the other, theory oriented equally the choices I made in the fieldwork. I assured all participants of anonymity, which is why there is only a pseudonym with each quote. I indicate merely the province in which the prison is situated and provide some characteristics of the prisons and of the urban area where I conducted my fieldwork. The sociological profile of the interviewees is summarized briefly to provide the essential information. In this book, I shall not make a detailed analysis of the innumerable quotes but rather use them illustratively, as if they were participating in telling my story.

As to the secondary data, I have carried out only a systematic analysis of one prison magazine. the only one to which I had full access. The statistical data derive from both publicly accessible information and estimates. The laws and rights referred to here were selected with a view to serving my argument. The overarching question that has guided my academic curiosity is the way in which

---

[91]   For the details of the questions, see my thesis: Irene Becci, *Religion and Prison in Modernity: Tensions between Religious Establishment and Religious Diversity – Italy and Germany* (Florence: European University Institute, 2006).

[92]   Cf. Barney Glaser and Anselm L. *Strauss, The Discovery of Grounded Theory: Strategies for Qualitative Research* (Chicago, IL: Aldine Publishing Company, 1967).

the meaning of religion is constructed in the context of relationships of meaning and institutionalized power relations.

The Fieldsites: Two Prisons and a Post-Socialist Urban Space

Some of the prison chaplains agreeable to interview in Berlin, Saxony, Brandenburg and Saxony-Anhalt supported me generously in obtaining authorization to enter the prisons where they worked. I visited seven of these (in particular the chaplaincy, prison cells, offices, chapels and libraries), but I recorded the interviews with inmates only in a prison in Saxony (Prison A) and in Brandenburg (Prison B). The halfway house[93] I observed more closely is part of a major secular association in Berlin that offers a wide range of rehabilitation programmes to ex-prisoners or to people who run the risk of being imprisoned. The following section offers a closer description of these three fieldsites, which comprise the empirical ground for the reflections I shall develop in the last chapter.

Prison A

This prison in Saxony was built originally in the eighteenth century as a house of correction, with space for 200 people, and later became a prison. It expanded quickly to make room for female inmates so that, by the end of the eighteenth century, about 500 people – criminals as well as the 'poor' or 'handicapped' – were kept there. In the following century it became a military prison, and during the Second World War it was the site of horrible executions. There are now just over 400 inmates in this prison; it is located in a suburb of a small town. The large room where the religious services were celebrated originally was transformed into a cinema where political films were shown during the era of the German Democratic Republic (GDR); today, this room is used for leisure activities, such as table tennis. The two chaplains who work in the prison – one Catholic, the other Protestant – adapted rooms close to the prison library, where they provide spiritual care; there is a kitchen, a prayer room and a meeting room. The smell of coffee invades the room. Paintings drawn by inmates hang on the walls.

During the war, this site was the destination for political prisoners. They were tortured, and some were killed and buried in mass graves. Today, a memorial marks the areas that were identified as former mass graves. In the last two decades of the GDR, some buildings of prison A were used as a workhouse for youth, called *Jugendwerkhof*, which functioned as a prison for minors. One chaplain remembers visiting the institution just before it was closed; he feels that what he saw then still resonates when he enters the building to provide spiritual care. The chaplain and an inmate present at the recorded conversation stated their views of prison A:

[93] A halfway house is a housing facility monitoring and supporting people who try to reintegrate with society, usually after prison release.

Chaplain Anton: The worst juvenile workhouse in the whole of the GDR.

Thilo: That's right…

Chaplain Anton: In general they [prisons] are terrible, but [prison A] was worse. If young people 'could not be educated' – as they would say – then Ms Margot Honecker would assign them personally to this prison. Terrible, I saw the juvenile workhouse just before it was closed down … You cannot see it any more today, there's only a memorial, it was horrible. It was a real prison, a real prison.

Thilo: Worse, even worse.

Chaplain Anton: … maybe it was even worse … and perverse … When the Wall came down, those who were still working there tried to redecorate the walls in order to improve the aesthetics of the place, what an idea – they were upholstering the doors, we saw that, the rest of the upholstering material was still lying around, those criminals … those [detained children] who came here and then came out after three to ten months … they told us what happened there. First thing when they arrived [was] they were beaten – that was called 'welcome greetings'.

I:[94] You mean by the employees?

Thilo: Yes, in GDR times, here in [prison A], it was like this.

Chaplain Anton: They were hosed down with water…

Thilo: That's right … I was 15, 15.

Chaplain Anton: We could see the single cells, you could not stand up in there, no windows, [it was] real dark.

Thilo: Yes, the cell was completely empty. At 9pm a mattress was handed over and at 5am it was taken out. They pulled the blanket away – [there was] nothing, [it was] completely empty…

Chaplain Anton: … one of the minor punishments was to have the kids duck walk up and down the stairs … You could not complain … You were told to 'sit in a row, come, you will do this'; nobody could choose any type of apprenticeship. Someone came [and said], 'You do this, you do that.' A terrible time.

---

[94]   Here and in the following cases, '*I*' stands for interviewer – that is, myself.

This interview extract makes clear, first, how important it was for the interviewees to give a personal testimony about the past of a building where they still worked. Although the conditions have changed drastically, it is a real challenge for East Germans to continue working in the very buildings where they experienced injustices.[95] Second, the interview extract is a good illustration of the complicity between inmates and some of the chaplains of the former GDR, with regard to the past.

Today, the prison has its own carpentry, tailoring workshop, garden shop, laundry, repair workshop and kitchen where inmates work. Some professional training possibilities exist as well as facilities for sports or music activities. The first time I entered this prison, I interviewed only the chaplain, in his office. I handed him a short text explaining the purpose of my research and my interest in conducting interviews with inmates. This text was distributed to other prison staff, such as art therapists and social workers. Thanks to their collaboration, some inmates registered for the interview and I obtained the governor's authorization with the help of the chaplain. Therefore, in this prison, not all the inmates were approached by the chaplain and only a few were involved in the activities organized by the chaplaincy.

When I met the governor of prison A in August 2003, he showed me a list that recorded the nationality of all the inmates: 83 per cent were German, 17 per cent were foreigners. About 25 per cent of the foreign inmates were Algerian and another 25 per cent were Vietnamese. There were 21 other nationalities, thus making for a wide range. The chaplains interviewed estimated that only about 7 per cent of the inmates were Protestant and 8 per cent Catholic, as many as Muslim. About 70 per cent of the inmates did not belong to any religion.

The profiles of the inmates can be summarized in the following way:

- *Thilo* and *Stefan* were in their thirties at the time of the interview. They had a average education level and no religious affiliation, socialization or practice. Thilo was close to his release; Stefan, a perky multi-recidivist bank robber, had a longer time to wait.
- *Kai* was in his twenties, had a average education level, and no religious affiliation or practice, but he affirmed a certain openness and curiosity for religious practices.
- *Franz* was a Catholic in his late thirties with an average education level; he did not participate in any religious practices.
- *Johan* saw himself as a 'Jewish Christian', was in his fifties, and attended the religious services regularly.
- *Jamal* was a Muslim originally from North Africa who came to the GDR as a specialized worker. His religious practice is limited to Ramadan. He has a average educational level, speaking many languages fluently.

---

[95]   See Anselma Gallinat, '"Menacing Buildings": Former Political Prisons and Prisoners in Eastern Germany', *Anthropology Today*, 22/2 (2006), 19–20.

- *Jakob* was a Catholic in his forties, not involved in any religious activities offered in prison and with an average education level.
- *Izmil* was a Muslim in his late twenties, originally from the Soviet Union, with limited religious practices (no prayers, partly Ramadan) and a low education level.
- *Bernd* was a well-educated recidivist, aged almost forty years, attending the religious services and other activities of the chaplaincy regularly. In his childhood he had followed some religious teaching in a Protestant parish, but at the time of his interview he had no religious affiliation.
- *Chaplain Anton*, with whom I had several in-depth interviews, was almost fifty when we met. He had been working half time in this prison since spring 1989 as a Protestant Lutheran chaplain. He is local to the area, and had studied theology in Saxony during the 1980s.

Moreover, I interviewed the governor and one art therapist in August 2003 in the rooms of the chaplaincy. I also met the Catholic chaplain, but I did not record our conversation. All the other interviews were recorded and lasted about one hour each. None of them was made under direct surveillance. All interviewees, besides the governor, were East German.

Prison B

Prison B is located in the province of Brandenburg; it, too, has a bloody past. The grey building was constructed during the Nazi regime as one of the most modern prisons in Europe, with space for about 1,800 inmates. During the war, it was occupied by approximately three times as many inmates as it was designed for; these prisoners were forced to make weapons. Thousands of inmates were executed in this prison during the war and hundreds died of disease.[96] The GDR regime continued to use the building as a prison. The conditions were very rough, as the Catholic chaplain Benedict remembers:

> During the GDR [era], an average of 3,000 [inmates] were in [prison B], with some peak periods when the number reached 5,000. And the inmates used to live either in inhuman [conditions] or in tiny, narrow single cells. The majority, however, were in the big cells containing up to 24 or 30 inmates. It was thus very, very inhuman and cramped.

The prisoners now live in various sections: high-security detention, pre-trial detention, open detention. The opportunities in terms of work, leisure and training are similar to prison A. There are three chaplains: two Protestants and a Catholic. Like prison A, prison B is located in the suburb of a small town and may be

---

[96]   Cf. Nikolaus Wachsmann, *Hitler's Prisons: Legal Terror in Nazi Germany* (New Haven, CT: Yale University Press, 2004).

reached by public transport. The prison is often in the news because of both right-wing violence among prisoners and violence between prisoners and officers. The chaplaincy is situated at the margins of the prison building, thus affording a view of the prison's parking lot. When inmates came for the interview, it was not uncommon for them to peek outside first and make comments about what they saw. My first visit to this prison involved participation in one of the chaplaincy's group meetings. The furniture in the waiting room at the entrance still bore the unmistakable GDR production style of the 1970s, while the chaplaincy rooms were full of plants. I introduced myself to the dozen inmates participating in the group meeting, explaining briefly what I was working on and that I wished to meet and interview them individually. During the following fortnight, the inmates were invited to communicate their interest in meeting me to the chaplain, and he would then ask for authorization. One month later, I returned to conduct the interviews with the inmates; I was then also able to interview two other Protestant chaplains and a Baptist minister who worked as a volunteer for a drug rehabilitation programme within the prison.

Of the inmates, 16 per cent were not German at the time I visited this prison, but came mostly from Poland and Vietnam. Only about 10 per cent of the inmates were Protestant or Catholic. At least two thirds of the inmates did not belong to any religion. One of the Protestant chaplains interviewed estimated that 5 per cent of the total prison population was Protestant. I interviewed seven inmates and four chaplains, all East German, in this prison:

- *Martin* was in his twenties at the time of the interview. He had an average education level, was Protestant, and attended the religious services regularly.
- *Justus* was in his thirties, had an average education level, and was converting to Catholicism.
- *Roland* was in his late thirties, had an average education level, and was converting to Buddhism.
- *Wim* and *Christof* were two well-educated elderly men attending regularly the religious services and other activities of the chaplaincy, such as group meetings. Neither had any religious affiliation. During their long detention they followed literature and economic courses. They contributed to the prison news magazine.
- *Lars* was in his forties and had an average education level. He stated that he had no religious affiliation, but he attended the weekly religious services regularly. For many years he had been involved in the prison news magazine.
- *Steven* had no religious affiliation, was about twenty, and had a low education level.
- I had a first long in-depth interview with *Chaplain Benedict* when he was in his mid-fifties. Coming originally from one of the Catholic enclaves in Brandenburg, he had studied Catholic Theology in Thuringia during the

late 1960s and early 1970. In 1988, some years after his consecration as a priest, he had started to work as a chaplain in prison B.

- *Chaplain Boris* was about fifty when I interviewed him. He had studied Theology in East Berlin and had been employed as a Lutheran prison chaplain as early as 1997.
- *Chaplain Bruno* was also a Protestant diaconal chaplain with ten years' experience of working in prison B. He was originally from West Berlin.
- *Sebastian*, a Baptist volunteer, was in his sixties when I interviewed him. Since 1993 he had been leading voluntarily a 'drugfree area in prison' offering detoxication classes for alcoholics with some religious instruction. He had grown up in a Baptist family but had become pious only after his imprisonment during the GDR times.

Moreover, I interviewed other ex-inmates of prison B, such as Ulrich and Manfred, later on in Berlin and Brandenburg.

The East Berlin Halfway House

In a halfway house, former prison inmates start a demanding and long-lasting process of resuming daily spatial, physical and social routines. Since its opening in the 1990s, the housing programme I observed, which is part of a larger association also offering support with employment issues, drug rehabilitation, and computer, language and arts classes, had hosted hundreds of ex-prisoners, giving them valuable support after their release.

During the period of the GDR, the area where the halfway house is located had been at the very centre of East Berlin and had thus been well known and visited for its commercial activities. Today, it is unpopular, as the media and the public discourse in Berlin portray it as a centre for right-wing[97] extremism.[98] Its five- to

---

[97] Deutsche Welle, 'World Cup Guide Highlights Germany's Racist Hotspots', 3 May 2006, at www.dw.de/dw/article/0,1991934,00.html, accessed 31 May 2012.

[98] For the notion of right-wing extremism in Germany, I refer to Hans-Gerd Jaschke, *Rechtsextremismus und Fremdenfeindlichkeit. Begriffe – Positionen – Praxisfelder*, 2nd edn (Opladen: Westdeutscher Verlag, 2001), 30. According to Jaschke, the following elements are contained in right-wing attitudes, behaviours or actions: a consideration of human beings as socially unequal on the basis of racial or ethnical considerations, the strive towards an ethnic homogeneity of people, a rejection of the UN human rights declaration, as well as value pluralism inherent in liberal democracy, a stress upon the priority of the community over the individual, the submission of citizens to the state, and the aim of calling off democracy. For the right-wing activities in Eastern Germany, see Richard Stöss, 'Rechtsextremismus', in Oskar Niedermayer (ed.), *Intermediäre Strukturen in Ostdeutschland* (Opladen: Leske+Budrich, 1996), 193–213; for East Berlin, see Claudia Luzar, *Rechtsextremismus in der Weitlingstraße 'Mythos oder Realität?' Problemaufriss im Berliner Bezirk Lichtenberg* (Berlin: ZDK Gesellschaft Demokratische Kultur, 2006).

six thousand inhabitants have a rather low income. Their houses, built originally for manual workers, are outdated and part of the state's comprehensive restoration plan. The unemployment rate is high, while the percentage of non-Germans, including non-East Germans, is well below 10.[99] Among the non-German residents of the area, the attention is mainly on Turkish shop owners – when they are the victims of right-wing attacks – or on the Vietnamese. In 1996 and 1997, the media reported widely of violent deaths presumed to have been committed by rival Vietnamese gangs.[100] Even today, the term 'Vietnamese mafia' resounds among the local inhabitants and people do not show great surprise when they see massive police operations accompanying arrests made in the area. Cigarettes on the black market are often sold by Vietnamese people at the entrances of underground stations, shopping malls and supermarkets.[101] The main concerns that have arisen here since post-Socialism include the concentration and increase of right-wing extremism in public,[102] black-market activities, and related violence and unemployment.[103]

I followed the activities of this house as a participant observer (with some restrictions)[104] for a year starting at the end of summer 2006. The halfway house is actually composed of two linked buildings: one at the front with five small flats for ex-inmates, the offices of the social workers, and the common dining-room,[105] and one at the side, where the eight ex-inmates have fully furnished studio flats and a common living room on the top floor. Some of the flats in the house at the front were rented to 'regular tenants', but as soon as one of them moved out, the social workers of the programme managed to have one of their former 'clients' move in.

---

[99]   TOPOS Stadtforschung, *Sozialuntersuchung Sanierungsgebiete Weitlingstraße* (Berlin: TOPOS Stadtforschung, 2007), 84–5. See also Franz-Josef Kemper, 'Restructuring of Housing and Ethnic Segregation: Recent Developments in Berlin', *Urban Studies*, 35/10 (1998), 1765–89, at 1771.

[100]   Cf. 'Schießerei unter Vietnamesen' (Gunfight among Vietnamese), *Berliner Zeitung*, 6 June 1997, at http://www.berliner-zeitung.de/archiv/schiesserei-unter-vietnamesen,10810590,9286610.html, accessed 2 July 2012.

[101]   These Vietnamese find themselves in a peculiar situation of illegality: after 1989, those who had been hired as workers by the GDR received no residence permits, contrary to the migrants coming from South Vietnam – they benefited from the refugee status. Cf. among others Pipo Bui, *Envisioning Vietnamese Migrants in Germany* (Berlin, Hamburg and Münster: Lit, 2003).

[102]   See Luzar, *Rechtsextremismus*.

[103]   For the different relations to space in Berlin with regard to right-wing extremism, see Nitzan Shoshan, 'Placing the Extremes: Cityscape, Ethnic "Others" and Young Right Extremists in East Berlin', *Journal of Contemporary European Studies*, 16/3 (2008), 377–91.

[104]   My participation was limited in the sense that I could be at the halfway house only during the day. For further details on restricted participation, see Kathleen Musante DeWalt and Billie R. DeWalt, 'Participant Observation', in H.R. Bernard (ed.), *Handbook of Methods in Cultural Anthropology* (Walnut Creek, CA: AltaMira Press, 1998), 259–99.

[105]   These rooms used to host a 'sensual massage saloon', meaning a brothel.

In order to join the programme, prisoners have to make a formal request. The social workers at the house evaluate each request, visit the applicants in prison, and come to a decision after examining individuals' motivations and eligibility. Ex-inmates are allowed to stay in the programme for up to two years. They are not required to abstain from alcohol altogether, but they are expected to refrain from drinking in the communal areas of the house. Ex-convicts participate on a voluntary basis and are motivated to desist from committing crimes. The programme is characterized by secularity, and has a pragmatic rather than moralistic orientation.

The ex-inmates were often bitter, their attitudes harsh and strongly gendered – either aggressive and misogynist or flirtatious and sexualized. Most of the inhabitants were multi-recidivists and (former) addicts of alcohol or drugs and had the experience of long-term imprisonment. With one exception, they were all East German. I had closer contact with the following ex-inmates of the programme:

- *Yanna* from East Berlin was in her late forties. As a child she had received some Protestant education and she had worked as a nurse for the elderly. While she was battered by her partner she also became an alcoholic. She had often been imprisoned, during and after the GDR, for violent offences against the police. Her strong body and the numerous scars on her skin reveal the experience of physical violence. Several years ago, as a client of the programme, she had arrived at the halfway house because she had followed her partner, also an ex-inmate. In prison, and during the programme in which she participated to obtain an early release from prison, she got to know the Salvation Army and became increasingly involved in the activities of the group. Her dream at the time of interviewing was to become a soldier in the Salvation Army and to receive the right to live with her two young daughters. She helped out regularly in one of the Salvation's support centres for the homeless and considered the other volunteers as her family.
- *Conrad* was almost seventy years old and belonged to the Catholic Church. While walking around the area, he had noticed the Apostolic church and asked me whether it was part of the Catholic Church. As I indicated a Catholic church located a little further away within the area, he seemed to be sceptical. As he was very withdrawn, I could never figure out why; I merely noticed that his being homosexual was part of that religious scepticism.
- *Ulrich* was born in Brandenburg in the 1960s as one of six siblings. He was illiterate and a dry alcoholic when he arrived at the programme. He had been married for 25 years and was the father of three young adults. Due to his alcohol addiction he had been imprisoned for many 'petty' crimes, such as driving without a licence (and thereby causing accidents and escaping), and some more violent ones, during 20 years. Hence he could be described as a multi-recidivist. Before he went to prison B, he had lived as a homeless person. During that time he had been badly beaten up by right-wing extremists and still suffered from the injuries. In prison, he attended the detoxification classes organized by *Sebastian*, where he learned some biblical maxims.

- *Manfred* was born in the 1980s in Brandenburg; he was one of five children. His father was an alcoholic, who was often in prison and violent towards his mother. Manfred had spent most of his childhood in children's homes and had attended school for nine years. Then he became homeless and was eventually imprisoned for armed robbery, extortion and aggravated assault. He was an alcoholic and displayed an anarchist and punk identity, looking aggressive and shy at the same time. Homes became his family, as he used to explain: 'I got simply alienated from my parents or from the life outside, one can say. My only family was the home.' In prison he participated in the Bible reading classes and wrote poems for the prison journal. A psychiatric report from the medical staff of prison B termed Manfred 'specifically dangerous' as his 'personality was inhibited but aggressive, his social competences were clearly lacking'. He was diagnosed as 'unable to stand conflicts, to solve problems, unsure and impulsive'.
- *Hans* was not living in this halfway house when I interviewed him in September 2006, but he attended some of the activities proposed by this association. He was in his early forties. During the time of the German Democratic Republic, he had already attended a Christian rehabilitation programme. In prison B, he started to become interested in religious questions despite his strong atheistic family background – his father 'was in the Party', as he put it, and 'at home, religion played no role at all', which was, he explained, the inevitable consequence of the fact that 'he grew up in East Germany'. In spring 1989, he was imprisoned for manslaughter, after having been sentenced to serve more than fifteen years.
- *Mathias* was in his late thirties and had grown up in Brandenburg, living with adoptive parents. He had never met his biological parents. He had been a multi-recidivist for felonies such as aggravated assault. Since a psychiatrist had diagnosed attention deficit disorder, Mathias was exempt from work. Due to his condition, he was unable to keep any commitments and could be impulsive and nervous. Wherever he was, people would notice his clumsiness. He had been a punk and had lived for years in central stations. His general scepticism was also directed towards religion.
- *Philipp* was born in the 1960s and raised in the 'East', as he put it. He had been a metalworker for 26 years during Socialism, but he lost his job when the political system collapsed and he became an alcoholic. Having committed a robbery while drunk, he was sentenced to seven years in prison but was released earlier because he agreed to attend detoxification therapy at an evangelical institution in the outskirts of Berlin. While at the halfway house, he suffered a stroke.
- *Doris*, a woman in her thirties, was responsible for the programme and the only permanent full-time member of staff. Three other people worked in the house in the frame of state-run occupational programmes; I spent hours with them every day.

Chapter 1

Modern Prisons in Eastern Germany: Between Secular and Christian Projects

In Germany, pastoral care in prison has existed as such since the end of the eighteenth century.[1] At the time, in Protestant areas the treatment of criminals became a combination of secular and religious individualized disciplinary practices: it combined hard labour, religious instruction, and isolation.[2] These were considered necessary conditions for achieving reparation for the crime committed and for freeing the criminal from carrying the burden of culpability. However, the philanthropic penitentiary projects that the positivists and Quakers initiated were too costly in a time of revolutions, poverty and general conflicts.[3] According to them, two essential elements had to be combined in

---

[1]   Cf. Sarah Jahn, 'Gefängnisseelsorge in der Bundesrepublik Deutschland', in Michael Klöcker and Udo Tworuschka (eds), *Handbuch der Religionen* (Landsberg and Munich: Olzog Verlag, 2011 [1997]), 1–22, at 2–3.

[2]   In Saxony by the sixteenth century, public punishment had slowly been replaced by public work. Convicts who were originally condemned to die and then had the 'grace' to work instead were reminded of their privilege by a burn mark on their skin, an image of the type of death they were supposed to undergo: the gallows, the sword or the wheel. See Erich Viehöfer, 'Zur Entwicklung des Strafvollzugs in Sachsen im 18. Jahrhundert', in Staatsministerium der Justiz (ed.), *Hinter Gittern. Drei Jahrhunderte Strafvollzug in Sachsen* (Leipzig: Staatsministerium der Justiz, 1998), at http://www.justiz.sachsen.de/content/683.htm, accessed 29 June 2012.

[3]   In the ideal prison, where at any moment of the day movements were ruled, normalized and codified in every detail, the Quakers hoped 'for religion to work as a technology of the self: Christianity was to work inside the individual. The prisoner was in other words to engage '"the other" inside himself, thereby reshaping his personality' – Peter Scharff Smith, 'A Religious Technology of the Self: Rationality and Religion in the Rise of the Modern Penitentiary', *Punishment and Society*, 6/2 (2004), 195–220, at 207. The Eastern State Penitentiary in Philadelphia, their first major realization of this ideal, rested on the principle of total solitary confinement. Once isolated, the inmate would be extremely receptive to moralizing voices coming from the director, the chaplain or the instructor. As Alexis de Tocqueville remarks, the prisoner, '[t]hrown into solitude … reflects. Placed alone, in view of his crime, he learns to hate it; and if his soul be not yet surfeited with crime, and thus have lost all taste for any thing better, it is in solitude, where remorse will come to assail him … Can there be a combination more powerful for reformation than that of a prison which hands over the prisoner to all the trials of solitude, leads him through reflection to remorse, through religion to hope; makes him industrious by the burden of idleness, and which, whilst it inflicts the torment of solitude, makes him find a charm in

prison to encourage rehabilitation through religion: first, a presupposed sense of being lonely; second, the possibility to live in accordance with the religion as presented in the institution. Neither the Quakers' ideals concerning penitentiaries nor the ideals of the *relative theory of sentence* gained any support in the German political arena. Some resistance came in particular from German Idealism and its influence on penal philosophy. Representatives of this philosophy, such as Immanuel Kant and Georg Wilhelm Friedrich Hegel, would advocate retaliation as a response to crime, which was based on a retributivist theory: a criminal act calls for a punishment that is proportional to the harm caused, without any other consideration being taken into account. Advocates of this approach opposed utilitarian ideas about sentences. Punishment is a categorical imperative necessary to treat every crime in the same way and to re-establish a juridical order. The correspondence between crime and punishment was presented as a neutral system that allowed for impartial judgement. In this intellectual atmosphere, attempts at introducing rehabilitative and philanthropic ideas relied strongly upon the churches and smaller Protestant denominations, such as Pietists and Jansenists. Only some reformers were able to introduce the idea of deterrence and retribution into the justice system, but the reality of imprisonment in German penal institutions at the turn of the century did not live up to the intentions of the prison reformers. There were gradual improvements in healthcare, hygiene and food provision, however, which contributed to a fall in inmate mortality.[4]

The process concerned not only Germany, as David Garland writes: at the beginning of the nineteenth century, 'a great criminal law reform swept Europe setting up codes, defining offences and scales of penalties, reorganizing procedure and jurisdiction'.[5] In Germany, however, the reforms, 'created a cruel

---

the converse of pious men, whom otherwise he would have seen with indifference, and heard without pleasure?' See Gustave de Beaumont and Alexis de Tocqueville, *On the Penitentiary System in the United States, and its Application in France; with an Appendix on Penal Colonies, and also Statistical Notes*, trans. Francis Lieber (Philadelphia, PA: Carey, Lea and Blanchard, 1833), 22, 51; quoted in Normann Johnston, Kenneth Finkel and Jeffrey A. Cohen, *Eastern State Penitentiary: Crucible of Good Intentions* (Philadelphia, PA: Philadelphia Museum of Art, 2000), 29. Part of the same passage is also quoted by Michel Foucault in *Surveiller et Punir. Naissance de la prison* (Paris: Gallimard, 1975), 274. The effects of solitude would predispose inmates positively to receive religious instruction. At the entrance prisoners were stripped symbolically of their identity: they had to leave behind their clothes and belongings and they were called by a new neutral term: see Johnston et al., *Eastern State*, 48–9. The entrance rituals also aimed at eliminating signs of previous criminal behaviour. As Erving Goffman has illustrated perfectly, this is now a defining feature of all total institutions: see *Asylums: Essays on the Social Situation of Mental Patients and Other Inmates* (Harmondsworth: Penguin, 1991 [1961]), 26.

   [4]   Nikolaus Wachsmann, *Hitler's Prisons: Legal Terror in Nazi Germany* (New Haven, CT, and London: Yale University Press, 2004), 23.

   [5]   David Garland, *Punishment and Modern Society* (Oxford: Clarendon Press, 1990), 142.

system of isolation and depersonalisation for most prisoners. Life inside German penal institutions was characterized above all by uniformity and strict discipline.'[6]

In Protestant Prussia, the organization of prisons placed an emphasis upon labour and military discipline: continuous hard labour and an ascetic life were considered necessary conditions to achieve liberation from sin, be it during or after life. Only in this way could the causes of criminal behaviour, laziness and pleasure from earthly goods, be removed from a person. Pastors in prisons were key figures in accomplishing the disciplining and punishing tasks because, as a German pastor wrote in 1866, in order to fulfil its functions the prison needed a Christian worldview. In his opinion, the prison

> had to be built to allow God's Word to fully deploy its efficacy. God's Word is the foundation on which the prison has to be constructed if we want it to become a sanatorium. It is not sufficient to have a church in the prison; the prison itself shall be the Lord's house![7]

Discipline emerged as a combination of outer and inner submission to authority. The prison administration was responsible for the former, the church for the latter. The German pastors conceived their work in prisons as a mission that was also oriented towards regaining some closeness to the lower-class people, a closeness that the Protestant Church had lost. The chaplains' role was to put the prisoners on the 'right path'. Together with the teachers, they 'believed that they should implant discipline, religious devotion and nationalism in the prisoners'.[8] According to the regulations of 1888 on pastoral care in Saxon prisons, religious celebrations had to take place every week and only inmates with a special authorization were allowed not to attend them.[9] Paragraph 74 of the regulations provided the right for Jewish inmates to fulfil religious practices on the Sabbath or other holy days. The Protestant chaplains were told exactly how they had to preach – that is, to expose in a 'most simple, short, precise and insistent way the basic evangelical truth about sin and mercy'. Their tone, however, had also to express their love and care for the inmates' salvation. Before allowing inmates to participate in the sacrament of the Last Supper, the chaplains had to be convinced that 'they were truly wishing to

---

[6]   Ibid.

[7]   Carl Wilhelm Haenell, *System der Gefängniskunde* (Göttingen: Vandenhoeck & Ruprecht, 1866), 43, my translation; quoted in Alexander Böhm, 'Zum 75-jährigen Bestehen der Evangelischen Konferenz für Gefängnisseelsorge in Deutschland', *Reader Gefängnis-seelsorge*, 11 (1995), 39–49, at 43. One further sign of the omnipresence of religion was the number of religious books in the prison library. For instance, in the prison in Bruchsal, of the 3,000 books available, 400 were bibles, 500 contained only church hymns, and 400 were religious books for school instruction and pietistic education.

[8]   Wachsmann, *Hitler's Prisons*, 23.

[9]   See *Seelsorge in Gerichtsgefängnissen* (Provinz Sachsen and Leitender Ausschuss der Gefängnisgesellschaft zu Halle a. S., 1888).

be saved'. The regulations also warned chaplains about the possibility of inmates abusing the sacrament. The noted aim of such pastoral care was to awaken in the prisoners the sense of guilt, to comfort and improve them. Chaplains needed to consider themselves spiritual friends of inmates and not their judges, so that inmates could trust them. The costs for the chaplains' salaries and for the Bible or the New Testaments were paid by state authorities. The daily schedule of the Waldheim prison in Saxony, which was, for instance, organized according to the Auburn model, contained several periods for prayers and attendance of religious services, alternating with periods of work.[10]

A similar understanding of how the tasks were to be shared by state and church actors equally emerged in the outer society. A range of associations proposed to meet social needs besides the state. The best-known examples from the Christian side are *Caritas*, which began in 1897 as an umbrella organization of Roman Catholic relief and social service agencies, or the *Diakonie*, which is the organized Protestant social welfare provision that started as an 'internal mission' as early as 1848. In 1925, the *Schwarzes Kreuz* – the black cross – was created as a trans-denominational network of committed Christians, comprising numerous volunteers with a free evangelical background and offering social help in particular with regard to addiction. Since the establishment of the Weimar Republic, the range of associations providing such services has been organized into larger associations, called *Spitzenverbände* (umbrella organizations), having professional organizational structures.

At the end of the nineteenth century, prisons became increasingly expensive and came to be perceived as unjustifiable by taxpayers, who viewed the state as financing unsuccessful prison experiments. There was no actual reduction in crime. The financial argument made the Auburn model seem favourable, as its advantage was that 'inmates laboring in workshops returned a profit that fully covered the costs of their incarceration'.[11] The idea that prisoners could produce something, rather than be costly and merely consume, prevailed. With the arrival of the twentieth century, the churches were forced to abandon the equation of the prison and the house of the Lord, and they confined their help increasingly to the areas of social needs and purely spiritual assistance. However, the general idea that prison needs religion has not disappeared; on the contrary, such thoughts still dominate, as Chaplain Anton stated: 'Since 1850 the pastor was the moral authority in prison; he was the second in command after the prison governor.'

Prison chaplaincy has also emerged as a means of control and a support to self-control, although motivated by humanistic and philanthropic aims. In 1919, the

---

[10]   The internal prison regulations in Saxony in 1883 prescribed compulsory participation in religious services for all inmates. Moreover, daily devotional exercise after breakfast and dinner was essential for all inmates, regardless of their religious affiliation. On particular days, a church member would hold the devotions, which were composed of songs and the reading of a Bible passage, a sermon or a prayer. See Viehöfer, *Zur Entwicklung*, 11.

[11]   Johnston et al., *Eastern State*, 54, 56.

Weimar Constitution introduced Article 141, explicitly about spiritual care. Such a care was not stipulated to be compulsory, but to be guaranteed in case a need for it was expressed:

Article 141

To the extent that a need exists for religious services and pastoral work in the army, in hospitals, in prisons, or in other public institutions, religious societies shall be permitted to provide them, but without compulsion of any kind.[12]

During this period, some prison reforms were made that aimed to strengthen social support for convicts, thereby weakening indirectly the role and importance of discipline and religious discipline in particular. The reaction of prison chaplains was immediate:

generally employed by the state and not the church, they reacted critically to aspects of the prison reforms advanced in the 1920s, arguing that the new policies did not force prisoners to confront their moral failings and guilt. In addition, the chaplains were clearly concerned that social workers would eventually edge them out of the penal institutions – just as traditional religious welfare organizations in the Weimar Republic at large feared that their moral and religious conception of charity was being pushed aside by the secular welfare state.[13]

Prison chaplains were not the only ones to act as a brake to reformatory trends that sought to introduce rehabilitative measures. According to Wachsmann, there were 'loud calls by journalists, politicians and prison officials for cuts in prison provisions and a return to stricter treatment … which was pursued with more vigour than ever during the depression.'[14] In 1924, the chaplains' role was reduced to celebrating religious services and to individual spiritual care. They could no longer interfere in the organization of the prison itself in terms of instruction or activities.

Nevertheless, the prison law of 1927 stated that every inmate had to be allowed to meet a chaplain or a minister of his/her religion. In fact, prisons 'still relied on teachers and prison chaplains to "reform" the inmates. In 1927, there were 864 state-employed chaplains (125 of them full-time) and 150 teachers (122 of them full-time) working in all the penal institutions.'[15]

---

[12]   Translated by Professor Christian Tomuschat and Professor David P. Currie, revised by Professor Christian Tomuschat and Professor Donald P. Kommers in cooperation with the Language Service of the German Bundestag, 2010.

[13]   Wachsmann, *Hitler's Prisons*, 33.

[14]   Ibid., 64.

[15]   Ibid., 31. A Protestant prison chaplains' association was created in 1927; since unification, its name has been *Evangelische Konferenz für Gefängnisseelsorge in Deutschland*.

The National–Socialist regime stopped penal law reforms and reinstated a system that was only intent on repression. Arrangements between the churches and the state guaranteed the presence of a chaplain in prison, but his authority lost importance and would depend increasingly on the prison administration. According to Wachsmann,

> in the early years of the Third Reich, slightly greater emphasis was placed on religious instruction. At the start of the Third Reich, prison chaplains hoped that religion, and with it their own role in penal institutions, would be strengthened, following concern that their status might be eroded by the Weimar prison reforms. They were not completely disappointed ... prison inmates were forced to attend religious services. Refusal to do so could lead to disciplinary punishment ... However, there was no religious revival in penal institutions in the Third Reich.[16]

At the same time, through their support of the resistance movement of the political prisoners that opposed the government, many other pastors led the basis for serious consideration during the post-war period.[17] Legally speaking, chaplaincy was considered to be part of the prison system, unless it was stated expressly that a particular prison did not offer any pastoral care. Where the National–Socialist regime allowed pastoral care, it not only reintroduced compulsory church attendance but also obliged inmates to attend Bible and religious instruction several days per week. Chaplains could visit inmates at any time, and they administered the libraries. They were also responsible for the inmates once they had left prison in terms of their finding a job and a home. During the Second World War, chaplains were the only remaining non-military employees admitted in prisons, but their presence could not change any of the devastating Nazi prison practices. In legal and institutional terms, nothing of this period has remained in place for prison chaplaincy. Therefore I do not elaborate further on it, but continue to some considerations of religion, imprisonment and release during Socialism in the next section.

Imprisonment and the Forcing of Secularization in Socialism

At the end of the Second World War, the occupation of Eastern Germany by Soviet troops and of Western Germany by the Allied Forces created a further split of the country, at a religious level. In the Federal Republic of Germany (FRG) Catholics predominated, whereas in the German Democratic Republic the majority of the

---

[16]   Ibid., 90.
[17]   Cf. Böhm, 'Zum 75-jährigen'. The life history of Dietrich Bonhöffer offers a clear illustration of this.

population were Protestants, with very low levels of religious practice.[18] In the FRG, churches enjoyed high moral legitimacy and were able to consolidate their authority;[19] in the GDR, churches' legitimacy was constantly attacked.

While there is no doubt that the general orientation of the GDR government was atheistic, in contemporary literature interpretations of its precise relationship with religious institutions vary. One of the two main contrasting claims[20] holds that the churches could keep a certain independence from the state and were not submitted to its complete control.[21] Contrary to the Soviet case, there was, for instance, an authorized (though tightly controlled) Christian Party in the GDR; however, it was not necessarily in step with the church. In the same vein, a 'Luther commemoration year' was celebrated – indeed, it seems no exaggeration to suggest that Martin Luther was one of the historical heroes of the German Socialist 'nation'. The opposite thesis argues rather that the state of the *Sozialistische Einheitspartei Deutschlands* (SED, the governing party since its creation in 1949) was totalitarian and that churches were submitted entirely to its domination or even supported it.[22] Various churches were destroyed for state purposes such as the construction of the Berlin Wall. And pastors, although members of an institution not only officially recognized by the state but also actively collaborating with it,

---

[18]   Cf. in particular Karl Gabriel, 'Déchristianisation et sécularisation. Aspects sociologiques et statistiques', in Paul Colonge and Rudolf Lill (eds), *Histoire religieuse de l'Allemagne* (Paris: Cerf, 2000), 333–48, at 338.

[19]   In the FRG, several parties that referred explicitly to Christianity were created after the war. The state sought the cooperation and partnership of the church on various issues, in particular in order to meet the social needs and demands of the population. The Protestants in the FRG united under the umbrella of the German Protestant Church (EKD). Its leading positions were occupied by the members of the 'confessing church', and the Protestant theology of that time was suffused with Karl Barth's writings. The debate on Penal Law resulted in reform in 1977: a large number of teachers and social workers were employed, which meant that the role of chaplains in the rehabilitation process was reduced. They continued nevertheless to play an essential role in spiritual and human matters. Catholic and Protestant chaplains remained employees of the state.

[20]   Cf. Herbert Heinecke, *Konfession und Politik in der DDR. Das Wechselverhältnis von Kirche und Staat im Vergleich zwischen evangelischer und katholischer Kirche* (Leipzig: Evangelische Verlagsanstalt, 2002).

[21]   This perspective is supported by the facts that, up to the 1980s, thousands of persons worked full time for the churches, be it as active clergy or in hospitals, homes for the mentally and physically disabled, old people's homes, orphanages, or nurseries, and that state universities included faculties of 'Protestant Theology' – see Sabrina P. Ramet, *Nihil obstat: Religion, Politics, and Social Change in East-Central Europe and Russia* (Durham, NC, and London: Duke University Press, 1998).

[22]   Gerhard Besier has supplied arguments for this position. Cf. for instance, Besier and Stephan Wolf, *'Pfarrer, Christen und Katholiken'. Das Ministerium für Staatssicherheit der ehemaligen DDR und die Kirche* (Neukirchen-Vluyn: Neukirchener Verlag, 1991); Besier, *Der SED-Staat und die Kirche 1969–1990. Die Vision vom 'Dritten Weg'* (Berlin: Propyläen, 1995); and Besier, *Der SED-Staat und die Kirche 1983–1991* (Berlin: Propyläen, 1995).

were spied on no less by the state police than were ordinary citizens. A variety of historical facts concerning the fate of religion at the time may be mentioned to support either of the two views. The situation of religion in the GDR changed over time and according to the various leaders in place (both in the party and in the church), some of whom were rather confrontational, while others looked for reciprocal adjustments. Distinguishing the different hierarchical levels composing a 'church' – for instance, single parishes or the consistory office (at some point, the Protestant church directorate was closely controlled by the SED) – also nuances the perspective, as does considering the socioeconomic conditions and, of course, the particular denominations. Additionally, the government's relationship with churches and religious communities would vary from one region to another.[23]

In the following section, I shall offer, on the basis of my informants' narratives, a partial historical reconstruction of the secularizing effect of church–state relations during the GDR period. These memories continue to direct and lend meaning to their social actions today, and thereby create continuity.

Although the first GDR constitution formally adopted the article of the Weimar Republic relating to religious freedom, subsequently the state put a lot of energy into disseminating an atheist worldview and confronting Protestantism. In Ramet's words, the government often gave two-edged guarantees: for example, the assurance that religion was a 'private affair' meant primarily that religious associations had no right to play any role in public life or to speak out on public issues.[24]

The bones of contention between the Protestant and Catholic churches and the government concerned a wide range of issues: education, discrimination at work, freedom of movement, the environment, national defence, and so on.[25] In the early 1950s, the SED was intent on breaking the inter-German links among churches – West German church periodicals were banned, for example. The government also weakened churches economically, by stopping almost all subsidies in 1953. Formerly, churches had had the right to collect taxes through the state, but the payment of church taxes was now placed on a voluntary basis and the financial services did not inform churches of willing church taxpayers. Churches had no right of access to the lists of taxpayers, and soon also lost the right to force the payment of outstanding church taxes. They were also prevented from carrying

---

[23]   Kristin Wappler illustrates this point by drawing on the example of schools in one of the Christian enclaves of the former GDR: *Klassenzimmer ohne Gott. Schulen im katholischen Eichsfeld und protestantischen Erzgebirge unter SED-Herrschaft* (Duderstadt: Mecke, 2007).

[24]   Cf. Ramet, *Nihil obstat*.

[25]   The constitution of 1968 dealt with the relationship between religion and state in Article 39, which was a shorter version of its counterpart in the constitution of 1949. It affirmed religious freedom, but insisted that it was important to exercise it in conformity with the GDR's legislative and administrative restrictions. The constitution prohibited expressly the use of churches for anti-constitutional aims and did not authorize the opening of new theological faculties or denominational schools.

out street or house collections. The most significant financial support came from donations by church members.[26]

Tensions between the two institutions culminated in 1954 with the introduction of the ritual of youth consecration, the *Jugendweihe*, a Socialist consecration ceremony for young people.[27] This signalled a shift of the state's battle against the churches from the organizational to the ideological level because the resemblance to the model of the Christian confirmation was evident. Both churches reacted very strongly against the youth consecration and excluded those who celebrated it from the equivalent religious ceremony.[28] Committed Christians found themselves in a double bind, as Chaplain Anton, born in those years, recalls:

> The youth consecration – that was a very hot issue, and the church, I think, reacted in a very strange way. That is, it forced people to choose: either the youth ceremony or confirmation. And this was, under the political circumstances of the time, a catastrophe for people – they had to decide when one actually could not really decide.

According to Karstein, Schmidt-Lux and Wohlrab-Sahr,[29] the genesis of secularization in East Germany revolves mainly around this kind of conflict, which resulted both from constant challenges by the Socialist regime and the equally constant but somehow more ambiguous resistance of churches, and from the way in which these conflicts were reflected in the choices, which had to be made again and again, between membership and ritual participation, between religious and Socialist morality, between scientific and religious worldviews. Religiously involved East Germans reacted to repression by differentiating, in their personal lives, between spheres of authenticity and the sphere of the state, typically deemed inauthentic: they tended either to exclude or to differentiate the opposing worldviews – for instance, by following Luther's doctrine of the two realms in identifying 'a father state and a mother church', which put their lives on

---

[26]   At the end of the 1960s, the churches received state funding for remunerating pastors, for the administration of the churches, and for the charitable services they offered. During the 1970s and 1980s, the Protestant churches received financial support from their sister churches abroad, in particular from the Protestant Church in the FRG and the Lutheran World Federation and the Protestant Lutheran Church in the United States. Additionally, the state financed the theological faculties existing at universities.

[27]   For a more detailed account, cf. Nikolai Vukov, 'Secular Rituals and Political Commemorations in Eastern Germany, 1945–1956', in Małgorzata Rajtar and Esther Peperkamp (eds), *Religion and the Secular in Eastern Germany: 1945 to the Present* (Leiden and Boston: Brill, 2010), 41–60.

[28]   It was only after the 1973 Dresden Synod that the Catholic Church reduced penalties for youth and their parents for participating in the consecration.

[29]   Uta Karstein, Thomas Schmidt-Lux and Monika Wohlrab-Sahr, *Forcierte Säkularität. Religiöser Wandel und Generationendynamik im Osten Deutschlands* (Frankfurt am Main: Campus Verlag, 2009).

dual tracks and made things complicated – or they tried to integrate ideologically Socialist principles with Christian principles, such as community, sincerity and work. Apart from the youth consecration, an individual's whole life (birth, marriage and death) in the GDR was marked by Socialist festivities reminding individuals that they belonged to a Socialist society and a Socialist state. State authorities interfered regularly in church events, harassing student congregations and student pastors. Being a Christian was certainly not easy during that period, as Sebastian remembers:

> I, too, experienced personally the persecution at school because I was a Christian, because my parents were Christians. We had the police at the house and so forth – I had the experience of all that.

A serious conflict arose in 1962, when the GDR introduced compulsory military service.[30] The Protestant Church pleaded for the introduction of a civic service as an alternative, but only managed to obtain a concession in 1964 when non-combatant construction units were created; these were controlled by the army and only open to those who refused to serve in the army for religious reasons.[31] This conflict entailed a long-term aggravation of the relationship between church and state. In 1969, the eight different Protestant churches on the territory of the GDR were obliged to unite and create the Union of Protestant Lutheran Churches of the GDR, and were detached from the West German Protestant churches.[32] This coalition had a clearly sympathetic attitude towards Marxism since it was rooted ideologically in the writings of Karl Barth and Dietrich Bonhöffer. On this intellectual basis, the Protestant Church organized campaigns on a large number of political fields: international politics (peace, NATO, civil service), ecological concerns (pollution, nuclear energy), gender issues (abortion, homosexuality), human rights (political prisoners,[33] freedom of speech and movement), and so on. In the 1980s, a church-

---

[30]   All males between the ages of 18 and 50 became liable for service in the *Volksarmee* (People's Army).

[31]   Cf. Lawrence Klippenstein, 'Conscientious Objectors in Eastern Europe: The Quest for Free Choice and Alternative Service', in *Protestantism and Politics in Eastern Europe and Russia: The Communist and Postcommunist Eras* (Durham, NC, and London: Duke University Press, 1992), 276–309, at 276. It was only at the end of 1989 that the GDR began to grant civic service as an alternative to military service.

[32]   The union had several names: 'Church for the Others' and 'Church in Socialism', which was the name by which it was known. Cf. Wolfgang Thunser, *Kirche im Sozialismus* (Tübingen: Mohr Siebeck, 1996), and Gregory Baum, *The Church for Others: Protestant Theology in Communist East Germany* (Grand Rapids, MI: William B. Eerdmans Publishing Company, 1996).

[33]   The banners of the demonstrations organized around Berlin churches in 1989 proclaimed, among other things, '*Mahnwache und Fürbitte für die zu Unrecht Inhaftierten*'. that is, 'solemn vigil and prayers of intercession for the unjustly imprisoned'. Cf. Ehrhart Neubert, *Geschichte der Opposition in der DDR 1949–1989* (Berlin: Bundeszentrale für

based opposition to the government developed to which subcultural groups such as punks, anarchists and hippies were also attracted. Depending on the type of protest and its content, the church directorate would support, depoliticize, individualize, or even contribute to state repression – for instance, by firing pastors. Church groups were infiltrated and the 'tensions within the church'[34] were manipulated until certain political groups were expelled from the parishes, as one former activist remembers.[35] Still, as many informants repeatedly told me, the churches were the only places where they could carry out cultural and political activity freely, to the point that church engagement and even religion more generally became synonymous with political action and opposition to the government, and also obviously with its inherent risks such as imprisonment.[36] The mobilizations and meetings had a secular–religious character: their frame was certainly religious, but the content was rather political, that is, secular; as the famous slogan '*Schwerter zu Pflugscharen*'[37] exemplifies, religion was adapted to the secular context, while secular values, present in politics, were translated into religious terms. A number of initiatives, such as the *Friedenswerkstatt* (peace workshop), which started in different towns of the GDR in the early 1980s, occupied the thin line between religious and secular concerns. These initiatives, branding pacifist topics, gathered large crowds that shared, in very collective ways, information, points of view and experiences, and formulated concrete political alternatives. The workshops took place in the Protestant churches of different towns. In the *Erlöserkirche* in Berlin-Lichtenberg, for instance, a religious service was always celebrated at the beginning and at the end of the *Friedenswerkstatt*.

As to the Catholic Church, there were significant peculiarities. It never really recognized the territorial separation or the Socialist regime and, as Goeckel rightly points out, relied strongly on the ties with its stronger West German

---

politische Bildung, 2000), and the interviews with various political activists made in 1990 and 1992 in Detlef Pollack, Hagen Findeis and Manuel Schilling, *Die Entzauberung des Politischen: was ist aus den politisch alternativen Gruppen der DDR geworden? Interviews mit ehemals führenden Vertretern* (Leipzig: Evangelische Verlagsanstalt; Berlin: Berliner Debatte, 1994).

[34]   My translation.

[35]   Elke Westendorff, 'Das war schon exklusiv', *Horch und Guck. Historisch-literar-ische Zeitschrift des Bürgerkomitees '15. Januar' e.V.* 57/1 (2007), 17–19, at 19. I met most of the quoted activists during commemorative celebrations of events linked to the *Wende*, such as the twenty-fifth anniversary of the *Friedenswerkstätte*, peace workshops in Berlin Lichtenberg.

[36]   Cf. among others, Birgit Müller (ed.), *Anthropologie der Wende. Kontroversen im Alltag der deutschen Vereinigung* (Berlin: Centre Marc Bloch, 1997), 84ff.

[37]   This is a citation of the prophets Micah's and Isaiah's verse, 'swords into ploughshares' (Mic. 4:3 and Isa. 2:2–5). The Soviet Union offered a statue symbolizing this metaphor to the United Nations during the 1950s. The civil movements chose it to symbolize the common concerns of religious and atheist defenders of pacifism.

counterpart.[38] The Catholic Church was able to train priests and make personnel decisions in conjunction with the Vatican. Through *Caritas*,[39] it provided help for the unemployed, the homeless, poor people, families of imprisoned people, and 'pariahs', as those who had applied to leave the GDR were described.[40] On a political level, Catholics followed the principle of political abstention with regard to the regime and adopted a standoffish attitude towards the Lutheran Church. As Silomon and Bayer argue, the repressive strategies of the government actually had a limited effect on the Catholic Church. It was able to maintain a relatively high level of regular church attendance: roughly 25 per cent of those affiliated.[41] As Gregory Baum writes, 'the majority of Catholics had settled in the GDR after World War II, arriving from German territories beyond the border, especially from Silesia'.[42] Within this small group of believers, the community ties remained strong, as Chaplain Benedict stressed when he recalled the historical background of the Catholic diaspora in Eastern Germany:

> We, the Catholics in this region, we received our religious socialization basically from the Christian families and from the couple of parishes who used to live together as a brotherhood, very close. It was our home. In the 1960s I went to high school – the equivalent of grammar school – and that was an exception because many Christians did not have the right to go to high school. I was lucky and could go.

In this situation, Catholics developed a particularly intense sense of belonging to their community that was their 'home', a home with strong ties lasting throughout

---

[38]   For details on Catholics and the Catholic Church during the GDR, see Robert F. Goeckel, 'The Catholic Church in East Germany', in Pedro Ramet (ed.), *Catholicism and Politics in Communist Societies* (Durham, NC, and London: Duke University Press, 1990), 93–116, as well as more recently Bernd Schäfer, 'State and Catholic Church in Eastern Germany, 1945–1989', *German Studies Review*, 22/3 (October 1999), 447–61.

[39]   *Caritas* is now active worldwide and has become an indispensable partner for state agencies in the provision of social care. Its activities were reduced, but not discontinued, during the time of the GDR – see Gerhard Bäcker, Reinhard Bispinck, Klaus Hofemann and Gerhard Naegele, *Sozialpolitik und soziale Lage in Deutschland*, vol. 2 (Wiesbaden: VS Verlag, 2000).

[40]   Cf. Christoph Kösters (ed.), *Caritas in der SBZ/DDR 1945–1989. Erinnerungen, Berichte, Forschungen* (Paderborn: Ferdinand Schoeningh, 2001).

[41]   Anke Silomon and Ulrich Bayer, *Synode und SED-Staat. Die Synode des Bundes der Evangelischen Kirche in der DDR in Görlitz vom 18. bis 22. September 1987* (Göttingen: Vandenhoeck & Ruprecht, 1997). In 1987, the Catholic Church had 1.05 million members, 1,300 priests, 6 bishops, 2,500 nuns, 7,347 employees, 1,037 churches, 11 seminars and retreat houses, 330 convents, 34 church hospitals, 1 theology faculty, as well as several nursing homes, homes for the elderly, kindergartens, orphanages, and homes for the disabled. Cf. Ramet, *Nihil obstat*, 55.

[42]   *Church*, xv.

the whole Socialist time. My next aim is to understand how the hostile yet somewhat ambiguous relationship between the government and the churches impacted on prison institutions and the treatment of ex-prisoners.

Prison Chaplaincy under Surveillance and the Tactics of Resistance

While no pastoral care at all was allowed in youth prisons, military prisons and internment camps, there was actually a legal basis for it in institutions where inmates served custodial sentences.[43] The role of the chaplains was defined in very strict terms. They were expected to limit their activities to religious services and to keep the prisoners calm. At the beginning of the 1950s, a restructuring process was set in motion. The government became increasingly suspicious towards chaplains and towards pastors more generally.[44] It was difficult for the government to control the numerous chaplains who worked in the GDR prisons. It wanted to reduce the number drastically to a handful of absolutely loyal pastors. To achieve this, it first put an increasing number of political prisoners in isolation cells and deprived them of any religious care. Second, it reduced the number of chaplains as intended, leaving only a few completely loyal pastors. The first full-time prison chaplain in the GDR was a pastor who had worked for the central secretary of the SED. When he escaped from the GDR in the 1950s, other chaplains were fired until only one pastor remained – he was a solid party loyalist who had received a bronze medal for his work for the state.[45] The activities carried out as part of prison chaplaincy were severely restricted and monitored. Chaplains were not allowed to relate what the inmates had told them to anyone inside or outside prison, nor could they accept any written notes from prisoners or transmit such notes to anyone inside or outside prison. Through *Caritas*, the Catholic Church was able to provide some pastoral

---

[43] The spiritual care offered within the framework of the chaplaincy in the GDR was basically of a Protestant and Catholic nature: in the observed prisons, as Benedict told me, 'every month there were these services, always at 8 o'clock the Protestant and at 10 the Catholic.'

[44] For instance, Harald Poelchau, a hero of the resistance movement against the Nazis, was a prison chaplain from 1945 to 1948, when he was fired, despite the spectacular growth of the number of inmates in that period, mainly because he disagreed with the government. Cf. Jens Röhling, 'Harald Poelchau', in *Reader Gefängnisseelsorge* (Berlin: EKD, 1999 [1995]), 35–8.

[45] This chaplain was supposed to provide spiritual care to all the prisoners in the GDR, of whom there were about 30,000 during the 1980s. He wrote a very controversial book in which he remained very elusive on many issues that could provide details about his collaboration with the Stasi. Nevertheless, it provides information about the reasons that were considered legitimate for inmates to meet a chaplain and allows – even if limited – insight into the practices related to religion in GDR prisons. See Eckart Giebeler, *Hinter verschlossenen Türen. Vierzig Jahre als Gefägnisseelsorger in der DDR* (Wuppertal and Zürich: Scm R. Brockhaus, 1992).

care to inmates and offer support to their relatives. Locally, some prison governors allowed chaplains to enter prisons in order to provide spiritual support, not as official ministers but as visitors.[46] This gave many chaplains the opportunity to help inmates on a personal level. Such opposition actions by prison chaplains may be interpreted in the light of Michel de Certeau's concept of tactics. The French social scientist opposed tactics to strategies, as they are an action lacking 'a proper locus ... The space of a tactic is the space of the other.' A tactic is deployed 'on and with a terrain imposed on it and organized by the law of a foreign power'. Those who deploy a tactic 'must vigilantly make use of the cracks that particular conjunctions open in the surveillance of the proprietary powers. It poaches in them. It creates surprises in them.'[47] The notion of the everyday is linked to that of tactics. Therefore particular attention is given to what everyday life comprises for the various actors in my fieldwork.[48]

Inmates saw the official chaplains as collaborators with the state security system, while, on the other hand, they considered the chaplains who came to prisons informally as deserving of their trust and thus entrusted them with confidential information. Lars, who was already in prison in the 1980s, revealed what type of relationship he had with these unofficial chaplains, one of them being Chaplain Benedict:

> [Chaplain Benedict] was, according to the terms of the time, a priest standing in opposition. His way of talking, of behaving – and I don't know if I can say that, [Chaplain Benedict] was as a Catholic priest under surveillance and he had to be careful and watch out because he could be persecuted. At the time you had only the right to write – I don't know – four letters. They were controlled, that is, read [by the staff]. Now, admitting you have a girlfriend, you want to write in a more intimate way to her, with feelings. But you would not dare any longer – this is how many relationships were broken – and [Chaplain Benedict] was always someone who would smuggle out a letter for you.

In the quoted interview extract, clearly the chaplain appears as a helpful person who is not afraid of siding with the prisoners. Interestingly, this inmate, Lars, is a very secular person who does not practise religion at all, which indicates that the positive perception of this chaplain is not the result of membership or denominational belonging. On the contrary, inmates also knew that some clergy

---

[46]   See Kösters, *Caritas*, and Josef Pilvousek, 'Caritas in SBZ/DDR und Neuen Bundesländern', in Karl Gabriel, Josef Pilvousek, Miklós Tomka, Andrea Wilke and Andreas Wollbold (eds), *Religion und Kirchen in Ost (Mittel) Europa. Deutschland-Ost* (Ostfildern: Schwabenverlag, 2003), 50–62.

[47]   Michel de Certeau, *The Practice of Everyday Life* (Berkeley, CA: University of California Press, 1984), 36–7, originally published in French in 1980.

[48]   I have given more details on my use of Michel de Certeau's concepts in a previous article on which my argument in this book draws: 'Tactiques religieuses dans les espaces carcéraux d'Allemagne de l'Est', *Revue d'histoire des sciences humaines*, 23 (2010), 141–56.

worked for the state security system. Ironically, as Ramet writes, 'collaboration with the *StaSi* did not undermine the Church's opposition activity: on the contrary, it may even have made that opposition possible.'[49]

Officially, however, what were inmates' spiritual needs in GDR prisons? According to Eckart Giebeler the prison chaplain in charge at the time,[50] inmates asked to meet the chaplain mainly to discuss questions relating to sexuality and suicide, to find out about people killed in their attempts to escape, to receive information about their families or friends who lived outside the GDR, or simply to know more about their imprisonment. Giebeler also writes about the many times when the Ministry for State Security (Stasi) tried – without success, as he underlines – to obtain from him information about the inmates or to persuade him to collaborate in intimidation techniques that were to lead to inmates' confessions or cooperation. Altogether, about 5 per cent of clergy and other church officials worked with the Stasi.

Another pastor, Heinz Bluhm, was employed by the Ministry together with Giebeler, but he was fired in 1956 after only one year in this post, probably for his involvement in the pacifist movement. Bluhm and Giebeler accepted the conditions set out by the GDR: they were not allowed to relate what the inmates had told them to anyone inside or outside prison, and they could not accept any written notes from prisoners nor transmit such notes to anyone inside or outside prison. However, in most cases, it was the security police that required them to break these rules, thereby putting them in a similar double bind as observed outside prison. In 1953, the state prohibited meetings between prisoners and chaplains without the presence of a prison officer. The employment of Bluhm and Giebeler as prison chaplains also meant that most of the other chaplains who had been working in the prisons could not continue their work. In May 1958, all the pastors who lived in the western part of Berlin were fired, as from then on only those living on GDR territory were deemed acceptable. Bluhm had never been replaced. This situation made it extremely difficult to obtain information about what happened in prisons and thus justify more spiritual care. Many pastors were very sceptical about their colleagues who had accepted the conditions for their work in prisons. Initially, this lack of solidarity increased the chaplains' collaboration with the prison authorities.

Given the spirit of the Socialist model, religion had nothing to do with the 'educational goal' of prisons: work, commitment to the party line, order, discipline and control were the top priorities. Conditions were very harsh and work was compulsory. The GDR had placed the prison department under the jurisdiction of the Ministry of the Interior, which implied that 'prisons were run on a police state model'.[51] As a consequence, the internal regulations were in the hands of the Minister of the Interior and the chief of police. During the 1970s, the attitude of

---

[49]   Ramet, *Nihil obstat*, 76.

[50]   *Hinter verschlossenen Türen. Vierzig Jahre als Gefägnisseelsorger in der DDR* (Wuppertal and Zürich: Scm R. Brockhaus, 1992).

[51]   Jörg Arnold, 'Corrections in the German Democratic Republic: A Field for Research', *British Journal of Criminology*, 35/1 (1995), 81–94, at 83.

the GDR government towards religion softened slightly on the surface. In 1973, religious minorities obtained some public recognition.[52] Legally, the dispositions assured spiritual care as a right, and pastors and priests made increasing use of this legal guarantee. Chaplain Benedict saw it as a way to increase pressure on a state that was seeking international recognition:

> In the mid-1970s – the political situation had changed drastically since the 1950s – the GDR was striving for recognition by the other states, it wanted to be included in the discussions, to be part of the UN, it wanted to be a recognized state, which respected human rights. And – I was at first surprised – there was a paragraph in the Penal Law of the GDR that spiritual care had to be admitted. And so I thought that the narrow prescriptions that the state had made had to be broken, because the state would not dare ban a Catholic priest from his job. At best it could say, 'This *man* has broken the rules, we can't keep *him*.' But they would let someone else take the job. The position itself was not in danger.

The distinction between the chaplains' position and themselves as people was possible because they were affiliated to an established church. The formal agreements between the institution of the church and the institution of the state opened a space for negotiation. This position gave chaplains strength and courage, as the following extract from the interview with Chaplain Benedict further illustrates:

> This way of thinking encouraged me and made me glad from the beginning –to go into the prison, also with the aim of breaking those rules. The first couple of times I was standing there with my small suitcase, with the cup and the vestments inside. One or two wardens would accompany me to the room where the religious service had to take place and the inmates were taken there. I could not say hello to them, I could not talk to them. I was merely allowed to hold the service and then had to leave immediately afterwards in the same way, under constant surveillance.

---

[52]   In 1975, the union of the Free Protestant Communes had 1,350 members, the association of the Old Catholic Church 1,200 members, the Seventh-day Adventists 11,300 members, and the Mennonites and Quakers less then 100 members each. Cf. Horst Dähn, *Konfrontation oder Kooperation? Das Verhältnis von Staat und Kirche in der SBZ/DDR 1945–1980* (Opladen: Westdeutscher Verlag, 1982), 198. In 1988, for instance, there were 80- to 100,000 members of the New Apostolic Church, 28,000 Methodists, 12- to 14,000 members of the Apostolate of Jesus Christ, 2,000 Catholic–Apostolics, and 2,000 Reformed Apostolics. Cf. Ramet, *Nihil obstat*, 56. There were only an exiguous number of non-Christian religious groups in the GDR. Johan told me how disadvantaged he felt as a member of a religious minority in the GDR: 'During the time of the GDR we did have a synagogue in *Xtown*, but it was closed by the GDR authorities in 1973. At that time, religion was despised, you know. It was not easy for us. In my case, it was difficult at school – and then at work.'

It was very significant for the chaplain to realize that the church was recognized by the state, as an institution with a territorial religious task – a legacy from the Westphalian model. The interview continued:

> *Chaplain Benedict*: I had no influence on who participated. Typically – which was actually good for us as church members – is to conceive of the church – and it was the same during the GDR – not to see participation in religious services as depending on a particular religion or denomination. At the time there were only a few Catholics, one or two, there were a couple of Protestants and many others. There were hardly any foreigners, the majority were German, but there were also some Africans who had been living here as students and who had got into trouble.

> *I*: Does that mean that the permission to hold services didn't depend on how many Catholics there were? You could do it because there was an agreement with the Church and chaplaincy had a position.

> *Chaplain Benedict*: There was a law, yes.

> *I*: But you didn't know if there were any requests for the service from inmates?

> *Chaplain Benedict*: Well, nobody was forced to participate.

According to the 1977 Prison Act, prisoners who were members of a church were granted, if they requested it, the freedom to carry out religious activities. Indeed, the fact that the church was recognized by the state as an institution with a territorial religious domain was very significant for inmates' demands for prison chaplaincy. However, the modalities and the general spirit of the regulations remained very restrictive. The government conceded that members of a particular church could request religious care from their church, but internal prison rules stipulated that 'religious services were to be allowed only if there were enough prisoners'.[53] This was not a big concession, considering the drastic decrease in church membership that the churches were witnessing: no more than 30 per cent of the East German population belonged to any Christian church at all.[54] Therefore, the number of prisoners who requested religious care was rarely high enough to warrant the organization of religious services. Locally, some prison governors allowed chaplains to enter prisons in order to provide spiritual support – not as official ministers, however, but as visitors. This allowed many chaplains to enact tactics of resistance to help inmates on a personal level.

As mentioned earlier, the Socialist model excluded religion of any 'educational' plan for society. To recap, work, commitment to the party line, order, discipline

---

[53]   Arnold, *Corrections*, 84.
[54]   Detlef Pollack and Gert Pickel, *Religiöser und kirchlicher Wandel in Ostdeutschland 1989–1999* (Opladen: Leske & Budrich, 2000), 9.

and control were the top priorities in both areas. In the prisons, the largest rooms that had traditionally been reserved for religious services were used to show propaganda films instead.[55] During their detention, prisoners were 're-educated' so that they would respect Socialist values through work, discipline and 'ideological training'.[56] The belief was that, as a result of this model, 'political–ideologically trained prisoners would commit no new offences'.[57] As a matter of fact, the Socialist model planned to put ex-inmates back into the position they had occupied previously in society. The Reintegration Act promoted far-reaching measures for the re-socialization of ex-inmates, revolving around working and housing in particular. Theoretically, released prisoners were to be integrated 'into the work collective in which the offender had been working before imprisonment', and local government authorities were 'responsible for providing accommodation for released prisoners'.[58] The idea behind these measures was that society as a whole was responsible for the reintegration of ex-prisoners. In practice, however, the picture was not as rosy. Workers' collectives sometimes refused to cooperate with ex-inmates, and 'the flats offered were frequently below the standards of decent human accommodation'.[59] The situation of ex-prisoners was hence far from unproblematic, and religious actors were unable to be very helpful in this context as they themselves experienced difficulties in terms of their social integration and could provide neither work nor housing.

Towards the end of the 1980s, some prisons allowed other local chaplains to enter now and then. Interviews with these chaplains, however, show that the notion of spiritual care was interpreted in a very different yet always strict way by prisons. Chaplain Anton, for instance, was allowed to enter the Saxon prison only once per month:

> Spiritual care in prison was basically a one-hour visit every month in the visitors' room. There was no religious service; it was a sort of Bible discussion with a small number of inmates, always under the surveillance of a warden. That's how I experienced it.

Some chaplains and priests asked to meet inmates without supervision, but their requests were refused. Therefore, many clergymen did not enter prison as official ministers, but as visitors. The experiences of Catholic pastoral care in prison were

---

[55]   None of the chaplains interviewed would use these rooms; the chaplaincy was placed in newly created spaces. The large rooms are only used for activities that require more space, such as playing table-tennis.

[56]   Arnold, *Corrections*, 85.

[57]   Ibid.

[58]   Ibid., 86.

[59]   Ibid.

extremely reduced.[60] From the point of view of Chaplain Benedict, this was due to the strict circumstances:

> *Chaplain Benedict*: There was also a Catholic chaplaincy, but only under very strict surveillance. Actually, you couldn't really say that it was real spiritual care, because it was only a religious service.

> *I*: Does that mean you had no place to go apart from the chapel?

> *Chaplain Benedict*: Exactly.

> *I*: There were no individual conversations either?

> *Chaplain Benedict*: No, none of that was allowed.

However limited the access to prisons was, it still made Catholic priests interesting interlocutors for the inmates' relatives, as they could not get any information at all from the prison administration. The priests were considered deserving of their trust and thus came to hold confidential information. The same Catholic chaplain remembers in this respect:

> I often overheard details about what was going on in prisons and had contact with some people who visited some inmates – sometimes family members – and they were under massive pressure: 'You cannot say anything about what you see there' and stuff like this. They were never sure – 'We do have an appointment, but I don't know whether they will let me in to see my husband, my son or whoever.' You never knew. At the time, one was very, very uncertain and afraid of going into a prison. I used to speak a lot with family members and I always heard that the chaplain observed the rules to the letter, that he didn't tell people anything about the prison and refused any contact with family members.

During the 1970s and 1980s, about 30,000 people were imprisoned, suffering the very harsh conditions in the GDR. Benedict experienced this situation in the prison where he was a chaplain:

> *Chaplain Benedict*: During the GDR, on average, there were 3,000 inmates in prison B, and during peak periods, 5,000 inmates. And the inmates used to live either in inhumane

---

60   Imprisoned Catholics reported that they had requested a Bible but could never convince the library to buy one. If a priest or monk managed to visit them, they were always under the surveillance of prison officers. See Amnesty International, *Amnesty International und die DDR. Die Arbeit für die Menschenrechte in der DDR von 1961–1989. Katalog zur Wanderausstellung* (Bonn: Amnesty International, 2003 [2002]).

or in tiny, narrow single cells. The majority, however, used to be in the big cells with up to 24 or 30 inmates. It was thus very, very inhumane and without any space.

I: How many inmates are there now?

Chaplain Benedict: Today, 840.

I: So were the buildings bigger before?

Chaplain Benedict: No – on the contrary, some buildings have been constructed afterwards.

The memory of the conditions in which inmates were living is still alive among today's prisoners. Kai, a young inmate in Saxony, for instance, can still see the traces of that time in his cell, which measures 8 square meters:

> During the GDR, there were up to five people in these cells, in 8 square meters. As soon as the door was open, nobody could sit on the bed. Bunk beds and in the middle, a boat – as it was called – could be pulled out. You can still see the imprints of those beds on the wall. In our cell, yes, you can still see them. Even those small holes for the screws, you can see everything. It's depressing. And it's small for two people up there. We have a space of about 2½ or 3 square meters for two people to move.

This young inmate has not had any direct experience of imprisonment during the GDR but seems nevertheless to have a vivid image of what it could have been. Imageries or language metaphors in the discourses of inmates and staff referred often to the GDR past and kept a powerful memory alive in everyday interactions. Hans, on the contrary, experienced detention at first hand during the GDR in prison B. I interviewed him after his release in Berlin and he told me about the conditions before the Turn (in German *Wende*, meaning the reunification) in 1989:

> *Hans:* Before the Wende, the religious services always took place under surveillance, there were always officers, it was not as open as after the Wende. We always had the impression that we were watched – it was also common to say: 'You only go to the religious service in order to receive some sort of gift.'

> *I:* Tobacco is often mentioned as an example…

> *Hans:* Tobacco, or a pastor regularly distributed chocolate … well, that was not the reason why I used to go, I was rather looking for something [spiritual] and also at that time, before the Wende, also to get out of the cell because I was with six people in 12 square meters – one is glad to have an opportunity at all to get out of the cell, and even if it's the religious service and you sit there and at least you're out of the cell for

an hour or an hour and a half ... hmm ... in particular on weekends there was nothing else anyway apart from one free hour and lunch.

Hans's narrative was very detailed and will often support my argument in the following chapters, in particular concerning converts and release.

Conclusion

This first chapter has offered a succinct overview of the ways in which successive political regimes have bureaucratized and routinized religion in prison, interpreting religious freedom in prison according to different historical contexts. The end of the Second World War and the collapse of the GDR changed the modalities of spiritual care in prison significantly as well as the support given to ex-convicts on their release. The historical link between religious conceptions and discourses on imprisonment (for example, discipline and solitary confinement) on the one hand, and the institutional strength of established religions on the other hand, have contributed widely to shaping, both structurally and discursively, the modern prison system in Germany as well as the organization of social support supplied to the needy. The twentieth century has inherited penitentiaries whose construction had been inspired by a discourse of re-socialization that resembled a spiritual conversion in all respects.

During the last years of the GDR, when outside prisons East German society was multiplying protests and opposition to the government, inside prison the situation was quieter. The strict control of communications between inside and outside could only be disrupted by chaplains if they made tactical use of their position. Chaplain Benedict's experience offers a vivid illustration of the way such tactics worked. While initially he accepted all the strict conditions imposed on his visits as a prison chaplain, slowly but steadily he became increasingly determined in his communication attempts:

> During the religious service, I broke the rules that were imposed. First, I shook hands for the peace message and thereby had contact with each inmate. The second or third time, I said, 'Well, we could at least say hello to each other.' I was already standing there, when they arrived – or when they left – and shook hands with everybody. The fourth time, I said, 'Now, I know what you look like, now tell me at least your name so that we can address each other.' After half a year this became increasingly longer, up to half an hour, and at the end of the service I transmitted information from outside.

The following illustrates that the fact that prisoners were not informed of the political mobilizations ongoing in the general population at the end of the 1980s encouraged Chaplain Benedict in his endeavour:

It was the time around the end of the GDR, there were peace vigils and prayers, and I told the inmates and they asked questions, all this under the surveillance of the police, who were not amused at all. Once a warden interrupted us and said, 'Now it's over, you're not allowed to talk to each other.' And I said, 'No, it's not over, it's part of the service, to exchange information', and in some way I concluded the discussion and made the benediction and said, 'Now the service is over.'

In the last sentences of this passage, the chaplain explains that he used the wardens' ignorance in terms of religious services to expand his freedom. These were the years when the church's role in harbouring political opposition to the regime became neater, an image that those who grew up in the GDR still have today. As an inmate told me, it was the result of a vague but certain feeling:

Thilo: Church people were in some way 'enemies' because, concretely, they demonstrated in the streets their opposition against the GDR. [Opposition] always started in the churches. That's what I heard, and the state knew that there was always the church behind those agitations because it had a different way of thinking. At school, one could never hear, 'You have to go there' [to the church], for instance. If it was considered as good they would have told us, 'Go there', as they used to tell us to join the Army for three years.

On the other hand, while outside prison the GDR strategies of intimidation created a general exhaustion and weakening of institutionally based opposition, inside, step by step, some chaplains were able to break the narrow conditions imposed on them to get closer to inmates, who were seen as dangerous enemies by the government but as victims of political repression by an increasing number of the population. When the Berlin Wall collapsed, prisoners became nervous since they obtained no clear information about how the situation would change for them. They started to agitate, and in some prisons inmates climbed onto the roofs to ask for an amnesty. Various chaplains played a crucial role in mediating between the administration and the inmates. Chaplain Benedict was one of them, but his support went well beyond mediation. In the following interview extract he describes another of his tactics:

Chaplain Benedict: On December the 5th 1989 there was a big press conference, in which the director participated, and even the chief of the prison chaplaincy from the Ministry for the Interior who supported him. Numerous, very critical, questions were asked, and it changed a lot for us working in prison. After this conference we could start with group meetings and things like that. We then had a very, very lively time; it was the time of the roof occupation that started from our group discussion. One evening, we were talking about a biblical theme; there were many people at that meeting, 40 or more.

I: Was it under surveillance?

Chaplain Benedict: No. That day it was a bit noisy. There were many inmates who wanted to go to the toilet and about one hour before the end of the discussion, one inmate said: 'You can see there are four or five people missing, it's because they are on the roof and protesting', and he read their demands and we were all very concerned. One inmate even said after a long silence, 'All we can do now is pray. Let's pray.' At nine we waited for the wardens to come and take the inmates back to their cells. Later we found out that they were watching a football game and that there was probably also some alcohol and so they did not notice that some inmates were missing from their cells. At half past twleve, the prison called me at home and told me, 'There are some inmates on the roof, could you come?' These were the last days of September 1990. October 3rd was the day of the German unification and the unification treaty was signed. The inmates knew very well that, 'If we don't obtain some kind of regulation we will be stuck in prison with our over-sized political sentences and we we'll be forgotten. We have to make sure that the GDR sentences are checked and reduced. If we don't do that before, they'll become applicable by law and we'll be sitting here maybe as innocents or certainly with too high sentences.' The inmates were very serious about drawing attention to this, and surprisingly the administration accepted it.

I: How long did they remain on the roof?

Chaplain Benedict: About three weeks. After a couple of days an agreement was met that they trusted each other a little bit. There were discussions with politicians – I talked to all of them and negotiated. The prison director also asked me to negotiate with all of them, and what I negotiated was then respected by the prison direction.

The pragmatic respect and recognition the chaplains obtained through their commitment during this important year was afterwards transformed into institutional recognition. Today, a Christian care service is institutionalized in prison in the form of the prison chaplaincy, which is starting to integrate non-Christian care. This new situation, however, also implied other less enchanting consequences for chaplains and churches. The next chapter aims to describe this development.

Chapter 2
Religion in Post-Socialist Prisons and Release Programmes

Various social scientific studies[1] emphasize that the shared experience of the radical transformation of social, political, economic, religious and cultural institutions has given East Germans[2] a distinct perspective of the world. It is in the authors' view a question not so much of substantial differences in identity, values or practices, but of the perspective from which these identities, values and practices are considered. Some of these authors emphasize the rather negative impact of the transformation on the local population, arguing in terms of loss.[3] Raj Kollmorgen, for instance, studies the institutional transformation process and argues that after the collapse of the Socialist government an 'exogenous top-down'[4] transfer of high-rank positions occurred in East German society. 'Ready-made actors' from the West replaced local ones in work-related associations and parties, but also in arts or sports. The territorial borders were redefined, and five new *Länder* were created.[5]

East German society is considered one of the most secularized societies in the world: it has reached the lowest levels of religious affiliation in Europe. Not only did the established churches experience a steady loss of members – between 1990 and 1992 alone, almost 60,000 people left the Catholic Church and

---

[1]   Cf. Wolfgang Engler, *Die Ostdeutschen als Avant-garde* (Berlin: Aufbau Verlag, 2002), and more recently Gert Pickel and Kornelia Sammet (eds), *Religion und Religiosität im vereinigten Deutschland. Zwanzig Jahre nach dem Umbruch* (Wiesbaden: VS Verlag, 2011); also Karstein et al., *Forcierte Säkularität*.

[2]   I use capital letters for 'Eastern Germany' to make clear that I do not refer to a geographical area in the eastern part of Germany, but to the German word *Ostdeutschland* – that is, the former GDR. Therefore, 'East Germans' here means 'former GDR citizens'.

[3]   Robert E. Beckley, H. Paul Chalfant and D. Paul Johnson, 'Germany's Reconstruction: The Role of the Eastern German Evangelical Church before and after Reunification', in William H. Swatos (ed.), *Politics and Religion in Central and Eastern Europe* (Westport, CT: Greenwood, 1994), 163–77. This qualitative study on pastors reports that lay participation increased after unification, but not as much as pastors had expected. The pastors interviewed felt relegated to second-class citizenship in the reunited church and they feared that the measures taken during the GDR when they had to accommodate a hostile state were not appreciated adequately by their counterparts in West Germany.

[4]   Raj Kollmorgen, *Ostdeutschland. Beobachtungen einer Übergangs- und Teilgesellschaft* (Wiesbaden: VS-Verlag für Sozialwissenschaften, 2005), 63–4.

[5]   Brandenburg, Saxony, Saxony-Anhalt, Thuringia and Mecklenburg-Vorpommern.

nearly 190,000 left the Protestant Church[6] – but East Germans do not even seem to follow the widely proclaimed trend of the 'return of the sacred'. A religious revival that many observers had expected after unification did not happen. Most East Germans were born into 'non-membership'; and even today, being the member of a church is considered unusual. Moreover, the percentage of elderly people was very high among church members and their educational level was below average.

Table 2.1   Religious affiliations (by percentage)

	GDR			Eastern Germany			Western Germany
	1949	1964	1989	1992	1996	2008	2008
Protestant Church	80.5	59.4	25	27	26	19.5	41.1
Roman Catholicism	11	8.1	4.5	4	5.3	3.7	34.3
Other religious affiliation	<1	<1	<1[a]	1.8	2	2.5	8.3
No religious affiliation	7.6	*c.* 31.5	70	66	66.8	74.3	16.3

Note [a]   According to Ramet, *Nihil obstat*, 53, there were 2,000 Muslims, 250 Jews and 15 Rastafarians in 1988.

According to Table 2.1, the overall trend clearly confirms secularization, but caution is in order since these numbers can refer to a variety of practices. I join Karstein, Schmidt-Lux and Wohlrab-Sahr in their more general argument about the emergence of a secular *habitus*.[7] They study empirically how such a *habitus* has emerged from the GDR experience and how it has remained the dominant approach to religion. Their conceptual distinction draws a line between secularization as a process that belongs to the past and secularity as a cultural frame of current East German society. Secularization was imposed by the political project of the GDR government, but social and family dynamics have maintained secularity tenaciously as a *habitus* after that government and its repressive authority disappeared. This persistence, the authors argue,

---

[6]   During the early 1990s, the number of people joining the Protestant Church was higher than in previous years, but well below the number of people leaving the church. Cf. Pollack and Pickel, *Religiöser und kirchlicher*, 25–6, and more recently Pickel and Sammet (eds), *Religion*.

[7]   In *Forcierte Säkularität*; cf. Pierre Bourdieu, *Le sens pratique* (Paris: Ed. de Minuit, 1980).

demonstrates that individuals embraced actively the plausibility of secularity despite the repressive context. The collective secular *habitus* frames local identities and individuals' most important decisions, as the following illustrates. When talking about his planned marriage, Bernd, a young inmate, said spontaneously that it was 'normal' not to belong to a religion or to have a religious marriage ritual:

> *Bernd*: I will soon get married.
>
> *I*: … And your partner is of which [religion]?
>
> *Bernd*: She's also quite normal.
>
> *I*: So no [religious affiliation] …
>
> *Bernd*: Yes …
>
> *I*: When you get married, will you have a religious wedding?
>
> *Bernd*: No … simply a normal wedding, the way you do it in here.

Karstein, Schmidt-Lux and Wohlrab-Sahr found of equal importance, however, that since 1989 religion had regained some also significance at a personal level, as a reservoir of stories and myths that offer moral guidance throughout one's life. Although according to these findings the guidelines rarely relate to the transcendent plane, they show the emergence of a category of people characterized by an 'agnostic spirituality' that contains neither explicit atheist views nor Christian beliefs but shows openness to ideas such as the individuality of the soul or reincarnation. East Germans of the younger generation display a higher level of religiosity in quantitative studies, but they rarely become members of a church or a formal religious community. Their personal aspirations often have a spiritual dimension (pilgrimage, yoga and meditation, for instance), which is also linked, however, to scientific explanations. The attraction of the churches for youth during Socialism, as providing an arena for political opposition, is now gone, partly because they had never been 'an agent of'[8] this opposition and therefore had lost to a considerable extent their position of trust within society. In East Germans' everyday life religion can be a set of ethical and moral principles that is disconnected completely from institutional belongings.

Moreover, religion survived in some regions – for instance, in Eichsfeld or Oberlausitz – often as a feature of regional, traditional or ethnic identity.

---

[8]   Daphne Berdahl, *Where the World Ended: Re-unification and Identity in the German Borderland* (Berkeley, CA: University of California Press, 1999), 78. Cf. also Pollack and Pickel, *Kirchlicher und religiöser*.

There, church members formed a social milieu with a sound social network, also able to contribute to shaping public life. This gave them an advantage after the fall of Socialism: some of those socialized in these milieus are now important figures in politics, cultural life or social service organizations.[9]

East German society is also characterized by other features that are linked indirectly to religion and important for my argument. It is, for instance, affected to a larger degree by unemployment, right-wing extremism and poverty. As far as foreign nationals are concerned, Germany counted 6,694,776 foreigners in 2009, which accounts for about 8 per cent of the total population.[10] However, in Saxony and Brandenburg, the two *Länder* that are the focus of my research, the proportion of foreigners was around 2 per cent in that year.[11]

After the fall of Communism and following the West German institutional model, religion was re-established at different social levels. In the prisons, both prisoners and chaplains received more extensive rights to exercise religious freedom. As in the West, religion is now viewed as able to make a significant contribution to rehabilitation.[12] However, East Germans participated in this rebuilding process and appropriated the new institutions from their own perspective – importantly, from the grassroots level, since most leading positions were taken by West Germans.[13] The rapidity of the institutional changes – for example, the West German currency was introduced as early as July 1990 – contrasted strongly with the slow pace of everyday life in East Germany. Religious institutions also underwent major transformations, and religion itself was given a new place in society. The religious communities and actors reacted in different ways to the new situation, resulting in a variegated picture. In the following section, I shall summarize the most important institutional changes that the *Wende* introduced to the realms of religion and imprisonment and offender rehabilitation. The East German case shows clearly that religion, as it is present in this society, can best be understood if it is compared with the predominating secularity.

---

[9]   See recently Alexander Leistner, '"Kirche muss Probiergemeinschaft sein". Typen des Verhältnisses von Religion und Politik in den Biographien von Friedensaktivisten', in Pickel and Sammet (eds), *Religion*, 325–41.

[10]   Germany has the highest absolute number of foreign nationals in Europe.

[11]   The five most common countries of origin are Vietnam, Poland, Ukraine, Turkey and Russia: see Statistisches Jahrbuch Sachsen 2006–2011, at http://www.statistik.sachsen. de/html/6669.htm, and Statistisches Jahrbuch Brandenburg 2006–2011, at http://www. statistik-berlin-brandenburg.de/, both accessed 19 December 2011.

[12]   Susanne Eick-Wildgans, *Anstaltseelsorge. Möglichkeiten und Grenzen des Zusammenwirkens von Staat und Kirche im Strafvollzug* (Berlin: Druncker & Humboldt, 1993), 65.

[13]   Details on the reproduction of elite positions can be found in Raj Kollmorgen, 'Ostdeutschlandforschung. Status quo und Entwicklungschancen', *Soziologie*, 38/2 (2009), 9–39.

The New Institutional Location of Religion in Prison

Unification introduced the West-German type of state–church relationship to the five newly formed 'East German *Länder*' as a model. This meant that the churches took the privileges that the establishment had given them in the Constitution of the Federal Republic of Germany of 1949. A complete assimilation did not occur, however: some peculiarities of the East German constellation of conditions remain, in particular regarding church tax, religious education and chaplaincy.[14]

In Germany, the legal status of the churches operates on two levels: the Republic and the *Länder*. The German Basic Law[15] – which is now also in force in the Eastern *Länder* – gives the churches the possibility to constitute 'bodies under public law' (*Körperschaften des öffentlichen Rechts*).[16] The law reinforces the freedom of conscience and religion by integrating the respective articles of the Weimar Constitution. It protects church property and allows the churches

---

[14] The controversy that flared up over a religion course due to be introduced in state schools in Brandenburg in 1996 is a good example: whereas religion in West German schools was usually taught from a religiously committed point of view, the new course in Brandenburg was designed to be taught from a non-denominational, detached perspective. Moreover, in the other four new *Länder*, students have been given a choice between lessons in Christianity and non-religious ethics. Today a secular teaching combines religion, ethics and social values. For details, cf. Imma Hillerich, 'Bildungspolitik und Religion. Die Diskussion um das Schulfach LER in Brandenburg', in Manfred Brocker, Hartmut Behr and Mathias Hildebrandt (eds), *Religion – Staat – Politik. Zur Rolle der Religion in der nationalen und internationalen Politik* (Wiesbaden: Westdeutscher Verlag, 2003), 199–222.

[15] The articles relating to religion in the German Basic Law of 1949 are 4 (Freedom of faith and conscience) and 140, which is based on the provisions of 136, 137, 138, 139 and 141 of the German Constitution of 11 August 1919. For the official English translation of the text, see German Federal Ministry of Justice, at http://www.gesetze-im-internet.de/englisch_gg/index.html, accessed 17 July 2011.

[16] Hans von Mangoldt's study of the constitutions of the new East German federal states shows that this collaboration is most clearly affirmed in Saxony, where churches and religious communities remain separated from the state but collaborate for the accomplishment of some tasks. He quotes the example of religious instruction in state schools. According to von Mangoldt, the state's motivation in searching to collaborate with the churches is 'to reestablish justice after the disorientation of the atheist state and to acknowledge the substantial importance churches have acquired during the peaceful revolution also through the people's will' – *Die Verfassungen der neuen Bundesländer. Einführung und synoptische Darstellung. Sachsen, Brandenburg, Sachsen-Anhalt, Mecklenburg-Vorpommern, Thüringen* (Berlin: Duncker & Humblot GmbH, 1997), 83. The distance between state and churches is greater in the other federal states, above all in Brandenburg.

autonomy with regard to contracts with employees.[17] The presence and services of the two churches are guaranteed in different state institutions, including prisons. All over Germany, the churches raise tax from their members with the help of the state.[18] Moreover, the state also pays a certain amount of money for the care of church buildings, for the organization of large meetings, and for some social, medical or educational tasks. All these arrangements entail a high level of establishment.[19]

The state recognizes and protects, among others, holy days,[20] the churches' internal forms of organization, the study of theology at universities, Protestant or Catholic teaching in state schools, state schools managed by established churches, church charity organizations, spiritual care in state institutions, church buildings and art, church property and the churches' autonomous management of it, and the need to communicate to churches information about citizens for tax purposes or other activities. Interestingly, the regulations also refer to the fact that the relationship between state and churches is friendly and that any kind of disagreement should be solved in an amicable way. The main Christian churches are prominent actors in politics, cultural orientations and social service provision, but for East Germans they are no longer 'alternative institutions'. As Müller and Pollack write,[21] East Germans have felt increasingly estranged from the church and religious beliefs. The human and social proximity to churches they had experienced during Socialism has faded. Expectations as to the kind of role the churches were to play in public changed

---

[17]   This is important, considering that in Germany churches form the second largest employer (after the state). This means that they have more employees than major German enterprises such as Siemens or Volkswagen. In 2007, about 1.7 million people were employed by churches: see Forschungsgruppe Weltanschauungen in Deutschland, at http://fowid.de, accessed 17 July 2011. Churches require their employees to varying degrees to act in accordance with their doctrines, in both their professional and their private lives.

[18]   Until about 1959, the tax was collected directly, in door-to-door collections. The state has now taken over this role, and the churches pay for this service. The amount paid in taxes is about 8–9 per cent of income tax and accounts for 63–80 per cent of the churches' income. The main religious organizations that collect taxes today are the Federal Union of the Protestant Churches – EKD, the Roman Catholic Church, the Old German Catholic Church, and the Jewish communities.

[19]   The constitution of Rheinland-Pfalz, which was rewritten as recently as 2000, is a good example. It states, in Article 33, that schools have to teach pupils, among other principles, 'Gottesfurcht' (godliness). Article 47 states that Sunday ought to be dedicated to 'religiösen Erbauung, seelischen Erhebung und Arbeitsruhe' (religious edification, spiritual elevation, and rest from work).

[20]   Cf. Wolfgang Vögele, *Zivilreligion in der Bundesrepublik Deutschland* (Gütersloh: Chr. Kaiser/Gütersloh Verlagshaus, 1994).

[21]   Olaf Müller and Detlef Pollack, 'Die religiöse Entwicklung in Ostdeutschland nach 1989', in Pickel and Sammet (eds), *Religion*, 125–44, at 132.

during and after unification,[22] which had an impact upon the way civil activists related to the churches. Once the Berlin Wall had been torn down, members of peace and environmental groups, who had used the churches for meetings and political mobilization, abandoned any involvement in religion. It was then more plausible to be involved in secular politics, as the churches stood no longer in opposition to the state and were no longer the only places where civil and political activism could find a sanctuary. New groups arose through the experience of the peace workshops, such as *Neues Forum*, *Demokratischer Aufbruch* and *Sozialdemokratische Partei*. Reference to and remembrance of that time still contributes to endowing identity to socially active associations and individuals nowadays.

As Germany is a federal republic, most of the legislation concerning religion is to be found at the level of the *Länder*. Their respective constitutions regulate the relationship with the churches. In contrast to religious minorities, 'the different Protestant land churches, plus some Orthodox ones, and the Roman Catholic Church' are, as Wolf Aires writes, 'bodies defined by the public law.'[23] Some *Länder* have concordats with the Catholic Church following the model of the *Reichskonkordat* of 1933. Here we find laws concerning religious education; theology departments at universities; pastoral care in the Army, hospitals and prisons; cemeteries; marriage; taxes; the media, and so on – as well as all the laws that regulate the position of the church in the public realm (for example, freedom to teach and preach, the administering of sacraments, guarantee of church property, and financial questions). After 1990, smaller religious groups were also recognized as public corporations: for instance, Adventists, Baptists, Buddhists, the Neo-Apostolic Church, the Anglican Church, and the Mormons.

Prisons are now under the jurisdiction of the Ministry of Justice. Some differences exist among the *Länder* concerning the regulation details of prison chaplaincy.[24] While the law allows all religious communities to provide spiritual assistance in prison, as a consequence of the guarantee of religious freedom, the established churches are guaranteed an institutional role within prisons.[25] In her book on the legal

---

[22]   For analysis of the changing church institutions, cf. Barbara Thiérault, *'Conservative Revolutionaries': Protestant and Catholic Churches in Germany after Radical Political Change in the 1990s* (New York and Oxford: Berghahn Books, 2004).

[23]   Wolf Aires, 'Germany's Islamic Minority: Some Remarks on Historical and Legal Developments', in James Richardson (ed.), *Regulating Religion: Case Studies from around the Globe* (New York: Kluwer Academic/Plenum Publishers 2004), 103–12, at 109. For broader legal considerations, see also Johannes Neumann, 'Die Kirchen und ihr Charakter als Körperschaften des öffentlichen Rechts', *Religion, Staat, Gesellschaft*, 2/1 (2001), 11–46.

[24]   Concerning the differences in the organizational structure at a national level and the theological self-understanding for the Protestant and the Catholic prison chaplaincy, see recently Jahn, 'Gefängnisseelsorge', 8–9, as well as Jürgen Ziemer, *Seelsorgerlehre. Eine Einführung für Studium und Praxis* (Göttingen: Vandenhoeck & Ruprecht, 2000).

[25]   Cf. two articles of the Basic Law, at the federal level: 4 on religious freedom and freedom of conscience, 140 about religious communities and the respect of holy days; as

aspects of the collaboration between state and church in German prisons, Susanne Eick-Wildgans notes[26] that both aim at transmitting to the prisoners the fundamental value of caring for peace, human dignity and the striving for justice, and freedom for all human beings. She finds that the churches have a neutral position in prison, and therefore they can do this much better than the state, she concludes. In order to grasp the implications of this point of view, it is necessary to understand that today spiritual care in prison is organized along two lines: the institutional chaplaincy (mostly Catholic and Protestant) on the one hand, and spiritual care on request for inmates belonging to religious minorities on the other.[27] In the philanthropic prison projects of the early twentieth century, the organization of religious practice was integrated into the proclaimed overall aim of prisons so that religion would favour inmates' personal repentance. Today, in a context of religious plurality, the guarantee of the individual right to religious freedom is independent and potentially in tension with the institutionally offered religion.

In every prison of the East German *Länder* one Protestant and one Catholic chaplain and one church or chapel is guaranteed, even where Catholics and Protestants are a minority.[28] The chaplains are required to be present for a stipulated number of hours per day; they are the only permanent employees whose task is to look after religious matters. They have their own office in the prison building; they can move around freely in the building (which is why they always carry a lot of keys); and they are protected by the right to keep their conversations with inmates confidential. The state directly or indirectly contributes to their salary, but it does not put them under the authority of the prison governor. According to Eick-Wildgans, the chaplain is part of the prison staff and his role is therefore not limited to giving advice but includes active participation in decisions taken by the prison administration.[29] He is the only religious agent who is part of the committee that decides upon the treatment of individual prisoners. The official tasks of chaplains in Eastern Germany include an almost overwhelming list of duties: to celebrate religious services, administer the sacraments, take confession, hold meetings with individuals and groups, have confidential meetings with willing inmates, provide spiritual care and material support for convicts' families and for all prison staff, contribute to the planning of prisoners' sentence programmes and reintegration after their release, organize leisure activities, and give their opinion about requests for pardon and early release.

---

well as art. 141 of the Weimar Constitution on religious instruction, and §§ 53 and 54 of the Penal Law on spiritual care and religious services respectively.

[26]   See *Anstaltseelsorge*, 65.

[27]   These inmates have the right to request a meeting with a recognized representative of their religious community. The latter, however, are not employed on a regular basis by the institution.

[28]   Legal perspective maintains that ideally one full-time chaplain should be employed per 250 inmates – see Eick-Wildgans, *Anstaltseelsorge*, 179.

[29]   Ibid., 182.

To sum up, prison chaplains now enjoy a much more comfortable position than during the time of the GDR. While prison structures have changed fundamentally, prison chaplains and prison officers have often remained the same, thereby creating continuity within the change. Their strengthened position allows prison chaplains to operate on a range of levels. Everybody in prison knows the chaplain and knows how to get in touch with him or her.[30] When I asked inmates how they find out on arrival in prison that there is a chaplain and what they can ask him, the answers were all similar. The principal source of information is the other inmates; then there are posters and advertisements on particular walls and in the inmate newspaper (if there is one); and, finally, there are the other employees, social workers, educators, and so on. Often the chaplains go to meet new prisoners when they arrive. Some answers were particularly revealing. 'Bernd' was a minor when he started robbing banks, for which he was repeatedly imprisoned. When I interviewed him, he was almost thirty years old; this time, he was in prison for holding up a bank. He thus had some experience of prison life, and although he was not a believer nor had any religious practice, he knew everything about the prison chaplaincy:

> There is one [chaplain] in every prison, you simply know it as an inmate that there is a pastor and that you can go and see him, if you want to talk … It's also written in the house plan … and in every unit, there is information about religious services and stuff.

Steven, a young and poorly educated East German inmate of prison B told me that, after he had been imprisoned, he had met an inmate who told him that

> one can also go to the church in here … And I thought he was kidding me and then I met the pastor and simply asked him, 'Can we really go to church here?' And he answered, 'Yes.'

Interestingly and understandably, it was a surprise for Steven to learn that there was a church in prison. Once this was a possibility for him and he had made contact with the chaplain, he participated regularly. The following discourse analysis of the extent and meaning of the activities of prison chaplains, as seen from the point of view of both chaplains and inmates, will show in more detail how such changes were approached in practice. The major changes in prison chaplaincy came either from the top – that is, from the newly employed West German prison governors – or from the growing number of non-German inmates who are more likely than East Germans to have a religious affiliation.

---

[30]   About 17 per cent of Protestant chaplains are women in Germany. See http://www.gefaengnisseelsorge.de/personensuche.html, accessed 17 July 2011. According to information received from the federal conference of Catholic prison chaplains, this proportion is just a little lower for Catholics.

Today, the representatives of all legally recognized religious communities are also entitled to offer spiritual support to their members within state institutions. Since prisoners have the right to religious freedom, they need to request such support. Despite this apparent legal equality, some disparities persist and are visible, for instance, in the terminology concerning religious needs.[31] In most cases, the established chaplains try to cope with requests coming from inmates of 'other' religions, such as the request for prayer rugs by Muslims:

> *Chaplain Boris*: Many ask me, for instance, to bring them a rug to pray on, and I bring one in from outside the prison. They are happy and use it. A couple of times they said, 'For some festivals we would like to go to the church, simply so that we can be together', for instance, after Ramadan, that they can be together and enjoy it, and so we provide the room and one of our colleagues supervises them, but the initiative comes from the Muslims.

So outside the Christian offer, spiritual care is offered on request. Therefore, the chaplain's personality plays an important role; his connections outside prison and his commitment to inter-faith dialogue are crucial. This mediation, or brokerage, as Beckford and Gilliat term it,[32] is problematic from the point of view of the 'others' since spiritual concerns are best addressed by those who share the same cultural relation to transcendence.

Relocating Religion in the 'Third Sector'

The demise of the GDR changed completely the terms of ex-offenders' reintegration and their relations to religious institutions and agents.[33] The notions of 'crimes' and 'prisoners' have now a different connotation: political crimes and prisoners have disappeared – at least in the sense understood by the dissidents of the time[34] – while drug-related offences, for instance, have increased. In some respects, the reasons have disappeared that impelled protesters originally to campaign against prisons. The *Wende* was associated with the long-awaited

---

[31]   For example, when legal texts refer to the attendance of religious services, they do not take into consideration that this terminology cannot be applied to other forms of collective religious practices such as prayers. Cf. Werner Wanzura (ed.), *Moslems im Strafvollzug* (Altenberge: Verlag für Christl.-Islam. Schrifttum, 1982).

[32]   See *Religion in Prison*.

[33]   This chapter is based partly on my working paper: Irene Becci, 'Collapse and Creation: The Rise and Fall of Religion in East German Offender Rehabilitation Programmes', Working Paper no. 109 (Max Planck Institute for Social Anthropology, Halle/Saale, 2008).

[34]   According to the SED's official information, there were no political prisoners in the GDR's prisons: cf. among others Wolfgang Rüddenklau, *Störenfried. DDR-Opposition 1986–1989* (Berlin: BasisDruck, 1992).

opportunity to democratize the justice system.[35] As Förster writes, the *Wende* 'opened the doors of the prisons and for the first time made imprisonment a little more transparent to the public – a topic that was taboo during the GDR was publicly discussed'.[36]

Hans had experienced this change first hand. He told me that he had been imprisoned in spring 1989 after having been sentenced to serve more than fifteen years. His sentence was reconsidered after the *Wende*, and he was released in 2000. With the help of the housing programme of a secular rehabilitation programme, he found a flat. Having been an alcoholic for years, he had attended a Christian rehabilitation programme during the GDR era, as a result of which he had become attracted to religious questions, although his father was 'in the Party', as he put it, which implied a strict atheistically oriented family background.

After his trial, he had been very afraid of prison, since he was to go to a prison in Brandenburg that had the reputation of being a particularly violent and desperate place. He remembers:

> I had mentally put an end [to my life] after I was imprisoned: 'Either I survive the time or not.' If the *Wende* hadn't happened, I would have remained in [prison B] for 15 years: nobody knows whether I would have survived that time ... then the *Wende* [came] and a lot of aid organizations entered the picture.

In Hans's reasoning, the *Wende* appeared clearly as life saving. Additionally, opening prisons to the public meant that the public would now start to deal with the problems surrounding imprisonment. However, many expectations about the public interest in prison were disappointed. The general population showed little interest in the new view of rehabilitation,[37] which saw religion as an important resource for rehabilitation, alongside education and work.

Activists who had a closer link with the church split into two sections: an institutional section (for example, *Caritas* for Catholics and *Diakonie* for Protestants[38], ecological groups and Fairtrade shops) and a kind of underground wing (for example, the anti-fascist and anti-militarist *Kirche von Unten*,[39] which provides an alternative space for political groups, punk concerts, soup kitchens,

---

[35]   The prisons were almost empty (by October 1990, the percentage of imprisoned people was one third of that in West Germany), but they filled up again quickly within a couple of months.

[36]   Thomas Förster, 'Beratung Straffälliger unter spezifischen Bedingungen in den neuen Bundesländern', in Raimund Hompesch, Gabriele Kawamura and Richard Reindl (eds), *Verarmung – Abweichung – Kriminalität. Straffälligenhilfe vor dem Hintergrund gesellschaftlicher Polarisierung* (Bonn: Forum Verlag Godesberg, 1996), 112–23, at 112 (my translation).

[37]   See Förster, *Beratung*.

[38]   These are among the six major organizations that provide social aid in Germany.

[39]   For *Kirche von Unten* (literally, 'church from below' or 'church at the grassroots'), see its website www.kvu-berlin.de, accessed 1 April 2012.

debates, and so on, in East Berlin). That religion had found a new place in East German society became clear by the time the so-called 'Round Tables'[40] had disappeared in 1993. While churches received remarkable juridical and political recognition (including some financial support) from the state, the majority of the population no longer belonged to any church. However, churches were expected to participate in public and political life, while keeping away from state power.

The German Constitution grants church-related organizations a privileged status so that they can shape and implement welfare and social service provision.[41] As had been the case in West Germany, the principle of subsidiarity[42] became the cornerstone of the welfare system.[43] This principle is rooted in Christianity's social doctrine;[44] its introduction meant that the entire organization of welfare provision was turned upside down and that a third sector – or voluntary sector – had to be moulded by a civil society that lacked appropriate structures. While the rehabilitation of ex-offenders had been organized in a top-down, centralized way during Socialism, the post-unification principle called for the social forces at the lowest possible level to provide such social services. However, as East

---

[40]   This expression refers to committees formed 'during the time of upheaval of the GDR in order to overcome a national state of emergency and which took over legislative and executive tasks, although they did not have a legitimate mandate authorised by a democratic election. Participants of all opposition forces faced the representatives of the old power as equal opponents at the round tables' – see http://www.chronikderwende.de/english/, accessed 17 July 2011.

[41]   Cf. also Articles 15 and 32 of the Unification Treaty and Paragraph 10 of the *Bundessozialhilfegesetz* (federal law relating to social aid).

[42]   In Germany, the *Subsidiaritätsprinzip* (subsidiarity principle) means 'the distribution of public tasks to different juridical agents', such as associations and other institutions, Dietrich Pirson, 'Subsidiaritätsprinzip', in Wolfgang Stammler, Adalbert Erler and Ekkehard Kaufmann (eds), *Handwörterbuch zur deutschen Rechtsgeschichte*, vol. 5 (Berlin: Erich Schmidt Verlag, 1998), 70–72, at 70. As long as smaller, local organizations are able to provide services, they should do so, while institutions at regional or national level intervene only when their capacities or structures are no longer sufficient. Jörg Bergmann argues that this principle is not only an abstract juridical measure aimed at limiting the state's intervention in private life, but it can also design a general rule of social interaction, according to which people first organize at their local level to solve problems before making requests to the state, Jörg Bergmann, 'Das Subsidiaritätsprinzip " zwischen Sozialstaat und Lebenswelt"', in Adalbert Evers (ed.), *Sozialstaat* (Gießen: Ferber, 1998), 240–63.

[43]   Gabriele Metzler, *Der deutsche Sozialstaat. Vom Bismarckschen Erfolgsmodell zum Pflegefall* (Stuttgart and München: DVA, 2003), 196–7.

[44]   The philosophical background of the principle of subsidiarity as a social theory is Aquinas' doctrine of *bonum commune* (the common good) – it sees individuals and smaller communities operating in the service of the common good and therefore receiving wide-ranging powers. John Calvin also referred to this concept in his social doctrine. However, it was only in 1931 that the principle was formulated explicitly in an encyclical letter of the Catholic Church: see Pirson, 'Subsidiaritätsprinzip', 70, and Bergmann, 'Das Subsidiaritätsprinzip'.

German society had had hardly any formally constituted associations at this level, the groups emerging from the civil movements, the churches and *Caritas* felt compelled to take on major initiatives. The introduction of the subsidiarity principle not only gave the main churches a privileged position, but other Christian churches and organizations, which offered social services, suddenly benefited from playing a highly valued role in society. Moreover, the subsidiarity principle clearly encouraged plurality so that the 1990s saw a veritable blossoming of the third sector.[45] However, as Helmut Anheier, Eckhard Priller and Annette Zimmer point out,[46] this transformation was fraught with tension and criticism. Critical voices argued that, while the new welfare associations had received extensive public funding for their intervention in the East, they continued to be based in the West. Hence East Germans did not

> regard these institutions as independent nonprofit organizations, but as public or quasi-public institutions … Furthermore, the two biggest welfare associations – Diakonie and Caritas – are church-affiliated institutions … Critics see the public support for Diakonie and Caritas in East Germany as a peaceful colonization in an effort to re-Christianize a secular society.[47]

The rehabilitation of ex-offenders has become a significant social problem since the collapse of Socialism. While it was organized following government legislation during the Socialist era, the introduction of the principle of subsidiarity turned the lines of command upside down, as greater importance came to be placed on civil and religious associations and organizations. Some secular and Protestant institutions simply extended their services to the East, but many East Germans used the change in policy to create secular and religious institutions. In my research, I focused on a number of institutions of this kind, especially organizations that had begun caring for ex-offenders during the 1990s. Values such as humanity and human dignity now guide the actions of both secular and religious East German agencies. East Germans who are active in the reconstruction of the third sector have endowed their practices with meaning and a distinctive and constructive moral orientation that is based on the experience of the *Wende*.

If associations fulfil the particular criteria set by a legal framework (such as not discriminating against people on the basis of religious adherence or targeting a legally defined category of people, and so on) and if they collaborate with the state administration (for example, regarding economic and political transparency), they receive public funding; however, this means that they have to be linked to one of

---

[45]   Cf. Helmut K. Anheier and Eckhard Priller, 'The Non-Profit Sector in East Germany: Before and After Unification', *Voluntas: International Journal of Voluntary and Non-profit Organizations*, 2/1 (1991), 78–94.

[46]   'Civil Society in Transition: The East German Third Sector Ten Years after Unification', *East European Politics and Societies*, 15/1 (2000), 139–56.

[47]   Ibid., 148.

the major associations (*Spitzenverbände*). Hence the manner in which providers of social aid to ex-offenders in Eastern Germany relate to one another is marked by competition rather than collaboration.

Thus, while religious institutions in the East received strong organizational support from the West, civil activists made a significant contribution by shaping the new fields of social aid from below, using their knowledge of what their 'target groups' needed. As a result, the meeting of religious and secular agencies was intermingled with East–West issues relating to an imbalance of power.

The field of ex-offender rehabilitation today includes state institutions and secular non-governmental associations as well as church-related associations and institutions.[48] Some had been re-created after unification, either by politically active East Germans (partly in connection with the initiatives of the Round Tables) or by West German agencies who had recently established themselves in East Germany; others are part of expanded West German institutions (for example, the *Universal-Stiftung*, a secular association founded in West Berlin by a committed actor, and Protestant social welfare organizations such as *Stadtmission*, focusing on urban social problems). Among the numerous programmes that provide offender rehabilitation in Germany,[49] about a quarter are located in Eastern Germany and a quarter of these have a religious (broadly Christian) orientation. The state administrations now consider established religions important partners for rehabilitating ex-convicts.[50] Usually Christian (Protestant and Catholic) support centres (*Caritas*, *Diakonie*, *Stadtmission*, *Schwarzes Kreuz*, and so on) are listed in prison newspapers and brochures, and on websites concerned with offender rehabilitation (these are issued by state

---

[48]   See also two previous texts of mine on which this chapter is based: Irene Becci, 'The Rehabilitation of Ex-offenders in Eastern Germany: A Religious–Secular Configuration', in Rajtar and Peperkamp (eds), *Religion*, 167–87, and 'Religion im Aufbau der Haftentlassenenhilfe in Ostdeutschland', in Pickel and Sammet (eds), *Religion*, 279–90.

[49]   According to the *Bundesarbeitsgemeinschaft für Straffälligenhilfe e.V.*, which is the federal umbrella agency for offender rehabilitation, over 300 organizations are active in the field throughout Germany. The number of such organizations is much higher in Bavaria than in Baden-Wurttemberg, for example. I draw on the following sources: my own research data, including data collected at a federal *Caritas* meeting, the documents produced by the observed association of support to ex-offenders, and socialnet website, http://socialnet.de/, an internet platform providing information on social services and non-profit management, accessed 1 May 2011.

[50]   Klaus D. Hildemann (ed.), *Die Freie Wohlfahrtspflege. Ihre Entwicklung zwischen Auftrag und Markt* (Leipzig: Evangelische Verlagsanstalt, 2004).

institutions and secular and religious non-governmental organizations[51]), while institutions led by other religious communities are rarely included.[52]

In the following section, I shall distinguish secular providers of social assistance, which operate in the field of ex-offender rehabilitation, from those that are anchored in Protestant or Roman Catholic churches. This exercise will reveal some similarities between the secular support of ex-offenders – including the self-understanding of the organizations – and some East German denominational agencies. This similarity, I argue, is the result of a secularized understanding of the way religious agencies relate to post-Socialist society.

Secular Rehabilitation Programmes

There are more secular than religious institutions in the field of ex-offender rehabilitation in Eastern Germany. I shall describe two associations that emerged from the *Wende* and still exist at the time of writing: one is located in Saxony-Anhalt, the other in East Berlin.

In 2006, I contacted the head of the *Landesverband für Straffälligen- und Bewährungshilfe Sachsen-Anhalt*,[53] a state-wide network of associations that offer offender rehabilitation.[54] My question about the role of religion in the field of offender rehabilitation almost shocked her: 'We are against it because we want people to take responsibility for themselves.' However, she then advised me to call a pastor who had played a leading role in an ecumenical working group created in 1990 for the prison in Magdeburg; it included socially active citizens, prison governors and church members. The pastor invited me to attend the opening of an exhibition in the Magdeburg prison. Prisoners had drawn numerous paintings, some of which had religious themes (such as orthodox churches, hands folded in prayer). Most of them, however, rather evoked what numerous prisoners craved: naked women, drugs, and so on. Figure 2.1 illustrates the painting that won the jury's prize.

---

[51]   The *Ratgeber für Inhaftierte, Haftentlassene und deren Angehörige* (guide for inmates, former inmates and their families), which is published by the *Arbeiterwohlfahrt Kreisverband Chemnitz und Umgebung* (Worker Welfare Association for Chemnitz and Surroundings), includes advertisements for, for instance, *Missionarinnen der Nächstenliebe* (Missionaries of Charity) and *Caritas*.

[52]   The website http://www.bag-straffaelligenhilfe.de/bereich3_2 refers to the Central Council of Muslims in Germany, accessed 1 May 2011.

[53]   Cf. http://www.lvsb.homepage.t-online.de/, accessed 1 May 2011.

[54]   This network now links over fifteen non-governmental associations and collaborates closely with state institutions. Its contribution to public debates in the Land has been very effective.

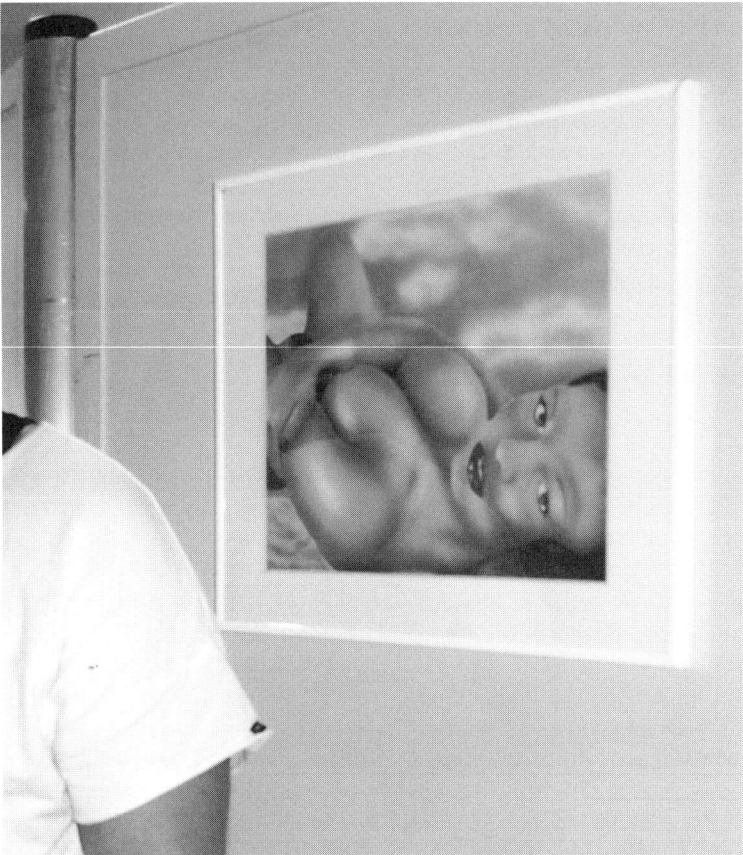

Figure 2.1   The painting, by a prisoner, that won the Magdeburg prison
               exhibition competition © Irene Becci, August 2006

On this occasion, the pastor introduced me to a former governor of the prison
and to social workers of the support centre for released prisoners. While we all sat
at a table, the pastor told the story of how the local support association for released
prisoners had been formed:

> Shortly before unification, the local association for offender rehabilitation was
> founded in Magdeburg, and shortly afterwards the regional association [was
> formed] … The church, because it was not integrated into the Socialist state, was
> the first contact for the independent initiatives. When the local association was
> created, there were only church people there, from the Protestant social welfare
> network, *Caritas* … Those active in the initiatives from the West contacted the
> church first. So the two associations were mostly founded by church people.
> This, however, changed right away because we thought the church should not
> remain in this position, but that the associations were free … the church can

only help with the birth [of something], so that autonomous associations and initiatives can develop ... and the local association changed very quickly in that way. The church people joined other initiatives instead – *Caritas*, the Protestant social welfare organization *Diakonie*.

If church people left the secular organizations once they were in place, the opposite occurred as well: secular individuals who had been active inside the churches around the time of the *Wende* began to leave the churches and launch initiatives of their own. Some of the most active and well-known associations in East Berlin resulted from this kind of process in the 1990s. Their posters and advertisements do not remain unnoticed in prison waiting rooms or in prison-related magazines. One of them, the *Freie Hilfe Berlin*, has a clear territorial and historical reference to Eastern Germany. Not only are its main offices located in East Berlin, it is also the result of initiatives that the *Wende* set in motion. Its creation during the early 1990s was a response to the needs of those who had grown up in the GDR and were now released from prison but did not feel comfortable with turning to institutions that they considered to be 'Western'.[55] Today, the *Freie Hilfe Berlin* offers a wide range of rehabilitation programmes to convicts and former inmates, focusing on work, computer skills, the arts, housing, and drug rehabilitation. Some are geared specifically towards migrants, others towards women or youth. The support offered is generally of a very practical nature, so that issues concerning values are not placed in the foreground. Prisoners and their families are aware of the association because of its prominent advertisements. Its brochure published for its tenth anniversary illustrates this affirmation:

> The birth of the *FREIE HILFE BERLIN* association came about during the middle of the 1990s, in the often recalled time of the *Wende*. In a variety of different places, activists met at round tables, in forums, groups and discussions, and lobbied for the organization of a new type of assistance and support for offender rehabilitation that would also take their previous experience into account. From a mixture of feelings and perspectives it was not easy to create something new that had not previously been possible and to embed it into strong existing structures that had long since been challenged, something that would reflect a meaningful and feasible conception of a needs-oriented association for the support of offender rehabilitation ... In this context, the people of the Pankow and Prenzlauer Berg districts who became involved more or less by chance joined together to found a non-governmental organization to support the

---

[55]   Cf. Freie Hilfe Berlin e.V., *10 Jahre Freie Straffälligenhilfe in Berlin. Festzeitung zum 10 jährigen Jubiläum des Freie Hilfe Berlin e.V.* (Berlin, 29–31 March 2000). The division of the clientele of these organizations in this way was widely shared. While talking to a Western representative of the Protestant Church in Berlin, I mentioned that I was following a reintegration programme in East Berlin. He commented that I was probably working with skinheads, as in his opinion East German inmates were primarily right-wing skinheads.

rehabilitation of ex-convicts. Metaphorically speaking, this is how the sperm
fertilized the egg.[56]

This extract connects with the metaphor of the 'help with the birth', which the
Magdeburg pastor mentioned earlier. Both this secular organization and the
Protestant pastor used metaphors relating to creative processes when referring
to the *Wende*. These activists continue to participate actively in public debates,
animated by the spirit of the Round Table, with the aim of improving the extent
of political participation among citizens.[57] For this rehabilitation programme,
religion plays a very minor role.

Protestant Institutional Support to Ex-offenders

Ex-offender rehabilitation and prison conditions in Eastern Germany are no
longer a priority for the grassroots activists of the Protestant churches. As church
organizations have moved closer to the state, they have become politically less
independent, but they have probably become more influential. A good example of
this is the Berlin Protestant social welfare centre – *Berliner Stadtmission*[58] – which
is located close to Berlin's main railway station and one of West Berlin's largest
prisons. In 2001, the centre started a programme called *Drinnen und Draußen*
(inside and outside), which provides support for inmates who are close to being
released (within two years of their release) and prepares them by finding housing,
offering training opportunities, mediating in conflicts with their partners, and so
on. The ex-inmates continue to receive support for a while once they have left
prison. The programme does not address East German ex-inmates in particular,
although they form a considerable percentage of the 'clients'.[59] I met various ex-
convicts, some of their closest relatives, and employees when I took part in the
activities of this programme, but only a few of them were indeed East Germans.
When the programme was launched in a Berlin prison in October 2006, I was able
to observe how close it was to state institutions. A state minister and the prison
governor said how grateful they were that the programme existed, and that they
placed great trust in it. The programme emphasized its role in conveying values
to ex-offenders, above all the values of family and responsibility. Although the
programme struggled with funding, it was able to rely on its strong ties with the

---

[56]   Freie Hilfe Berlin e.V., *10 Jahre*, 4 (my translation).

[57]   For instance, the debates on 'The Prison as a Place of Violence?' in the newspaper
Die Tageszeitung in Berlin, on 13 November 2007.

[58]   This type of Protestant support organization for ex-offenders also exists in Saxony
and Saxony-Anhalt.

[59]   According to information given to me by staff, they number about 200 every
year. The word 'client' has come to replace the word 'user' in social work, illustrating the
paradigmatic shift towards a more managerial language in social care.

Protestant Church, which had promoted it as a denominational agency. The often-mentioned strength of the Protestant churches in the provision of social care in Eastern Germany has to be reconsidered with regard to ex-offender rehabilitation, since many East German Protestant agents see themselves better placed in secular organizations. I argue that this shift of religion into the secular world is a typical pattern that Protestantism follows in Eastern Germany.

Aid from the Catholic Side: Change and Continuity

The main Catholic agency in the field of offender rehabilitation is the *Caritas* association. As mentioned above, *Caritas* already existed during the Socialist era, but by the time the GDR had collapsed it had become clear that the East German *Caritas* had transformed into something 'completely different' from what it was in West Germany, as an employee expressed it when I interviewed him in Berlin in January 2007. He said, 'Caritas has just emerged here from the parishes', much more than had been the case in the West. The parish was indeed the organizational anchor for *Caritas* during the GDR era, as it would have been impossible to organize a legally registered association at the time.[60] In the Socialist environment, *Caritas* allowed Catholics to 'invoke Christian charity without speaking'[61] – that is, without using a religious vocabulary. This understanding of its role, as a provider of social assistance, continued after the *Wende*, as the interviewed *Caritas* employee explained: 'the structure came from the West but many things, our understanding of our work or of the "provision of services" as they [the Westerners] say, to understand how I do what I do, this is still strongly rooted in the East.' In this way, he outlined the importance for East German Catholics to appropriate Western structures.

The employees of the *Caritas* offender rehabilitation programme in Eastern Germany know each other well and meet on a regular basis. One of its most important centres is located in the town of Frankfurt (Oder) in Brandenburg. Most of the social workers involved in the programmes that the centre organizes got to know each other during their social work studies at the Catholic University for Applied Sciences, which was founded in Berlin immediately after unification.[62] During my 2007 interview with one of the coordinators of this centre in Berlin, he explained how working for Caritas meant continuity to him:

> After the *Wende* I had the opportunity – I had always been interested, but didn't have the necessary diploma, since I had not taken part in the *Jugendweihe* [Socialist youth ritual] – ... to attend a Catholic school. It was again about questioning values – I find that important – and broadening my point of view.

---

[60] Pilvousek, 'Caritas', 54.
[61] Ibid., 59.
[62] Cf. http://www.khsb-berlin.de, accessed 17 July 2011.

Today, I still rely on what I experienced there … After the *Wende*, in my first
semester, people took the opportunity again – we were questioning what the
professors from the West presented, not only in terms of knowledge, but also in
terms of values. We were all in the middle of our lives and we had all experienced
the *Wende* in such a conscious way that we were questioning a lot of things. It
really was a time of uprising, it was really great as we tried so hard to contribute
to shaping our school. I was just talking about that recently, we still make use of
the contacts and the experience of the time.

For these social workers, their schools remain 'points of identification'. In
2006, the office in Frankfurt Oder celebrated its tenth anniversary by organizing
a gathering at the centre, a multi-level building that houses offices, a chapel, a
nursery and a large church. Prison wardens, representatives of the Protestant and
Catholic churches, and local politicians were invited, and a local theatre company
performed a play about imprisonment. The politicians spoke and praised the
work of *Caritas* in the area: the presence of *Caritas* was, one official said, 'a
sign that Frankfurt's prisons are humane ones.' On various occasions – during the
anniversary celebrations, but also when I met those involved in other contexts –
the words 'humanity' and 'Christianity' were used interchangeably.

The posters on the office walls presented the history of the programme,
showing continuous activity since the 1970s when the first *Caritas* assistance
programme for released prisoners in Frankfurt was created. Until the end of the
GDR, the few people active in the organization kept in continual contact with
the inmates and the priests who were allowed to visit them. After 1989, however,
the activities depicted on the posters multiplied: housing programmes, training of
volunteers, debt management, school presentations, photo exhibitions, and so on.
In 1990, the organization was part of a Ministry of Justice commission charged
with reorganizing the prison system. In 1996, an office (with a staff of three
employees) was set up to assist released inmates looking for accommodation, with
other offices following throughout the state of Brandenburg. It was interesting to
see the display of continuous activities in the office, from the GDR period until
the reopening in 1996. Often staff stressed continuity between the Socialist past
and the present as evidence for their experience and current competence. In 2007,
the opening of a photo exhibition in a Frankfurt church gathered local officials and
ministers. With the support of *Caritas*, a photographer had worked with inmates
for several months and their pictures were then exhibited in the church. While
the ministers praised the collaboration with churches for offender rehabilitation,
a member of the local authority commented that East Germans had a particular
relationship with walls. The aim of exhibiting the prisoners' photographs was, he
said, to show in public what happens 'behind the walls. In the GDR,' he continued,
'we all have experience with walls and know how important that is.'

Caritas has survived unification almost unscathed and was actually invigorated
by the experience. After the difficulties during Socialism, the restructuring of

Caritas as an association 'went without any major problems'.[63] *Caritas* employees did not associate the change with a decline of religiosity or with a shrinking of the political dimension of religion. On the contrary, since unification the religious community around them has been strengthened.

The 'Free Evangelical' Offer

An important Christian association working in the field of offender rehabilitation is the *Schwarzes Kreuz*[64] – *the black cross* – *which was discontinued during the GDR and allowed again only after the Wende* in the East. In Brandenburg, Saxony and Berlin it was built up following the West German structure. Its volunteers are particularly active in prisons and only to a limited extent outside of them. It is basically an association guided by committed Christians – such as Baptists – that aims at linking together volunteers and social workers. It trains volunteers and organizes help to inmates to prepare their release. It supports them in finding an apartment or a job. In its public (real or virtual[65]) appearance, its Christian orientation becomes very clear: Bible verses are quoted at length or Christian prayers and songs are encouraged at every meeting. Being a very large but loose network for the moment in East Germany – the volunteers of the network are present on a wide territorial area, but they are quite dispersed –, its influence remains modest.

Ex-inmates can also find support in other Christian institutions that are not conceived directly for offender rehabilitation but for related problems, such as family conflicts or drug addictions. Some associations of this type are located in East Berlin: the *Evangelische Beratungsstellen*, helpdesks for persons in distress or experiencing life crisis, that opened in East Berlin in 1991; the Salvation Army; and *Ichthys*, a centre for the rehabilitation of alcoholics founded in 1992/93 by a couple of Baptists coming from West Germany. These associations present themselves ostensibly as Christian and they describe their work as the necessary contribution to the re-evangelisation of the East, often provoking scepticism among East Germans.[66]

Conclusion

In this chapter, I have attempted to illustrate, on the one hand, the institutional strengthening of the churches after Socialism and, on the other, the simultaneous withdrawal of the state from social functions, which made for a complete

---

[63]   Pilvousek, 'Caritas', 60.

[64]   See www.schwarzes-kreuz.de, accessed 17 July 2011.

[65]   Cf. their monthly newsletter, 'News'.

[66]   Mathias and Philipp were first released into one of these institutions for alcoholics. They told me that only a few days later they escaped because they could not stand the insistence on Christian morality put forward all day long by the leader of the institution.

reorientation of all agents involved in social assistance. In post-Socialist Eastern Germany, the different ways secular and religious actors relate to the time of social change, now known as the *Wende*, and its aftermath reveal variations in the understanding of secular–religious configurations. While Catholics were able to adapt to the new structural environment by building on their experience during the Socialist era, Protestant and secular agents experienced a much more incisive change. For them, the events that took place around the time of unification laid the foundations for what is now viewed as specifically East German. While the relationship between the secular and the religious had become increasingly conflictive during the GDR era, the *Wende* has changed this relationship fundamentally. Analysis of the reformation of the institutional landscape of social assistance for ex-offenders in Eastern Germany finally reveals that, in a way, the secular and religious agents can be seen to have emerged from one another. The demographic changes in religious diversity, combined with the introduction of establishment, enabled spiritual care to assume an important presence in state prisons. Certainly, it has also become more individualized. The degree to which those requesting spiritual care hold secular attitudes alters significantly the way chaplains interpret their mandate. They still communicate without using an explicitly religious vocabulary that would not find any understanding, while emphasizing, as in the secular discourse, the universal character of their message. The analysis that follows draws on different empirical cases that together offer an explanation of the ways in which all these changes were experienced by religious actors, inmates and ex-inmates.

Chapter 3
Transformations of Religion during and after Imprisonment

Prison: A Total Institution in Society

Prisons are total institutions – that is, structures that in Erving Goffman's sense tend to define the totality of human agency.[1] In this section, I shall address to what extent the prison context affects religious practices and discourses. In order to do so, it is necessary to combine the concepts that I have discussed previously with regard to the relation between religion and state, such as secularization, individualization, or pastoral power and pastoral care, with those deriving from the social study of prisons.

Religion occupies a particular place within prison. In Europe, prisons are state institutions, places in which the state keeps people who were sentenced for having committed crimes in detention, limiting their freedom and thereby punishing them in the name of the society it represents. However, religion is in principle part of a protected private sphere, that of religious freedom, which is a human right, even in prison. European prison institutions are not permitted to deprive individuals of their most fundamental rights, such as the right to health and to life, and their freedom of conscience or religion, although a particular frame of security and deprivation is set. I shall set out in this chapter how this paradoxical situation – freedom in deprivation – is dealt with and experienced by the different actors concerned, most of all by chaplains and inmates. A social constructionist perspective[2] offers plausible methodological tools to approach this apparent contradiction.

It is true that every prison is different, but it is also true that all prisons are the same in some way. The prisons I visited, not only the ones in Germany, looked very similar to me in many respects, although each one was simultaneously unique. Some features are common to prisons, and these are best described by using the concept of the 'total institution'.

There is a lengthy debate about the 'totality' of prisons that remains inconclusive, either the study of prison as a society or the study of a society in relation to what prisons reveal about it. A Goffmanian perspective tends to stress the differences between prison society and wider society and to concentrate on the particular character of total institutions and how it affects human behaviour. There are numerous authors who imply that any generalization is misleading. Others

---

[1] See *Asylums*.
[2] Beckford, *Social Theory and Religion*.

have studied prisons from a so-called 'diffusionist' perspective,[3] which means that social life inside prison is considered to be linked to outside society and that understanding the prison system helps in understanding society itself. Such an approach was adopted by Michel Foucault, for instance.[4] His study of the French penitentiary system has proved useful for analysis of various types of disciplinary settings that are located beyond national or temporal borders. As the first chapter of this book sought to document, the creation of the modern prison is linked to far-reaching developments in society, also with regard to religion. Religious actors were present from the very beginning and never really left the world of prisons, not even during the strictly atheistically oriented management of prisons during the GDR era. Over time, the churches have developed experience with prisons that other social institutions would find hard to match. They have become very skilled at adapting their presence in prisons to the various discourses on penal theory and prison life: punishment, discipline, humanization, rehabilitation, and so on. It would be misleading to interpret this change only in terms of secularization and imply that religion is fading also in prison. Rather, the role and place of religion have changed, as it now coexists with a set of new needs and arrangements. Analysis of the presence and management of religion in prison over time reveals much about the general place of religion in society. Studies on spiritual care, conducted in England and Wales, elucidate continuity between prisons and wider society.[5]

In prison, where control and resistance are in evidence every day, religion plays a role that goes well beyond the question of allowing prisoners to avail themselves of their right to religious freedom. In order to understand what role spiritual care and religion may play in prison, one needs to be aware of the social conditions in which inmates find themselves. These conditions are, in my view, set both by the internal world of the prison and by its link to the society outside. Some of the elements that account for the particularity of prisons actually depend on the way crime is managed outside prison. The fact that some social groups – such as immigrants and the poor – are now over-represented in the prison population indicates ongoing processes concerning social control in general. The prison society has a particular socio-demographic profile. Sociologists regard various social institutions, such as the justice system, the police, the job market, public policies (in particular, migration policies), and the economy, as more or less conducive to particular sections of the population committing crimes and being imprisoned. The prison population, for instance, consists to a very large extent

---

[3]   See Combessie, *Sociologie*, at 68.

[4]   See *Surveiller*.

[5]   See Beckford and Gilliat, *Religion*; Beckford et al., *Muslims*. For the situation in France, cf. Beckford et al., *Muslims*, and for the situation in Norway, cf. Furseth, *Muslims*. More European cases are treated in the April 2011 issue of *Archives des Sciences Sociales des Religions*.

of men. A majority of these are young men, non-nationals, with a noticeably low level of education. Many are drug addicts and alcoholics.[6]

As we know from scholarly work in the social study of religion, all these structural factors have an influence on religion – in terms of the frequency of religious practice, spirituality, and religious affiliation. In the sample on which this investigation is based, the inmates more likely to be religiously involved tended to be unmarried. Less than half of the inmates and ex-inmates interviewed had some kind of religious socialization (generally within the nuclear family) and participated in some religious practice. The educational levels of the interviewees varied: one prisoner had a university degree, others had A-level education, while still others had low levels of education, with some cases of illiteracy among the ex-convicts. Only two of the interviewees were foreign. Unfortunately, there are no reliable data on all the socio-demographic factors mentioned in relation to the whole prison population in Germany, nor in relation to the two prisons in this study, but prison is certainly a particular place of society in this respect, as it amplifies the degree of national diversity.[7] In Saxony,[8] on average, the proportion of foreign nationals was no higher than 3 per cent by the end of 2005, while in Saxony's prisons foreign inmates accounted for 12.5 per cent of the prison population in 2007 (having decreased from about 25 per cent in 1997). The majority are Polish (13.7 per cent), Vietnamese (11.8 per cent), Algerian (10.7 per cent) or Czech (10.5 per cent) nationals.[9] In the prisons of Brandenburg, the percentage of foreign inmates was around 17 in 2005, which is about ten times higher than in the wider society.[10]

Religion in prison – the experience of religion as well as the management and use of religion – is both specific and linked to, and signified by, wider developments. Every prison has some particularity in terms of actual facilities that allow some activities to run more or less well, such as education or vocational training, sports,

---

[6]   I do not consider systematically the crimes committed by the inmates interviewed. In fact, it would direct the research towards a biographical approach, whereas I deal with the links between the structural settings of prison and society and inmates' religious experience. The choice was motivated also by methodological concerns. Having only a limited possibility to interview and spend time with inmates, I avoided mentioning their crime expressly, suspecting that this would have oriented and monopolized the whole interaction.

[7]   Non-German inmates are affected particularly by imprisonment. See Mechthild Bereswill and Werner Greve (eds), *Forschungsthema Strafvollzug* (Baden-Baden: Nomos, 1995), and Loïc Wacquant, '"Suitable Enemies": Foreigners and Immigrants in the Prisons of Europe', *Punishment and Society*, 1/2 (1999), 215–22.

[8]   Here, the most common foreign nationality is Vietnamese, while in Brandenburg it is Polish: see Statistisches Jahrbuch Sachsen 2007 and Statistisches Jahrbuch Brandenburg 2006, at http://www.statistik-berlin-brandenburg.de/produkte/produkte_jahrbuch.asp and http://www.statistik.sachsen.de/html/6669.htm, both accessed 24 May 2011.

[9]   See http://www.justiz.sachsen.de/smj/content/959.php, accessed 9 April 2011.

[10]   The percentage of female prisoners in Brandenburg was 4.1 in 2010 (source: Amt für Statistik Berlin-Brandenburg, Potsdam Kulturbuch Verlag, 2010).

or spiritual care. Still, I maintain that religion in prison is, to a large extent, but not completely, determined by the character of the total institution. The conditions of detention, inmates' criminal experience, the way they relate to everyday struggles for freedom – in terms of space, time, their own bodies – and their social relations to other inmates create a situation in which religion gains a particular meaning. In prison, individuals are confronted with existential questions in a particularly intensive way. The inmate society is to some extent irregular and yet also endlessly monotonous. All this influences, in different ways, inmates' religious feelings and practices. However, other issues relate mainly to the general experience of imprisonment.

What allows me to extend my considerations beyond the prisons I visited, at least with regard to men's prisons in Eastern Germany, is that the inmates I interviewed had long-term sentences – that is, sentences of at least four years – and most of them therefore had experience of different prisons. Moreover, only some of those I observed as ex-inmates came from prison B. Aspects of my investigation that may be treated as general points are the symbolic meaning of religion and chaplaincy or the discourses held by chaplains and inmates about religious conversion. In the following exploration of how inmates develop religious practices and constructions in prison and how they change these after they leave prison, it may be shown that there are links between the outside and the inside of prison, but that these are intricate and complex.

In order to describe the elements that have to be considered as specific in the study of religion in prison, I shall concentrate on characteristics of the prison institution itself. Prisons create particular situations in which individuals act differently from the way they act outside, including with regard to religion. The total character of prisons leads to deprivation and alienation in many respects, and thereby influences social relations and identity formation. Prisoners have particular channels through which news from the outside world is relayed into the institution. Prison walls not only filter people but also news, messages and ideas. I see these consequences as the differences that are generated inside prison. Due to its particular place in prison, religion opens up a space where creative action and spontaneous tactics (in Michel de Certeau's sense) are possible. These conditions cease to exist materially for inmates at their release, but, as I shall illustrate, they may be prolonged by different factors.

Erving Goffman's study on asylums provides a conceptual tool kit for analysing 'total institutions'.[11] His definition is rather inclusive, as it refers to the facts that, in such organizations, (1) all 'aspects of life are conducted in the same place and under the same single authority', (2) each 'phase of the member's daily activity is carried on in the immediate company of a large batch of others, all of whom are treated alike and required to do the same thing together', and

---

[11]   Some of the results presented in this chapter have been published in my article 'The Curious Attraction of Religion in East German Prisons', in Courtney Bender and Pamela E. Klassen (eds), *After Pluralism* (New York: Columbia University Press, 2010), 296–316. Reprinted with permission of the publisher.

(3) 'all activities make sense within the proclaimed aim of the institution'.[12] This definition thus points to space ('in the same place'), time ('phase of ... daily activity'), and the heteronymous character of inmates' action. The last part of the definition includes in my view two kinds of consequences: the alteration of inmates' relations to themselves (body) and to other inmates. Prisons are certainly total institutions, insofar as a central authority determines all aspects of the lives of those who are incarcerated – their movements in space, their activities during the day, their opportunities to take care of their bodies and to some extent their social relationships. In short, I shall keep in mind the specificity of prisons in terms of space, time, body, and the social relations among inmates and with the outside world. Using these elementary categories enables me to include a wide range of factors; however, the list does not include every factor that shapes prison as a particular institution in society. To be exhaustive in this sense is impossible, since the experience of imprisonment is also influenced by the inmate's personal and individual perceptions and biography.

A consideration of how chaplaincy is embedded in these aspects within prisons A and B will allow me to define the role of religion for inmates and religious actors. I shall also provide some information about these four aspects at national and local level.

Space

Space is scrupulously subdivided in prison. The way this is done reflects the hierarchies of the different sections in prison: for inmates, space is certainly a rare commodity. The cells are narrow and dark. When I interviewed Stefan, a former bank robber, it was a hot day in summer and I wondered what it was like to be in his cell. He said:

> Now it's fine, but two weeks ago it was bad. The temperature was as high as 31 degrees [Celsius] at night, no draught; what can you do, if the door is closed?

There are enormous disparities between the German *Länder* in terms of density of prison occupancy. In most cases, prisons located close to big cities have a greater density of occupancy.[13] According to official statistics,[14] conditions are acceptable in Saxony (A), where the level of occupation stands below the foreseen limit. In

---

[12]   Goffman, *Asylums*, 17.

[13]   In Berlin, prisons are often crowded. Its largest prison, Tegel, officially has 1,571 places, but at the beginning of 2009, 1,581 inmates were in fact imprisoned: see http://www.berlin.de/jva-tegel/02_UeberUns/03_Statistische_Angaben/Statistik.pdf, accessed 9 April 2011.

[14]   See www.justiz.sachsen.de, accessed 31 December 2011.

both studied prisons some inmates share their cell with one or two persons, while others are more than happy to be alone:[15]

> *Franz*: When I was given a single cell – I closed the door and that was it. I don't want to have nothing to do with anybody else any longer, because they go 'blah-blah-blah-blah' – shit, a lot of rubbish.

Another crucial issue concerning space is that, in prison, inmates depend on the institution and its agents for all their movements. This physical dependency also entails serious psychological consequences, as it conveys to inmates that they need to be obedient and submit to the state's rules and thus have little autonomy or responsibility. The following quote from the conversation I had with Chaplain Anton is a good illustration of the extent of this dependency:

> The [inmates] can't go out of their cell alone, they can't leave their section alone, they need authorization, they can't do anything on their own … It's interesting, when an inmate sits where you sit now [in the chaplaincy] and he says, 'I have to go to the bathroom', and here outside, he needs to go out of this room, round the corner, there's a bathroom, and I say, 'Well, just go outside', and he remains standing in front of the door, he thinks it's locked [!], actually, that's a catastrophe.

The East German chaplains I encountered all felt that dependency was such a big problem that their role should consist of reducing dependency – at least physical dependency, but really psychological dependency. This was their way of translating religious values into secular action. In theological terms, this meant that they met inmates' early religious enthusiasm or requests for baptism with sound scepticism and reluctance, fearing that an early conversion would reproduce patterns of dependency.

In order to move around in prison, inmates are obliged to follow precise instructions. Even the so-called *Freistunde* or free hour is only free in the sense that inmates do not have any predefined activities, and they are confined in a precise space, the courtyard or the hall. They do not possess any keys and become accustomed to living in narrow spaces. Released inmates have great difficulty during their first weeks in crossing a busy street or driving a car again. Indeed, for Ulrich, one of the first physical challenges after his release was to cross the street, as he was afraid of cars and unable to judge how far away they were and how fast they drove. Ex-prisoners often leave the doors of their apartments open and feel

---

[15]   According to German prison regulations, inmates have the right to decorate their cells to their own taste. However, this has to be done within the limits that the administration sets (§ 19 Abs. 1 StVollzG.), which in some cases may be experienced as arbitrary. Izmil, for instance, found that the way in which decisions were taken about allowing him to grow a plant in his cell was unfair. He thought that German inmates had much bigger plants in their cells than he did.

ill at ease in crowded spaces. The spatial conditions in prison certainly infantilize inmates' behaviour and also limit their religious freedom. One may easily imagine how the strict rules about movement tend to hamper certain religious practices that are different from the traditionally known ones. When I asked Chaplain Anton what he thought could be improved regarding spiritual care, he gave me an interesting answer:

> I imagine that inmates could, for instance, come up here and pray on their own. I would find it good to have a room in this building, a small chapel, where inmates – I wouldn't say at any time – but at some times had access … without complicated procedures or without passing through all the weary controls and without being accompanied, it would be good if that were possible.

Chaplain Boris wished he had the possibility to offer meditation classes in order to give inmates the possibility to experience silence in community. In prison A, Stefan had noticed Muslims praying during the recreation hour in the yard, a place that was not designated officially for religious activities but that counted as a public space in prison. This made them visible to him as a religious group. He described what he saw as a public affirmation of faith:

> *Stefan*: When he [the inmate leading the prayer] prayed, they are always so loud and sing or say, I don't know, the Qur'an. All the faithful, the Muslims who were in the yard, joined them. You could see it was different from the German Protestants or Catholics, they hide it, I find. They don't go to church, they go to their leader. And they [the Muslims] don't hide it, they pray in the yard, put their carpets on the floor and are not interested in anything else; in some way they are more public and stand for it, really.

The collective prayers made this prisoner aware of the 'Muslims' as a group. The discrete investment of the space in prison that chaplaincy has constructed since unification hence has a reverse side. It is less visible and is perceived by some inmates as if it were hiding.

Time

As Pierre Bourdieu argued in the last chapter of his *Pascalian Meditations*,[16] being in control of the time of others is a sign of power. Absolute power is in the hands of those whose actions cannot be predicted by others and who own their own and other people's time. Waiting for someone else's permission to use one's own time means being subordinated. In prison, time is controlled totally by the administration. It decides how the days and the hours are structured. In the prisons

---

[16]   (Paris: Seuil, 1997).

I observed, the day starts with the wardens doing a roll call; in prison B they do this at half past five in the morning. How the day continues depends on whether inmates work, follow a course, or have no planned activities. Martin talked about his day as follows:

> Well, at half past five they count [us], then 1 hour and 20 minutes later I am let out to school. At around half past eleven I am back in my cell, wait for lunch, I get lunch and then I watch TV, or I play with my play-station, then [there is the] free hour, then dinner and then more TV, depending on what is on, a book or a newspaper, or I take my school stuff and see if there is something to do, study a little, and then it's night again.

Not even weekends or festivals are considered different or special; on the contrary, they often cause additional stress because fewer activities can take place, as weekend staff offer a minimal choice of occupations. Lars explained what it meant for him:

> *Lars*: Well, the weekends are a little different from the point of view of the daily routine.
>
> *I*: How precisely?
>
> *Lars*: Well, the free hour is a little earlier and the cells are closed earlier.

In prison A, the day starts a little later, with a roll call at half past seven. Thilo's description goes as follows:

> I wake up at 7, when the alarm rings; at half past seven the cell is opened up. By then, I have washed and had breakfast. At about a quarter to eight I have finished drinking my coffee and shortly before 8 I go to vocational training to prepare for my release, because I will soon be released … [that goes on] until about 11 o'clock, and then I have lunch and at 12 I go back there [to the training] until 3, then I prepare for the free hour that starts at a quarter past three until a quarter past four. Then, I come in again, there is dinner and then they open the cells again from 5 to 7 or from 7 to 9, depending on the section … and we have a chat with the other inmates and – this is confidential – we smoke or drink, you know? It's nicer in company…
>
> *I*: What about the officers, they don't notice that?
>
> *Thilo*: They, we are discreet about that … and then they close the cells again at about 7, I watch a little TV or write some letters if needed or read.

The vocabulary used in these interview extracts shows that inmates often adopt the terms used in the regulations ('the free hour') – they are not their own. This, as I shall demonstrate later, tends to change when they speak about religion, indicating a process of appropriation. Inmates nearing their release, such as Thilo, organize their whole time according to this event. The perspective of release gives the time spent in prison a meaning and an aim, yet also increases feelings of anxiety. Otherwise, days strongly resemble each other; and for many inmates, not to think too far ahead is a tactic to protect themselves, as Kai, a young inmate in prison A, put it:

I: Is every day the same?

Kai: I try to express it this way: of course, every day is different, but in some way they are all the same. I think most people here – that's so for me and it's my observation – try not to perceive the prison really as real, do you know what I mean? It's almost like being in a trance. In here, one tries in that sense not to think too far ahead, to get every day over as quickly as possible. You know? There are also people who feel it very intensively. I remember one guy. He got 22 years, that's quite a lot. I think he did not take things as they come, he thought too much ahead, he was aware of every minute of his sentence. Some weeks later when I met him again, he was really changed. You could not talk to him any longer. Psychologically. He had destroyed himself. I think it is a sort of self-protection not to feel or think about every single day. You know?

One further particularity of time in the context of prisons is provided by the high unemployment rate. Work is compulsory in German prisons, but on average only about 20 per cent of the detained population actually have work.[17] Working in prison has always been a highly arguable issue. Indeed, it cannot be conceived of as a voluntary commitment, since it is generally not an alternative to any meaningful activity and is very poorly remunerated.

Time counts as a major factor insofar as the inmates usually feel they do not have any control over the time for which they are convicted. This, of course, creates a great sense of dependency and stress.[18] When I asked Jamal how much time he was due to serve in prison, he answered that he did not know and did not want to know:

Jamal: I don't know. No idea.

---

[17] See paragraphs 37 and 41 of the German Prison Act. The work should correspond to the inmates' competences and be profitable (§ 37 Abs. 2 StVollzG). The wage, however, is less than 1 euro per hour, which is much less than the lowest wage outside prison, representing about 20 per cent of this. A third of it is put aside and given to inmates when they leave prison. The law states that, if the institution cannot provide enough work for the inmates, they can occupy themselves otherwise. No further details are given.

[18] For a more detailed discussion of the stress linked to the time dimension, see John J. Gibbs, 'The First Cut is the Deepest: Psychological Breakdown and Survival in the Detention Setting', in Robert Johnson and Hans Toch (eds), *The Pains of Imprisonment* (Beverly Hills, CA: Sage Publications, 1982), 97–114.

I: Why?

Jamal: I don't ask, Madam. I prefer them to come one morning and tell me, 'Prepare your stuff.' I'll be happier than if I know when I will get out.

Time in prison does make for repetition, routine, boredom and, at the same time, stress. Do these set recurrences have an impact on religious life in prison? Or, to turn the question the other way around, does religion provide a rhythm to time in prison, and if so, how exactly?[19] We shall see that the question of how to fill the day in prison is crucial for understanding inmates' recourse to religion. The rhythm that religion can bestow upon a day, a week or a year connects inmates to a community that exists outside prison. Belonging to that community allows inmates to follow a different rhythm from that set in prison. The religious rhythm interrupts the bureaucratic routine of prison; its structured time sequence removes inmates from an undifferentiated temporal fluidity or 'this amorphous mass of time', as Wim expressed it:

I could most clearly observe the impact of having lost control over time at the halfway house. After the first week, during which the former prisoners of the programme were kept busy with all kinds of activities that are part of settling down (registration at the unemployment office and elsewhere, organization of basic things in the flat, and so on), they often find themselves confronted with the fact that they are alone and that they have no commitments. After the endless boredom and at the same time stress of prison detention, finding out how to spend the day is a tough task for many ex-convicts, also because only a few find a job. The most frequent occupation ex-inmates engaged in was games: darts, cards, dice or crosswords – activities in which they were well trained. The few who had a job usually worked in areas that can be described as being at the margins of society: they cleaned up leaves in cemeteries, collected items for recycling, helped to clear out abandoned houses, or were employed by the rehabilitation association for some restoration work in one of its houses, which were the same kind of activities that were organized in prison. Following their own agenda in an autonomous way was something ex-inmates needed to learn again, as in prison the guards had always reminded them of meetings by coming to accompany them. I was surprised to note that those who had been eager to find a job and managed to be called for interview did not then go to the interview, because they 'forgot', as they said.

---

[19]   Religions may be built upon one, the other or both senses of time – one cyclical, the other linear. For instance, in Hinduism there is a prevalence of cyclical time, whereas in Christianity both types coexist in the temporal linearity of salvation and the cyclical repetition of the commemoration of Jesus' life.

Body

Prison is a place where the experience of suffering and despair is particularly intense: the tangible evidence for this is the suicide rate in prisons. In 2007 about 11 people out of 100,000 committed suicide in Germany, while for prisons this figure was as high as 94. Fortunately, suicide is still an exception. What happens on a daily basis is self-mutilation, sometimes taking the form of scars, tattoos and injuries. Tattoos are not necessarily the consequence of inmates harming themselves; sometimes they are used to express memories and affinities. Many tattoos I saw on inmates in Eastern Germany were crosses; however, they were not religious symbols, as Sebastian explained to me:

> *Sebastian*: When I was imprisoned at the age of 17 … I was a sort of gang leader … I was not a Christian, but I nevertheless had a cross tattooed – why that? Well, normally it should say 'In Memoria Mori', but I haven't finished it.

> *I*: Does that mean it was more of a symbol for death?

> *Sebastian*: Yes, a symbol for death.

During our conversation, Thilo painted a blueprint for tattoos on a sheet of paper, in order to show to me which one is often found in prison. He called it 'cross on a hill with sunshine'.

Thilo had a lot of tattoos on his arms, legs, shoulders and throat, all of them made in prison by him or other inmates: 'I've tattooed many myself, wherever I could reach.' He had a letter tattooed on every finger; when he closed his hand in a fist, the letters read 'HATE' (in German, *HASS*). He said that this expressed his feelings towards the whole state. Tattoos make the body a medium that fixes moments, and transmits or expresses emotions or ideas about others or about oneself. They also belong to the 'cultural milieu' that develops in prison, and thus they vary from prison to prison; they also reflect developments in wider society. Crosses are now less popular; the prisoner commented: 'The older inmates have that [a cross]. The younger ones prefer skulls.' While the cross apparently used to signify death, the symbol for death now tends to be a skull. Interestingly, this is reminiscent of the practices of sixteenth-century Saxony, when inmates who were forced to work instead of being killed were branded with the symbol of the instrument through which they would have been sentenced.[20] There is an analogy between the former and present practices of using tattoos, in the sense that tattoos still symbolize the inmates' own death. Their own death was a topic that often emerged spontaneously when talking to inmates and ex-inmates. Frequently, their near-death experiences in prison were the starting point of a conversion process.

---

[20] Cf. Viehöfer, 'Zur Entwicklung', 2.

Figure 3.1   'Cross on a hill with sunshine', tattoo drawn by Thilo © Irene Becci,
                August 2004

Besides death, prisons increase also the probability of falling ill. Many inmates
are drug addicts or HIV-positive. Several inmates told me that they actually became
alcoholics while in prison. The prison institution increases health problems in
a number of ways: the living conditions in prison are particularly rudimentary
and requests for medical assistance entail bureaucratic and time-consuming
procedures. Often inmates request medical assistance, but they know that they
first need to persuade the officers that they are genuinely unwell in order to obtain
such assistance.

Not only does the body react to prison in terms of health, but it is also shaped –
in aesthetic terms – to fit prison requirements. Erving Goffman documents well the
physical rituals that inmates undergo on arrival: having to abandon one's clothes
goes together with a symbolic impairment of one's identity.[21] Much has changed
since Goffman's study, but in prison A the inmates' physical appearance was still
homogenized: all the inmates were expected to wear the clothes provided by the
institution, whose colours differentiated some prison categories from others, such
as working inmates, unemployed inmates, and so on. This homogenizing process
does not allow family members to provide inmates with personal clothing. One of
the reasons for this is 'security', as the Saxony chaplain explained:

> *Chaplain Anton*: If relatives or friends want to send a T-shirt, they face many
> obstacles – basically it's impossible. The prison provides the basic material. The
> blue people you have seen, that's the prison dress. Well, there could be many

---

[21]   Cf. the concept of the moral career in the second chapter of Goffman, *Asylums*.

other ways, but then everything has to be controlled, and it's difficult to control, because you can easily convey a lot of things with clothes.

That experience of imprisonment affects inmates physically, and their taste becomes strikingly clear when they are released from prison. The difficulties of life outside prison begin immediately, and the first days outside are known often to be 'a time of acute stress'.[22] When together with a staff member of the observed housing programme I picked up Manfred after his release from prison B, the first thing he wanted to do was to eat a doner kebab. So we drove to a Turkish kebab house to buy one for him. He was very happy, but unable to eat even half the kebab. The taste, he told us, was now too strong for him, as he had become used to the bland food in prison. During the interview I conducted with him a couple of weeks later, he explained further about the physical difficulties he had experienced after his release. It was hard for him to deal with his new life, 'because everything was strange outside', he said. Apart from problems with eating and sleeping – Manfred was dependent on prescription medication to fall asleep – it was very hard for him to be away from his small flat in the first weeks. He found it too crowded elsewhere and, for weeks, he left his flat only when it was strictly necessary. He said:

> all those people around me ... that is strange because in prison I was in a cell for two ... and there weren't many people coming to see me ... and now here I see, let's say, downstairs, for instance, there are, let's say, five, six, seven men or so ... or yesterday, when I went to that office, to the job office or job centre or whatever they call it now ... we were waiting for five hours and there were about 50 people ... that's too much...

In prison the body gets used to and probably becomes dependent on routine, confinement and mono-gendered relations.[23] Another ex-inmate dreamed of being able to drive a car again after his release. The only person who would lend him a car to do so was his former prison chaplain, Benedict, when he visited him at the programme. These examples illustrate the extent to which prison life affects the most basic aspects of the inmates' selves: the control over their own body.

Social Relations: The Prison Culture

Figure 3.3 was on the cover of a brochure published by a rehabilitation programme in Brandenburg. It depicts a situation in which an inmate – 'Herr Knack'[24] –

---

[22] Marc Renzema, 'The Stress Comes Later', in Johnson and Toch (eds), *Pains*, 147–62, at 142.

[23] As a reaction the inmates' imaginations, women are often over-marked by feminine attributes. Cf. figures 2.1 and 3.3.

[24] The word 'Knack' is in prison slang synonymous with 'long-term inmate'.

Figure 3.2   An ex-convict at the halfway house © Irene Becci, March 2007

mentally translates words that probation officers tend to use into prison language. The probation officer is a young lady wearing sexy clothes, and the inmate is a 'tough guy' who smokes. On the one hand, the prison artist uses the stereotypical idea of the inmate by drawing himself and his fellow inmates similarly, as people who cheat, try to escape, hide what they really think, and so on. On the other hand, the probation officer uses standardized language, acts according to written rules and files, and the features of her female body are exaggerated, which makes her appear unreal. In my view, it is a good illustration of the different aspects of Donald Clemmer's concept of 'prison culture'. This arises from the very interaction between inmates' ideas of themselves and of how they relate to others. As study of religion in prison also needs to take full account of these dynamic cultural processes, in the next section I shall draw on the studies by Clemmer, Gresham Sykes and Erving Goffman.[25] Having worked as a prison governor himself, Clemmer was engaged in the day-to-day tasks of the prison and analysed

---

[25]   Similar to the majority of social studies of prisons, Clemmer's and Sykes's studies are concerned with male prisoners. The situation is different for female prisoners, in terms of social roles, main problems, and types of crime. Moreover, women represent less than 5 per cent of the prison population in Europe: cf., among others, Rose Giallombardo, 'Social Roles in a Prison for Women', *Social Problems*, 13/3 (1966), 268–88, and Roy Walmsley, *World Female Imprisonment List* (King's College London: International Centre for Prison Studies, June 2006).

André P., JVA Frankfurt (Oder), 10/2006

Figure 3.3   A drawing by an inmate in Brandenburg; the Caritas programme
put it on the cover of its invitation for the celebration of their tenth
anniversary © Irene Becci, March 2007

the effects of imprisonment on inmates' personalities. As the title of his important book indicates, Clemmer observed a *community* in prison. Those imprisoned create a culture of their own, which is not determined simply by the disciplinary setting of the institution but in fact develops in opposition to it. One important question that Clemmer examined was the high rate of recidivism (40–80 per cent at the time, a percentage that persists), which he tried to explain not only via social–structural factors, but also by means of cultural influences. Clemmer observed that the prisoners tended to distinguish different types of groups within their community. Apart from the distinction between staff and inmates, as pointed out by Goffman in *Asylums*, inmates organized themselves by differentiating between an 'elite class' or a 'middle class', or between geographical origins and between criminal types:

> the confidence men and embezzlers constitute one class of the total structure; the bank robbers and advanced thieves comprise another segment; the abnormal sex offenders are a type; the aggravated assaulters are another, and so on … the 'politicians' and trusties compose a part of the structure, while the ordinary working convicts comprise another segment.[26]

A further viewpoint might categorize the population according to those whose sex behaviour in prison is considered normal, quasi-abnormal or abnormal. Yet another categorization might place recidivists in one stratum and non-criminalistic offenders in another. Still another structural delineation might refer to the personality differences resulting from the regional influences of pre-penal conditioning.[27]

All these distinctions are of course not rigid but undergo changes according to the social intercourse of the prison population. Despite many distinctions between prisoners regarding their social and cultural backgrounds and despite their positions within prison hierarchies and social groups, commonalities develop among them as a result of what Clemmer calls,

> symbiosis, by which is meant a living together so that a benefit exists which is mutual for the parties involved. This occurs in spite of the ruggedness of individualism among the inmates, and, while symbiosis does not rule out impersonalization, the need for a degree of cooperation in coping with an unfriendly environment keeps individualism from becoming too rampant.[28]

Clemmer argues that this symbiosis changes inmates' behaviour: they are 'prisonized', which means 'the taking on in greater or less [*sic*] degree of the

---

[26]   Clemmer, *Prison*, 295.
[27]   Ibid., 296.
[28]   Ibid., 297.

folkways, mores, customs, and general culture of the penitentiary'.[29] This culture, the 'prisoners' world', Clemmer describes as follows:

> It is dominated and it submits. Its own community is without a well-established social structure. Recognized values produce a myriad of conflicting attitudes. There are no definite communal objectives. There is no consensus for a common goal. The inmates' conflict with officialdom and opposition toward society is slightly greater in degree than conflict and opposition among themselves. Trickery and dishonesty overshadow sympathy and cooperation ... It is a world of 'I', 'me', and 'mine', rather than 'ours', 'theirs', and 'his'. Its people are thwarted, unhappy, yearning, resigned, bitter, hating, revengeful. Its people are improvident, inefficient, and socially illiterate. The prison world is a graceless world. There is filth, stink, and drabness; there is monotony and stupor. There is disinterest in work. There is desire for love and hunger for sex. There is pain in punishment. Except for the few, there is bewilderment. No one knows, the dogmas and codes notwithstanding, exactly what is important.[30]

Although this description dates from many years ago, it still fits quite well with the observations I made among prisoners and ex-prisoners. Despite all the differences that exist between inmates, there is a clear tendency to adapt to the subculture.

Most of the literature on prisoners that followed Clemmer may be viewed as variations of his findings.[31] Gresham Sykes's work[32] on prison as a 'society of captives' is a milestone in the discipline: it looks more specifically at the language used by inmates to refer to the different social roles they play in prison, such as 'rat' or 'squealer' – 'the man who betrays his fellows by violating the ban on communication',[33] as opposed to 'real men'.

The prison institution exposes inmates to two major processes: isolation on the one hand and homogenization on the other. In this context, it is particularly difficult for individuals to affirm their personal diversity, while group creation and affirmation is easier. I observed that prisoners and ex-prisoners mentioned others frequently in terms of groups, such as 'Arabs', 'Vietnamese' (*Bernd*), 'sex offenders' (for whom there were many vulgar nicknames), murderers, or *Glatzen* (skinheads). These observations call for interpretations based on relational approaches, as the one offered by Goffman's study on stigmatization. It provides useful tools to illuminate this situation. For Goffman, groups 'in the broad sense

---

[29]   Ibid., 299.

[30]   Ibid., 297, 298.

[31]   A recent study of internal hierarchies and group formation is by Léonore LeCaisne: *Prison. Une Ethnologue en Centrale* (Paris: Editions Odile Jacob, 2000).

[32]   *The Society of Captives: A Study of a Maximum Security Prison* (Princeton, NJ: Princeton University Press, 1971 [1958]).

[33]   Ibid., 87.

of like-situated individuals'[34] inform individuals' personal points of view. Rightly, Goffman points to the double mechanism at work in the generation of group affiliations, one coming from outside, the other from inside. A group's standpoint is built gradually in the interaction between those who are within it and those who are outside it. Fake oppositions arise in that the differences between those within a group are removed and differences between groups are accentuated. I shall come back to this point in the last part. For now, I shall elaborate on what scholars inspired by Erving Goffman's work have found as an additional crucial characteristic of prisons: the high barriers to social intercourse with the outside.[35]

Contact with the Outside

Although prisons are closed institutions, there are many ways to make contact with the outside world. One way is through the people who come to the prison every day: the prison officers who control and supervise inmates. Then there are staff associated with rehabilitation: teachers, social workers, psychologists, and so on. Apart from professional relationships, inmates have contact with volunteers who visit regularly or at particular times of the year, such as Christmas, often in collaboration with the chaplaincy or as part of activities organized by religious communities. The main purpose of volunteers' activities in prison is to supply what visiting rights alone hardly provide – human and affective relationships. Therefore chaplains, who also face enormous psychological challenges every day, appreciate their support immensely.

The closer the place of incarceration is to inmates' homes, the more visitors they are likely to have. In general, their visits are not very frequent and diminish over time. As Rachel Condry argues in her study of family members of serious offenders,[36] it is a common pattern that family members turn away as soon as the offender is arrested. Those who remain in contact are mostly the closest women in the family – mothers or partners. This very much corresponds to what the inmates and ex-inmates I met told me. Moreover, where inmates are moved from prison to prison (which takes weeks each time), keeping regular contact with the outside

---

[34]   Erving Goffman, *Stigma: Notes on the Management of Spoiled Identity* (Englewood Cliffs, NJ: Penguin, 1990 [1963]), 137.

[35]   See, among others, C.A. McEwen, 'Continuities in the Study of Total and Nontotal Institutions', *Annual Review of Sociology*, 6/1 (1980), 143–85, and Christie Davies, 'Goffman's Concept of the Total Institution: Criticisms and Revisions', *Human Studies*, 12/1 (1989), 77–95.

[36]   Rachel Condry, *Families Shamed: The Consequences of Crime for Relatives of Serious Offenders* (Cullompton: Willan Publishing, 2007).

world is almost impossible. Moving inmates from one prison to another is also a strategy to break existing networks of inmates.[37]

A less personal channel to the outside world is the media. Compared with people outside prison, inmates are overexposed to television and radio but often do not have the financial means to choose or subscribe to particular news media. Almost every cell now has a television or radio, which is often switched on during the day. The role that the mass media, and television in particular, play in prison is amplified by the closed character of the institution. Inmates told me that they mainly watch the news and discuss this again and again with other inmates.

Some inmates – unless they are illiterate – may subscribe to a newspaper, but this is rarely the case among foreign inmates. For them, foreign newspapers are a luxury, but it is not uncommon, as Jamal told me, for chaplains to bring in foreign newspapers: 'For instance, he takes newspapers, for instance Arabic newspapers, foreign newspapers. That's right. The chaplain does that.' In summary, prisons are not entirely cut off from the outside world, but they filter carefully the links between inside and outside. Inmates who have substantial economic capital and local connections clearly take more care in developing their links with the outside.

The five defined factors that make prisons different places will now help in identifying the role that religion plays in such contexts. I shall point to the different roles religion has in prison, depending on the standpoint from which it is examined. We may then be able to answer the question, what exactly generates religious involvement in prison? I shall consider whether it is true that religious involvement is greater in prison than outside and I shall describe what it looks like.

The Chaplaincy: A 'Free Space' in Prison

As described previously, what the chaplaincy provides to inmates is not just limited to spiritual care: its provision ranges from material support (tobacco, books, and so on), to prayers, to contact with family members. During my enquiry I focused particularly on the observable facets of interactions between inmates and chaplains:

- What were the topics of their discussions?
- What material help was provided?
- What were the spatial and temporal constraints with which the chaplains had to contend?
- What services were accessible to the different 'users'?

---

[37]   Christoph Maeder's discourse analysis of the strategy of moving inmates shows the disciplining effect such practices have on the inmate population: 'Narrative Zivilisierung im Strafvollzug. Die Macht der Versetzung', in Hubert Knoblauch (ed.), *Kommunikative Lebenswelten. Beiträge zur Ethnographie einer geschwätzigen Gesellschaft* (Konstanz: Universitätsverlag Konstanz, 1996), 125–43.

- How tight were the bureaucratic constraints in the context of a prison environment?
- How wide was the range of people involved in the chaplaincy's work?
- What difference did the chaplaincy make in relation to the outside world?
- Did the chaplaincy facilitate inmates gathering in a way that would usually be impossible?

After addressing these questions, I shall present the conclusion that the chaplaincy represents a space of freedom in prison and a space that bridges the gap between the inside and the outside.[38] Analysing the chaplains' answers to my question as to what their job was like, I found that, regardless of their respective denomination, the largest part of a chaplain's time is spent providing individual care for inmates:

> *Chaplain Anton*: What occupies a lot of space is, of course, individual spiritual care.

Only the frequency of the religious services seems to differ among denominations, with Protestant chaplains celebrating services less frequently, as chaplain Boris indicated:

> *Chaplain Boris*: Basically one religious service per month.

The main focus of the chaplains' attention is therefore their relationship with the inmates and the latter's relationships with each other, as one Protestant chaplain pointed out:

> *Chaplain Anton*: Spiritual care is about relationships, I construct a relationship with people, that happens a lot here: a relationship that has no precondition – nobody has to achieve anything or bring anything. I am like that and of course that works in prison.

Personal relationships are best dealt with in private, such as in one-to-one meetings. Chaplains are able to arrange such meetings in prison, as they represent established religion, and they make full use of their position to cultivate their relationships with inmates:

---

[38]   Ralf Günther, today himself an (East German) pastor, made a linguistic analysis of discussions between chaplains and convicts in his Theology dissertation (University of Leipzig, 2002). He drew similar conclusions with regard to the role of chaplaincy as a free space: *Seelsorge auf der Schwelle. Eine linguistische Analyse von Seelsorgegesprächen im Gefängnis* (Göttingen: Vandenhoeck & Ruprecht, 2005).

> *Chaplain Anton*: Inmates come and really want to talk about their problems
> with me and they work through the whole story of their lives. Often it is inmates
> who are not here for the first time and who already have severe problems. I also
> meet inmates regularly, every two weeks at a particular time, for 60 minutes,
> and we talk.

Chaplains affirm openly that the principal aim of chaplaincy is helping to maintain
relationships. They do not see this as a deviation from the traditional purpose of
pastoral care in the strict sense – caring for convicts, for the needy, is a biblically
rooted duty for any Christian:

> *Chaplain Bruno*: Unlike other types of chaplaincy, prison chaplaincy is based
> on two passages in the Bible: 'I was in prison, and ye came unto me', and Jesus'
> crucifixion with the two criminals next to him, the benediction.

According to the chaplains I interviewed, the care they provide is not primarily
religious or practical, but comprises relationship guidance. This is, to some extent,
a secularized form of pastoral care. The chaplains who identified this as their main
activity did not express the need to legitimize it. Their secular intervention is taken
for granted. Chaplains stressed both the importance of relationships and the task of
organizing a system of assistance involving a number of volunteers or sometimes nuns.

A closer look at the various activities that chaplains organize reveals an
interesting feature: for those who find themselves in a situation of imprisonment,
the chaplaincy symbolizes a space of freedom in relation to a number of aspects.
From the inmates' point of view, the chaplaincy allows them to reach beyond prison
with respect to space, time, material goods, and communication. The chaplains
also find it easier to overcome bureaucratic barriers and deal with sources of
potential conflict, such as the relationship between staff and inmates. I call these
two aspects 'bureaucratic freedom' and 'relational freedom'. I start with what I
have already reconstructed, which is that the relationship between chaplains and
inmates is closer than that between inmates and any other professionals in prison.

Social Relations: Communication

When inmates meet the chaplain, they may talk about anything they choose.
The chaplaincy thereby creates a space of *communicative freedom*. Not only are
inmates permitted to discuss any topic with the chaplain, but they do not even have
to justify any lies they might tell, nor do they run the risk of not being believed by
the chaplain. People who experience imprisonment after a crime and a trial have
encountered many instances when they were not believed. What they said had to
be proved, word for word. Therefore, for them, not being questioned has great
symbolic and emotional importance. Chaplain Boris stressed precisely this point:

It's mainly about listening – that is, to accept the other person completely, based on what he tells me. I don't set any criteria as to how truthful what he says is, but I assume that he tells me something in a certain way, that he just wants to tell me that, and he probably has good reasons for telling me his story, his biography, in that way. And first of all, I accept that and try to enter into contact with him.

Such an acceptance can go as far as continuing a relationship with an inmate in spite of his calling you names, as Ralf Günther himself relates in the foreword of his *Seelsorge*. The discursive freedom arises also from the fact that the chaplaincy is a protected place, a place of trust – probably the only such place in prison, as inmates as well as chaplains confirmed:

> *Chaplain Anton*: The chaplaincy is one of the few places where one can speak openly and the inmates know that I have the right to keep things confidential, I can keep the secret of the confession … There's at least an advance on trust [*Vertrauensvorschuss*]. That opens up many possibilities. All the other staff members can be constrained to testify in court; I have the right to refuse to do this and this protects me and obviously helps when I am in contact with inmates.

The chaplains' position in the prison institution also allows them to offer inmates an 'authentic' or genuine relationship. This option stands in stark contrast to that which other staff members may afford, insofar as the chaplains do not issue orders; they have no obligations; unlike officers, for instance, they do not have power. They make hints or suggestions, as inmates described, but do not dictate:

> *Justus*: If he gave clear orders, that would bother me – if he was putting pressure on me by saying, 'You have to do this.' Instead it's, 'You can do this.'

Frequently inmates compared the chaplain's function with that of the psychologist, which helps to understand the specific character of the chaplain's role:

> *Jakob*: The discussion with the psychologist is always about elaborating guilt. In the discussion with the chaplain you talk about your own problems, he listens, nobody is obliged to do anything. It's spontaneous … I prefer talking to him rather than to the psychologist.
>
> *I*: Why?
>
> *Jakob*: Because I realize that he simply listens to me. He does not put pressure on me, he does not ask any questions or try to find things out that I don't want to talk about.

Inmates who participated often in religious activities noticed these differences in particular. Those who attended meetings and services, which the chaplaincy organizes, greatly appreciated the chance to be open:

Johan: In prison, in your unit, with other inmates, you need to put on a face, although it is false. You cannot give someone a kiss, show feelings, and so on. It's a mask you're wearing. By contrast … with Brother X or [Anton], you can talk to him, say what you think, show your feelings. And that means a lot. For me personally it's a sign that you don't need to pretend.

Goods for the Body and the Soul

Another task of the chaplains is to offer *material* support to all inmates, whenever possible and regardless of their religious affiliation. Chaplains may provide inmates with small items that they cannot get in prison because they have neither money nor authorization, such as newspapers, books, tobacco, coffee, socks, underwear and stamps. Chaplains tended to legitimize their provision of material help more than the support they provided in terms of relationships. Their accounts of legitimacy evoked the wide reach of their chaplaincy, its openness and its range:

Chaplain Boris: As chaplains we're much more than simply representatives of the religious sector. Our position is also very peculiar. We have some freedom, and bringing inmates some stuff from outside is part of that, what we consider their needs, we don't refuse and say, 'Wait', as if we were thinking, 'Give them an inch and they'll take a mile' We are in a different situation, we have some freedom here and inmates know it and … the issue is more that bit of freedom in the totalitarian system of the prison, that they associate with us. That's why I think they look for us and then that also works out on the human level, if we understand each other, the contact is easy.

The chaplains' dual role of providing material help and spiritual care gave rise to controversy. As one chaplain pointed out, for a number of inmates, particularly for those who present themselves as strong and unbreakable, it is not easy to be open about seeing the chaplain. It means admitting to a weakness, which is not beneficial in the hierarchical structures of the prison population. For these inmates, the material help they may get from the chaplain may be a pretext for seeing the chaplain for other reasons:

Chaplain Boris: Also, inmates have a threshold. Many overcome it by saying, 'I only want tobacco from the chaplain', or, 'I can make my telephone calls there.' I think, in their cell, when they get back, they are teased.

In fact, given the East German context of forced secularity, inmates do not look too favourably at participation in religious activities, which makes justification for doing so important. The inmates interviewed gave different accounts of their intentions and feelings with regard to their participation in chaplaincy activities and of how they thought that other inmates perceived this. A number of inmates were convinced that their commitment was sincere, but that other inmates took advantage of the situation and were thus insincere:

> *Christof*: I can see that there are sometimes material needs, that one can run out of tobacco or things like that, but I don't think the task of the chaplain is to help in a material way. He has to help the mind. The reason for going to the chaplain is not to receive material things, but I can also get material help when I meet him first of all for spiritual/psychological matters.

Among inmates these fine distinctions are not sufficient to excuse behaviour that some deem inappropriate in the religious realm. Johan's opinion reflects this strict division when talking about inmates who behave differently inside and outside chaplaincy:

> *I*: Some say that inmates become more spiritual in prison, is that true?

> *Johan*: Yes, but I think it's very much a utilitarian matter.

> *I*: Why do you think that?

> *Johan*: Because I think that what I say when I'm up here [in the chaplaincy] cannot be changed when I am in the units. I cannot say completely different things there.

The chaplains were aware of these viewpoints and tried to make their point clear. It was important for them to 'serve everybody' and to reserve special treatment for those affiliated to their respective denomination. In any case, the chaplain has considerable freedom with regard to bringing things into the prison. He does so openly, with the eyes of the prison administration on him. During one of my visits to prison A's chaplaincy, I observed that an inmate came to ask for tobacco and that the chaplain gave him a small portion of it. After they had exchanged a couple of sentences, the inmate left. The chaplain commented:

> *Chaplain Anton*: What I just did with this inmate, that I gave him some tobacco, well, I do that when he comes in here and asks, but usually I go with the inmate to the unit officer and tell him, 'Mr X has little money at the moment and no tobacco, so I've offered him some tobacco from the chaplaincy.' So I try to be very transparent so that they don't get the impression that the chaplain is hiding things. The prison director knows and actually everybody here knows that there are some people who think the chaplain does strange things.

Chaplains make a great effort to show that what they do is transparent, and they direct this endeavour towards both inmates and prison staff.

Space

An additional important factor that allows chaplains to provide such wide-ranging help and intervention is that they have *freedom of movement* within the institution, which is much greater than for most prison staff. This freedom makes it possible for chaplains to cope with any kind of situation and to have confidential meetings with inmates, which also suits the institution. Chaplains apply different tactics to guarantee that inmates have an environment where they can speak in confidence.

> *Chaplain Boris*: If they are in a cell with others, I tell them, 'You come to my office.' In unit [X] there are only single cells, to get here [to my office] would take too long, so I usually go to their cells.

There are hardly any spatial obstacles for prison chaplains, which allows for a freedom they make the most of. The inmates benefit as the chaplains offer them the possibility to leave their cells, even if only for a short time. Thilo summarized this, saying that the chaplain, unlike other staff, 'takes us out of the cell'. Inside both prisons, processes of reappropriating the space are ongoing. For instance, in both prisons A and B, the chaplains created new spaces after 1990, which are dedicated to the chaplaincy. Contrary to all the other rooms to which inmates usually have access, chaplaincies are carefully decorated places that transmit an atmosphere of welcome and peace. There are generally flowers and/or plants, colourful pictures, the smell of coffee and biscuits.

Chaplains carry keys that unlock most of the prison doors and gates – in many cases, they also unlock the inmates' cells. Inmates said that chaplains may help with obtaining *Lockerungen*, meaning the possibility to leave the prison for a day, for special occasions – for instance, when a relative has died or a child is born into the family. Additionally, chaplains break through the barriers by assisting inmates with their relationships with people on the outside – family, friends, colleagues, and so on. This aspect plays a major role in the way inmates perceive the chaplain.

Time

The chaplains' presence is a regular part of inmates' lives, their help is immediate, and the relationships they build in a prison may last for years. Therefore, the *temporal* dimension plays a significant role in prison. Some chaplains extend their care for inmates to the various institutions where they may be incarcerated, thereby creating strong and long-lasting personal ties. Most convicts experience the breakdown of relationships throughout their lives, due to varying periods or places of incarceration, their need for or choice of secrecy, or because of their crimes. Such conditions give long-term perspectives particular importance. The following interview extract indicates that this aspect of the inmates' relationship with the chaplain actually counts more than religious matters:

> *Roland*: Obviously I have a very close relationship with [Chaplain Benedict], but that has nothing to do with the fact that he's a Catholic or not a Protestant or whatever. It's just because of him as a person, because he's accompanied me in some way since the beginning of the 1990s, he's always come to see me when I was [detained] in isolation and every time I was moved to another prison, he could come and see me there.

Both inmates and prison officers appreciated greatly the regularity of the chaplains' services. The chaplain thus becomes a person they can count on. For an institution governed by routine and repetition, this reliability facilitates interactions:

> *Chaplain Bruno*: [Inmates] don't write any longer, they say, 'Chaplain, come', and it's clear that one week later, I'll be back and, if I cannot go one Monday because there's something else on, I go on Wednesday, but they know they'll see me in that week, they assume that they will.

Even inmates who do not attend religious services or participate in any of the chaplaincy's activities know about the regular presence of the chaplains:

> *Thilo*: Every two weeks, [there is a] Catholic and [a] Protestant [chaplain]. So there is someone here every weekend.

A chaplain is not just a prison employee. He is different from other employees in several respects. It is very significant to consider how inmates express the differences with regard to timescales when they talk about their relationship with the chaplain. For various reasons, an inmate from southern Germany was not able to complete any therapy. Only his relationship with the chaplain guaranteed stability:

> *Franz*: With the first [psychologist], I had left this institution after two months. OK. I can understand that. The second psychology service has been restructured so that instead of taking care of 10 or 20 men, he [the psychologist] now has 'only' [ironic] 50. Thus some have to be dropped. But I have already had meetings with him for half a year. Now I have the third psychologist and I'm starting where I had basically started with the first one. I have to tell them why, how come, what feelings … personally I find that, pfff… With the chaplains I don't have any problems at all.

For inmates, everyday interactions in the institution involve continuous waiting: for the cell doors to open, for visiting time, for the time when sports activities happen, for letters, for food, and so on. This seemingly timeless spiral is interrupted by the presence of the chaplain, not least because he is almost always available. This aspect clearly distinguishes the chaplaincy from other services offered in prison. It is a definite advantage and creates the kind of conditions that allow for a private dialogue with inmates. Chaplain Anton told me:

> There are no long discussions [between staff and inmates]. There are some, but I know that the psychologists would like to see more of them, but they are under pressure and simply have to move on. This gives me the possibility to enter deeper into the inmates' life stories.

Chaplains thus use the freedom they have as to how they use their time to establish deeper and longer-lasting relationships with inmates. They also organize special events to mark Christian festivals, such as Easter or Christmas. Usually they give a parcel to every inmate on these occasions.[39] As in the wider Catholic community, Catholic chaplains celebrate minor festivals in the ecclesiastical calendar, such as the commemoration of a particular saint. This synchrony creates a link between inmates and the church community and suggests that the prison population is part of a larger community – in this case, the Catholic Church.

As chaplains spend a lot of time in prison, they see what needs inmates have. Having noticed the low levels of education among the inmates he cared for, a chaplain in Brandenburg decided to teach them how to read and write:

> *Chaplain Bruno*: I don't do that every week, but I regularly offer one-and-a-half-hour classes … so that people learn to read and write.

Institutional Constraints: Bureaucracy

A further dimension of the 'free space' that the chaplaincy represents relates to prison *bureaucracy*. For instance, in prison A, attendance of the Sunday service does not require complicated written requests:

> *Chaplain Anton*: If people want to come to the religious service, they don't have to register. When I arrived, I could introduce that. There's nobody here who has to register in a written form. There is a poster, people can come but – theoretically, 500 inmates could come! [*laughs*] When there are important ceremonies for festivals … I have to limit the number, only … then they register in writing because a lot of people are expected. And the security officers check whether there is anybody who could be dangerous or whatever. Then it's also in my interest that they say so. Otherwise the religious services are very open.

In some prisons, the Sunday services are also open, in the sense of not being supervised, especially when chaplains have not requested supervision. This was

---

[39]   The German prison law states in Paragraph 33 that inmates have the right, under certain security restrictions, to receive personal parcels three times per year.

also the case for a group meeting that I attended in prison B. In fact, it is often the prison governor who requires chaplains to go through complicated procedures and take several religious services in different sections of the prison, as the inmates of these different sections are not supposed to meet. The chaplains' attitude is that they will comply with such requests.

In a total institution where it is hard for inmates to get any requests fulfilled, the removal of bureaucratic obstacles means a lot to them. Prisons have the perennial problem that operating them is very expensive and therefore choices have to be made in setting priorities. Investment in rehabilitation is often more expensive in the short term so that the enhancement of security issues takes top priority. Unless considered absolutely urgent, every request that inmates make needs to go through numerous security checks, thus requiring weeks to be answered. However, the procedure for arranging a private meeting with the chaplain is quite easy. One reason why it is easier for chaplains to overcome bureaucratic barriers is that they are on good terms with the prison administration.

A chaplain's network of connections is very wide, as she or he deals with all the staff in the prison institution. Generally inmates see the chaplain as a 'a teacher, a good friend' (Justus), someone who can be trusted. In any case, their feelings towards him are positive. Another inmate appreciated that the chaplain was there when he needed him, when he needed to talk about his soul (Martin).

Chaplains take care of relationships among inmates and also of inmates' relationships with their families, whenever possible. For example, Jamal told me that he sometimes asked the chaplains to give something to a fellow prisoner whom he could not reach otherwise:

> if someone is in section X and I am in section Y, I cannot go there and get something from him, a CD for instance, so we ask the pastor, and he helps.

Not only is the chaplain responsible for the wellbeing of the inmates – as guaranteed by the right to spiritual care in prison institutions – but he is also supposed to provide spiritual support to members of the prison staff. However, prison officers do not often approach the chaplain. In fact, the German word *Gefängnisseelsorge* (prison chaplaincy) clearly refers to the institution, not to the inmates, as the Protestant chaplain of prison B reminded me. Although the number of staff members who request the chaplain's spiritual care is very low, the principle of the inclusive nature of the chaplain's role is clear. I asked Chaplain Boris whether he liked the expression that qualifies his job as *Gefängnisseelsorge*. He said:

> I am quite content with the expression 'prison chaplaincy' … because the narrow term would be 'prisoners' chaplaincy', but my ambition is to think about the prison institution and not only about individual prisoners.

As one might expect given their Socialist heritage, most prison officers were socialized to have a hostile attitude towards religion; therefore, they rarely contact chaplains about spiritual care:

I: Does that mean that you also take care of prison officers? Is that part of your job?

Chaplain Boris: It is my intention, but in practice it happens very seldom, because there are gulfs between chaplains and officers. It's as if … an officer does not want to come to the chaplain as inmates do, he does not want to be on the same level. He has colleagues who would tease him if he went to the chaplain. They have built some kind of protection against the chaplain, and to break through that, they need to have really particularly difficult problems before they come and talk to me. Since I have been here, it has happened five or six times … Even when I can see that officers need spiritual care as much as the inmates do and that they are in the worst position in prison … It's a hard job, I wish they received more spiritual care, but I think it's unlikely to happen.

Since most of the officers who worked in GDR prisons have remained in their positions after the fall of the Berlin Wall, they are not particularly sensitive towards religion. For many officers in Eastern Germany, the GDR remains their dominant cultural background, as Décarpes's analysis demonstrates.[40] Clearly, the new generation brings in a different attitude, but both inmates and chaplains indicated that their relations with prison officers are influenced by a mixture of ignorance and distrust.

Moreover, the chaplaincy makes it possible for inmates to meet; the rules of the institution would normally not allow this. Thus, in some cases, the chaplaincy allows connections among inmates that are otherwise forbidden, such as meeting with people of the opposite sex. Some chaplains are well aware of this, and most of them understand very well what goes on. I asked Chaplain Anton whether he minded that religious services were used for purposes other than the ones they were meant to serve; he answered:

I would do the same. If I were imprisoned in Switzerland … I would go to the chaplain and say, 'Well, I would like to talk to my friend who is over there and whom I cannot meet otherwise.' I do it here, I let inmates meet who otherwise would never meet because they are in different units or simply because of the circumstances. I ask them to come here, so they can meet – of course.

---

40   Pascal Décarpes, 'Der DDR-Strafvollzug vor und nach der Wende. Die Umgestaltung des Gefängnislebens zwischen Herrschaft, Rechtsstaat und Willkür', in Sandrine Kott and Emmanuel Droit (eds), *Die ostdeutsche Gesellschaft. Eine transnationale Perspektive* (Berlin: Ch. Links Verlag, 2006), 88–103.

For chaplains, it is generally acceptable that the inmates' motivation to participate in chaplaincy activities is to meet other inmates:

> *Bernd*: For me, that simply means meeting other people. Often there are also people from outside, one can often speak with people about different things, because every day it's the same people here in prison and in particular for those with long-term sentences … they come from different units and the church is for many some kind of point of convergence because otherwise you cannot meet these people. And here it's possible.

Under these circumstances the chaplaincy also becomes a place where inmates can escape from the daily routine or feel less isolated:

> *Jakob*: Maybe it's also some kind of escape. Maybe some come to the service because they don't have any contact across the units. Here they can meet each other and share something, talk to each other. There are also many who are in high-security units.

The inmates know that the chaplain does not question them about what exactly happens during the religious service. There is an implicit agreement not to enquire, provided everything is kept quiet and order is maintained. The following quote from an interview with an inmate illustrates this point:

> *Bernd*: As long as there aren't any major problems, the chaplain does not notice anything or he does not know what happens here, I don't know.

Traditionally, isolation in prison has been associated specifically with spiritual experience. Interestingly, in the very first Christian communities, isolation was conceived as inducing the risk of individuals being tempted by evil forces. Being all alone – for example, in a place like the desert, as the biblical narrative recounts –, the individual is exposed to the wiles of the devil and thus needs to resist temptation with formidable strength. On the other hand, isolation allows for deep spiritual questioning. Chaplains still feel particularly responsible for inmates who are detained in isolation, whatever the reasons. However, the availability of chaplaincy creates not only the conditions of freedom; as discussed in the Introduction, freedom under modern conditions always has a conjoined twin, which is discipline and control.

Established Religion in Prison: The Logic of Universalization

As noted earlier, prison chaplaincy is an institution that was created originally according to a territorial logic, at a time when territoriality roughly coincided with demography. Therefore, if a prison is located in a particular territory, the inmates are guaranteed the same religious rights that they would have outside prison in that territory. Formally, the regulations relating to territoriality (the parochial system) also apply inside prison. As shown, the link between outside and inside prisons is very important to the chaplains. They find the rules that apply outside prison a source of legitimacy for their strong presence in prison, although this presence is out of step with the demographic composition of the inmate population. The discourse of prison chaplains thus shows that they have distanced themselves from demographic criteria. The comments of Chaplain Anton provide an example of this:

> When the Ministry published those statistics five or six years ago, we were afraid. They showed how many Protestant and Catholic inmates there were in Saxony's prisons. And there are always people who – at least that was our suspicion – want to measure our posts in relation to that. And you can't do that, nobody does that on the outside. I am the pastor of 800 church members on the outside, but I am in contact with many more people, the same is true here, and that's why I am very happy that these statistics don't come up any longer.

In Eastern Germany, the pastors learned to justify and affirm their presence in prison as historically rooted, irrespective of demographic composition. If the chaplains in the East German *Länder* were responsible only for inmates affiliated with established religions, there would be no justification in their being employed on a permanent basis, as Chaplain Anton pointed out:

> If you want to measure the chaplaincy that way, we would have to go out of here immediately and could come back as volunteers once a week for those 17 people, whatever the number is.

This chaplain also sets his East German understanding of the churches' role against an interpretation that is closer to the idea of *Volkskirche* present in Western Germany. When I asked Chaplain Boris whether the inmates he supported were mainly Protestants, he answered as follows:

> *Chaplain Boris*: I have almost no Protestants. In the [last] 20 years, I have been taking care of about 20 Protestants, not more.
>
> *I*: What percentage is that?
>
> *Chaplain Boris*: About 5 per cent, maybe less, probably less.

As discussed before, chaplains are responsible for the whole institution and see this as perfectly justified. These privileges and duties are a consequence of legal arrangements, as Chaplain Bruno summarized in the following formula:

> That's because of the German constitution. It says that only the two big churches
> can provide chaplaincy because their secret of confession is recognized by the
> state. Now also the Russian Orthodox Church is recognized, the others not yet.

Besides these two kinds of justification – demographic and juridical – a third
kind was often mentioned. It refers to theological and historical factors that
make Christian chaplaincy intrinsically the best provision for what is needed
in prison. This implies that only Catholic and Protestant Christianity practises
universality, an openness to everyone in its care for the soul. While this openness
is in fact a recent development within the two churches, different interlocutors
– not necessarily chaplains – tended to consider it a substantial and original
characteristic of the churches' respective doctrines. Universalization in theological
terms means that Christianity extends the alliance with God to an alliance with
the whole of humanity, thus breaking with the Jewish idea of the chosen people.
Universalization implies that God does not refer to one particular people any
more, but to each individual as a person. For prison chaplaincy this translates into
an openness to everyone, as one chaplain explained, and it is this very openness
that distinguishes it from other religions:

> *Chaplain Bruno*: Chaplaincy in itself is not defined as accepting only people who
> are church members – that is, believers or whatever –, but it welcomes everybody.
> I hold the principle that I take everyone, also Mohammedans [*sic*] or whatever,
> for individual meetings or for group meetings. We also have several groups for
> foreigners, but we have people who are Russian Orthodox or Greek Orthodox, in
> the Rumanian Church, Hindus, and so on. Vietnamese – we take everyone.

A further question is what the inmates think about the chaplains helping everyone
– all inmates and prison staff – without making any distinctions. The answers
to this question indicated rather negative feelings, particularly as expressed by
inmates who conceived of themselves as religious and sincerely faithful in their
participation of the chaplaincy's activities. They would prefer it if the chaplains
were more attentive to them and less attentive to others. These inmates are not
among those who consider their relationship to the chaplain as utilitarian, as a
means to obtain benefits from the institution. This relates also to the fact that they
do not view the chaplain as close to the institution.

   These small yet significant changes in the adaptation of pastoral care to the
new situation reveal, on the one hand, the capacity of established religions to
respond to a changing environment. On the other hand, making these changes
allows them to demonstrate their universal reach and to justify their privileges
and duties. Another aspect in this discourse of universality concerns the relation
to territory. Despite the fact that the establishment of a church in principle entails
limitation to a precise territory, the churches' discourse on that territory aims
towards universalization. The following extract from an interview with Chaplain
Boris illustrates the notion of what I call the logic of universality:

> I think for the Imam and for the Orthodox priest, spiritual care is something else. For them it is a more restricted action of religious instruction and work on religious problems … As a consequence, they are oriented very much by a religious sense, and not by a wider sense as we are here, also including the body and other elements. That you need that simply to feel human is something they don't understand. For us, spiritual care also means that someone simply tells me something and I listen to him, but then I don't need to pray with him, to conduct some rituals with him.

In other words, in this chaplain's view, it is not the fact that sessional chaplains are not given the opportunity to run a chaplaincy that limits their action; it is the case that their action is inherently limited. The influence of the established religions thus derives from their unique position, which is defined by the interaction between two longstanding and powerful institutions, both of which have universal ambitions. In fact, establishment includes two main elements: church and state. This is why the 'other' religions may be those lacking either the religious or the political dimension. The following example elucidates my point. I asked an established chaplain how he related to sessional chaplains. Interestingly, he answered that he found it particularly difficult to relate to ministers from foreign countries. For him, the Polish priests were not 'complete chaplains', unlike the German ones:

> *Chaplain Bruno*: The priests who come from Poland don't do any conversations, they only offer religious services, confessions, and that's it.

In the end, it seems that through establishment boundaries are drawn and a specific religious tradition appears as universal. A similar understanding of the role of Christianity emerged from my fieldwork in ex-offender rehabilitation programmes in Saxony-Anhalt. The church actors who created the programme that helps ex-inmates considered themselves to be 'a help with the birth' and expected to leave once the new structures were born. During the group discussion mentioned earlier, the democratic commitment of the East German religious actors was openly articulated. The pastor underlined, for instance, that, for him, the first article of the constitution – 'Human dignity is inviolable' – was a fundamental value that could be justified theologically. For him – and this was the basis of his motivation to care for prisoners –,

> Each person deserves to be loved, even if he is the lowest dog that has to be incarcerated for life. But – somewhere, somehow – every person has a value. And this is crucial for me, the value that took on its concrete character through God's becoming a person.

By putting forward such values as comprehension, forgiveness and humanity, this pastor demonstrated his universal concern for the good of society as a whole. According to him, the church's task is to contribute to building a 'free society with a democratic state, where the values we find important are preserved.' A non-denominational social worker responded enthusiastically with the remark, 'When I hear such a statement, I feel so close to the church!'

The comments by both pastor and social worker exemplify the widespread understanding of the place and role of the Protestant churches in East German society: the churches have to be morally upstanding yet independent, and they need to keep a critical distance to the state in order to allow for the democratic functioning of secular society. While the discreet and modest presence of religion in the public sphere seems to be accepted, at a personal level it remains almost taboo. The social worker who contributed to the discussion in Saxony-Anhalt insisted that she 'never considered ... worth finding out' what were the religious affiliations or beliefs of other people:

> I am a child of the GDR ... I decide my relationship with the church for myself
> ... religious affiliation has no importance for me in my work. It is also okay that
> church people have left our organization.[41]

In this overall secular society, however, there are niches in which religious practices and worldviews may develop more easily. Prison chaplaincy seems to be one of them, since it develops as a free space. At the same time, however, through its very location within the total institution, this space may also easily develop into a space of control.

Rehabilitation and Control

When I interviewed the chair of the international association of chaplains in Germany in 2003, I noticed the association's poster on the wall, which read: 'Challenging despair, creating hope'. Certainly, as we now have a better understanding of how far-reaching the chaplaincy's symbolic and material action is in prison, we see that the chaplaincy may indeed 'create hope' by creating a space of freedom. However, this is not an entirely unambiguous endeavour in prison. In a total institution, a space of freedom means a space of humanity. Christof expressed this very clearly in terms of his expectations:

> When ... I have private conversations with the chaplain, I want my problems to
> be solved, I want to empty my soul, I want to have someone who hugs me or
> whatever, something human.

---

[41]   Interestingly, she makes an exception only when she deals with Muslims: 'I know of course, when it comes to Muslims, it is no longer a minor issue, when we need to solve basic problems or problems related to marriage, and so on, religion cannot be left out, I know that well.'

A woman chaplain in Saxony-Anhalt[42] stated that the relationship she establishes with the inmates is also of great symbolic importance. The chaplain, she said in an interview in 2006, is not like other members of the prison staff – she deserves trust. If the chaplain tells an inmate that it is possible to be forgiven, to start his life all over again, and so on, this has a strong, one could say even a charismatic or mystical, impact on believers. This might be a crucial moment that inmates with a strong sense of guilt need to experience before they are able to imagine repentance and rehabilitation. Chaplain Boris described this process in terms of a burden going away:

> The individual meetings are very different. Sometimes it's all about having someone who listens to you and sometimes says, 'Yes.' Others want to get rid of their burden … by saying it, not to just anybody but to the chaplain, and thereby the burden goes because of the hope for forgiveness, because they themselves don't believe it, can't even imagine it.

All the special conditions in which chaplains operate in prison favour the construction of relationships on the basis of certain affinities in character. What is at stake in these relationships is often connected only loosely to religion in a denominational sense. In a context such as Eastern Germany, where the levels of religious affiliation, participation and knowledge are very low, the religious content of the chaplaincy – its mission to evangelize – can become completely irrelevant. As the following quote illustrates, the aim of the contact between chaplains and inmates is often simply to create the conditions for a different, an extraordinary, kind of experience:

> *Chaplain Anton*: I tell inmates: 'I'm not here to convert you, I don't care if you're a member of the church or not, what counts for me is dialogue, contact, to have the possibility' – and they do have the possibility here – 'to look at our lives from another perspective, the Christian perspective, the perspective of the Bible, of God.' That is what counts for me. But maybe it's also the possibility here in such a secular space to say openly that people are looking for that contact … There are also inmates who experience something completely different here. There were also inmates who said, 'That's not how we imagined the church. It's completely different.' I like that … Even the type of religious service we have here – we sit in a circle and have multimedia technology and openly focus on something. Recently an inmate told me … 'That was good for me here, simply to be quiet for an hour, to listen, it's completely different from sitting in a church and

---

42   This chaplain and pastor grew up and studied Pedagogy and Protestant Theology in Thuringia. She moved to Saxony-Anhalt with her family as early as 1989, and started to work as a chaplain in a women's prison there in 1990. Four years later, she took over the men's section. When I interviewed her in 2006, first at her home, than in the prison where she worked, she was almost sixty. In prison she was employed part time.

singing the old church songs.' Well, he apparently had an idea of church that was not very positive. There are also inmates who say they experience church here in a completely different way ... Once an inmate told me, 'You're not a real pastor!'

Chaplain Anton takes as a compliment the observation that he does not correspond to the widespread image of church people. Moreover, trust plays a crucial role. All the inmates confirmed that they trusted the chaplain much more than the other prison employees.

> *Lars*: Spiritual care is very important to me, to have someone to whom I can tell everything and I know I can trust. Because, as far as I am concerned, I have developed a huge mistrust in prison, first towards inmates, then towards officers. And for me chaplaincy is simply an opportunity to express my deepest feelings without risking being seen as ridiculous. For instance, I talk about many things for which I accept I'll be criticized.

One aspect that promotes their trust in chaplains, inmates say, is their perception that chaplains are detached from the prison institution. Inmates feel that they do not have any allies within the prison hierarchy. Martin, for instance, appreciated the chaplains' discretion in particular:

> They don't spread around what you tell them, they keep it to themselves, while the social workers, they meet other social workers and chat.

The chaplaincy helps inmates to gain some inner distance from the prison. Those who perceive the chaplain to be independent from the institution are most likely to take part in the activities, meetings and services that the chaplaincy offers. For them, the chaplaincy is the only place in prison where the idea of *rehabilitation* becomes real, as Wim pointed out:

> Spiritual care is the only accessible offer of rehabilitation for inmates, the only one, there's nothing else. Otherwise, prison is purely about revenge.

The chaplaincy conveys its message about rehabilitation most strongly when the chaplain intervenes in moments that inmates find the most painful, which inevitably occur in prison:

> *Chaplain Boris*: Those who are in the high-security section have done something bad, either attempted suicide or whatever, they are in a crisis and if in their helplessness they want to talk to someone, it's the chaplain.

Some inmates find support and help in the chaplaincy, and look for the reasons for their incarceration in personal mistakes rather than in social circumstances:

> *Kai*: Through the chaplaincy people learn to understand themselves better: why is it hurting, where did they make a mistake? I think this positive effect, that you feel better afterwards, simply comes from the fact that one knows what mistake one has made. That you don't make it again. That's the effect on people who consciously go there and talk openly about themselves and also somehow hope they will recognize the mistake and not repeat it.

The chaplains' influence on inmates is therefore beneficial in terms of preventing destructive situations or motivating inmates to look for the mistakes they made in the past. However, this influence can also be read in a different way, as a kind of self-*control*, as Bernd suggested:

> Chaplaincy for inmates? For those who think it's important to talk about oneself, it's an important step. For themselves. In order to control themselves a little bit. Because here you easily lose control, in every way, socially, regarding violence or whatever.

For some convicts, the chaplaincy does indeed provide the possibility to focus on ideas that are not related to violence nor lead to illegal action:

> *Martin*: Since I have been coming here, I have not had any violent thoughts and can get over all the mess I caused, I can get out of it … One gets a clear conscience if one comes here a couple of times and says what one thinks and what one does not think, and of course I would suggest to anybody to come here a couple of times and to participate. Sometimes we really have good themes for discussion … In some way you can say it puts me on another path, on the right path so that I don't make a mess of things any longer, as I usually do. My life has simply changed since I've come here.

By encouraging self-control, however, spiritual care contributes necessarily to stabilizing the total institution. This is also one of the conclusions of Ralf Günther's study.[43] In order to be able to play such a stabilizing role, chaplaincy needs to stand on solid ground, at best outside the delicate balance between different forms of power in prison. To consider chaplaincy as located outside prison is the ultimate consequence of the metaphor of the 'free space'. Some inmates, mostly those who attend many of the chaplaincy's activities, therefore consider the chaplain as 'someone who stands out from the prison system' (Justus). The chaplains themselves promote greatly the understanding of their role as positioned outside the power relations between the inmates and the prison institution. My question as to whether chaplains stood on the side of inmates or on the side of the institution received an unambiguous answer:

---

[43]   *Seelsorge*, 322.

Roland: The chaplaincy is independent, has nothing to do with the prison, they don't judge me, don't catalogue me or whatever. They are simply there, when you're bad, and help. They're neutral, don't assess and analyse everything.

Only some inmates saw the chaplain as an ally against the prison administration. There are indeed situations when the chaplain has to fight for the liberties mentioned earlier. Sometimes, staff do not seem to accept that chaplains have more freedom than other staff members:

Chaplain Bruno: We have more freedom than social workers, and some officers don't like that.

It also happens that chaplains experience pressure from the prison administration – for instance, when new security measures are introduced that could undermine the confidentiality between chaplains and inmates.[44] This tension relates to the inherent discord of the prison institution, with its proclaimed official function – rehabilitation – on the one hand, and actual practice that is more inclined to control and punishment on the other hand. Chaplaincy and prison administration depend on one another, but the administration certainly has the advantage now, as it is in control of the means that organize prison life. Sometimes the way things are organized puts chaplains in tricky situations. For instance, with fewer prison officers on duty during weekends, allowing inmates to attend the Sunday service has an impact on the organization of the whole institution. When the officers escort the inmates who attend the service to the chaplaincy, they have to leave their positions; this means that the inmates they supervise must be locked in their cells earlier. The following quote from an interview with an inmate illustrates this:

Christof: If, for instance, in our unit they lock the cells … those inmates who don't go to church are mad, but it's simply our right.

I: Why are they mad?

Christof: Because the cells are locked earlier. That's a bad habit here, that some receive a penalty because others are allowed something. But that's the way it is here. They simply say, 'We have to lock up here' … The inmates understand that so they don't complain.

I: Does that mean that each time there's a religious service … the others have to be locked in their cells?

44   See Irene Becci and Joachim Willems, 'Gefängnisseelsorge in der sich wandelnden ostdeutschen Gesellschaft. Eine Analyse der kulturellen, theologischen und sozialen Spannungen', *International Journal of Practical Theology*, 13 (2009), 90–120, at 111.

Christof: They have to go to their cells, yes, because there are fewer officers on weekends.

I: Just for an hour?

Christof: No, they don't open their cells again, because we're here for an hour, have the service, then we have coffee. And so they don't open [the cells] again.

The prison institution constantly puts chaplains in a double bind. For instance, if there are not enough prison officers on duty on Sunday so that inmates may attend the religious service, the chaplains are not allowed to have the service. The same applies when other activities are organized that the prison administration considers more important, such as meetings – these have to take place at times when religious services normally happen.

From the point of view of the inmates who attend the chaplaincy's activities, the chaplains and the volunteers who assist them appear to be as dependent on the institution as they themselves. In any case, the chaplains appear to do their jobs for purely altruistic reasons and for no personal gain.

All the chaplains told me how they resisted the power of the administration. To some extent, this is a daily struggle in that they try to push further and further the limits set by the institution. We may recognize in some of the strategies how, as Foucault wrote, the power configuration works. The law is often the basis on which the struggle for more autonomy takes place:

Chaplain Boris: It has to be decided for each single case, when do I have to put in a request, when do I not have to put in a request. There's a kind of polite mistrust, but I know the penal law says that I can take in things that are part of religious life … Sometimes chaplains and officers stand on very different sides, the gulf is very wide …

I: Does that mean you feel you are more on the side of the inmates?

Chaplain Boris: Of the inmates, yes.

There are many occasions when the chaplain has to choose which side he is on and when it becomes clear where he stands. The administration appears to try all kinds of approaches in order to obtain particular knowledge that the chaplain has accumulated through his experience with and proximity to inmates. All the chaplains spoke at some point about the difficulties or tensions they had experienced with the prison administration; the following account provides an example:

Chaplain Boris: If I want to take out some prisoners for one week, they [the prison administration] often want a report afterwards. And I always refused, saying, 'It was not in the agreement I had with the inmates that I would write a report.' … But one inmate wanted it because he knew it would help him. So

I wrote it. There are many inmates with whom I have a very confrontational relationship and it happens that the unit officer wants to talk to me and says, 'How can I solve this? Can you suggest how I can have a peaceful relationships with him or can you propose this or that?' These ... things often happen and I always have to decide when I should do it and when not. And sometimes I might have overstepped limits, it's a minefield, it's easy to step on a mine, and if you mess up your duty to keep things confidential in some way, you have messed up everything here, if the inmates think in some way or have the impression that I tell the administration something about them.

Chaplain Boris's metaphor of the minefield is certainly evocative of the daily stress with which chaplains are confronted in prison. The way in which chaplaincy and administration interact is a clear indication that the chaplain represents a part of the institution outside the institution's control. The chaplains with experience of the GDR regime were particularly suspicious:

Chaplain Anton: The chaplaincy is still regarded with suspicion ... by the officers and the governor and the administration ... The chaplain is the one person here you cannot really control in what he does. It's all very strange sometimes. Sometimes I am searched, I have to allow them to look in my bags – which I find a bit too much. It does not happen often, about twice per year, when the officer comes and says, 'Mr X, I have to look in your bag today.' I am searched ... It's because we distribute tobacco ... 'How can you do something like that, reward inmates, those criminals?' That's the opinion here. Or, 'They only go to the chaplain because they want coffee or cake.' That's why the chaplaincy is always a little bit on the margins, half illegal, and that's viewed with suspicion, I guess ... often officers would like to know more, I guess; inmates are interrogated – 'What is the chaplain doing with you or what happens there?' ... At the conferences when it is decided every year how the imprisonment time is to be organized individually for every inmate, either he has a long sentence and they check whether he can work ... [or] be released; what possibilities are there for giving him permits to go outside. I seldom participate in these conferences because of my duty to confidentiality ... I also know much more about the inmates than the officers do and don't want to be in the situation where I am asked to give information about inmates. I deliberately stay out of it. I participate in many conferences when I think it's useful, in order to get a realistic assessment of an inmate, when it concerns a release, for instance. 'I don't think he is dangerous, I don't think he would escape, and so on.' ... When we had that inmate whom we wanted to take to his father's grave because he had not been able to go to the funeral, we said, 'It's important for him, because he never had the chance to say goodbye.' I had prepared that with the psychologist ... I remember a situation when the security officer said, 'We're going to create a group on subculture and talk about subculture.' I thought it was great that they were doing something like that and decided to participate.

I registered and went along. There were a couple of psychologists, social workers and security officers, and I was shocked when he said, 'Well, now tell us where the alcohol is made, you know, you have the right contact with the inmates!'

Within the church, there is appreciation for the work prison chaplains do, but being a prison chaplain is certainly not a highly sought-after position. Although the prison administration appears ever willing to charge chaplains with disciplining tasks, which the church does not officially oppose, it seems that the chaplains themselves object to this. On the one hand, chaplains rely heavily on the institutional position they have, thanks to the establishment of their churches, but, on the other hand, they act as individuals who meet inmates independently from the prison administration and who are able to use the personal space they occupy to resist any attempt to submit their position to the disciplining power of the prison administration. However, analysis of the interview transcripts and observation notes shows also that inmates who do not really participate in the chaplaincy's activities think that the chaplain is a channel through which they may influence the decisions of the administration. Thilo, a very secular recidivist bank robber, had a clear opinion about this:

I always think, if you are really credible, that you belong to the church and that you have the faith, you have the chaplain on your side, then you have a 99 per cent chance of getting out after [serving] two thirds [of your time].

From this point of view, the chaplain appears to be on very good terms with the prison direction and administration. As most chaplains and the two prison governors I interviewed stated, it is true to some extent that chaplains receive little material support from the administration. However, it is plausible that the latter's relationship with the chaplains is good because their presence has a calming effect.

Most chaplains are also very active outside prison with regard to issues related to incarceration. They present papers at conferences,[45] relate their experiences, and publish articles in ecclesiastical newspapers and in political arenas. Chaplains are often against politics facilitating incarceration and in favour of alternative measures. They demand more support, means and attention from both the church and the state. Whether they were religious or not, all the inmates told me that they would empower the chaplaincy and never replace it with any other type of activities:

Kai: Also, for those who don't use the chaplaincy, it is simply good to know that they can use it, that they have something like this as a backbone … in case they

---

[45] See, for example. Friedrich Ebert Stiftung and Forum Berlin (eds), *Gemeinnützige Arbeit statt Knast* (Berlin: Friedrich-Ebert-Stiftung, Forum Berlin, 2002), publication of papers at the conference of the Friedrich-Ebert Foundation in Berlin, 24 and 25 January 2002.

crash, I mean psychologically – there are many people who attempted suicide. In the end they refer to God and the church, and simply knowing that there is such a possibility in prison gives you a good feeling. Whether you believe or not, whether you use it or not, you have it in your mind.

The chaplaincy, in sum, strengthens the inmates' capacity to survive the prison experience, yet without questioning the experience itself. Rather, chaplains encourage inmates to face the crimes they committed as individuals and to take responsibility for themselves. The prison administration is tempted to use the chaplaincy as a tool that helps to mould inmates in accordance with prison requirements. This does not mean that the commitment of chaplains and inmates is not genuine or that the chaplain's role is not appreciated. On the contrary, since self-control, human relations and the ambition to leave prison and be free again are crucial for prisoners, in symbolizing a space of freedom the chaplaincy becomes a tangible source of support.

Conclusion

In this chapter, I first identified what establishment entails for the institutional position of chaplains in Eastern Germany. In many respects, the chaplains act – especially when compared to other prison staff – as intermediaries in prison. Their action is directed to the whole institution, as they bridge gaps and tend to stand on the side of the inmates. Their relations with prison officers still suffer from a lack of recognition and from mistrust. For inmates, the chaplaincy represents a wide range of possibilities: it is a space of freedom within the boundaries of the prison. My findings are close to those of Rachel Sarg and Anne-Sophie Lamine[46] in France, concerning inmates making a strategic use of religious activities and chaplains in order to meet other inmates, to contest authority, or to contact their family. However, I also point to the fact that in Eastern Germany the perception of how the chaplain relates to the administration is highly important: she or he may be independent, outside the daily routine and bureaucracy of the prison, on the inmates' side, or functioning as the extended arm of the institution's controlling and disciplining regime. We have seen that these options are really alternatives. As soon as the chaplain participates in rehabilitation procedures, he is also an agent of control. This is why the chaplaincy finds itself in an ambivalent position: it stands for both the inmates and the prison administration, and this is a direct consequence of establishment.[47] Given certain conditions, the chaplaincy without

---

[46]   Rachel Sarg and Anne-Sophie Lamine, 'La religion en prison. Norme structurante, réhabilitation de soi ou stratégie de résistance', *Archives de sciences sociales des religions*, 153/1 (2011), 85–104.

[47]   For the definition of 'ambivalence', I refer here to Marc Augé's distinction between 'ambiguity' and 'ambivalence'. The latter is used, he argues, when a person, an attitude, a

doubt contributes to something akin to rehabilitation for some inmates. For others, it simply enforces the 'pastoral power' of the institution. The freedom that the chaplain is given by the administration is therefore like a gift with a price tag: the price to pay is to legitimize and reproduce the institution. The chaplaincy is on the dividing line between the prison direction (which the chaplain sees as controlling) and the inmate population (which the chaplain sees as in need of help). The chaplains are in a position in which they are free from many administrative constraints, but which makes them at the same time dependent on the administration. The inmates' perceptions of the chaplain vary greatly in accordance with the way they relate to the administration and in accordance with their religious affiliation with established or non-established religions.

The overall redefinition of the relationship between church and society led to new types of tension for East German prison chaplains in their daily work. First, they are now strained between on the one hand the denominational definition of their activity by the current institutional setting, and on the other hand the expectations of the highly secular society to act in a universally comprehensible and acceptable way. Second, their experience of being a minority and politically active church during the GDR stands today in contrast to expectations of cooperation with the state.[48]

---

statement or a situation combines two contradictory qualities – liberating and constraining, for instance. The term 'ambiguous' is used when someone or something is neither of two alternatives: neither right nor wrong, for instance. Cf. *Le Sens des Autres. Actualité de l'anthropologie* (Paris: Fayard, 1994), 54–5.

[48]   For a comparison between religion in schools and prisons in Eastern Germany, with more details on the chaplains' perspectives, see Becci and Willems, 'Gefängnisseelsorge'.

Chapter 4
Inmates and Ex-Inmates' Relations to Religion

Having analysed the ways in which the logic of establishment leads religious actors to adopt a logic of universalization and to create a space of freedom, yet also control, I turn now to the other perspective and focus on inmates and ex-inmates. According to Rachel Sarg and Anne-Sophie Lamine in 'Religion en prison', the ways in which prisoners relate, subjectively, to religion, faith and beliefs may be diverse. Their observations in various French prisons indicate that, besides the strategic usage of religion as a way to resist prison authority, prisoners may use it as a norm to structure their lives, to give a meaning to it, or to tranquillize or self-rehabilitate. Numerous criminologists,[1] mostly in the United States, where religious programmes in prison are very frequent, have studied the therapeutic effect of religious practice on inmates. These functions are to some extent mentioned also by the religiously involved inmates I interviewed. What I consider to be a further major element, however, is that, in the context of a total institution, the personal relation to religion is influenced necessarily by the institutional location of religion and therefore by the relations between chaplaincy, prison direction and inmates. My focus thus shifts to the following questions:

- How do inmates and ex-inmates experience religion?
- Which issues do they associate with religious practice?
- To what extent does religion contribute to their daily experiences?
- How do they approach religious diversity day to day?

According to what I have addressed so far, there seem to be important specificities concerning the ways in which religion is experienced inside versus outside prison.

---

[1] Recently, for instance, C. McDaniel, D.H. Davis and S.A. Neff, 'Charitable Choice and Prison Ministries: Constitutional and Institutional Challenges to Rehabilitating the American Penal System', *Criminal Justice Policy Review*, 16 (2005), 164–89; B.R. Johnson, 'Religious Programs and Recidivism among Former Inmates in Prison Fellowship Programs: A Long-term Follow-up Study', *Justice Quarterly*, 21/2 (2004), 329–54; T.R. Clear, P.L. Hardyman, B. Stout, K. Lucken and H.R. Dammer, 'The Value of Religion in Prison', *Journal of Contemporary Criminal Justice*, 16/1 (2000), 53–74; K.R. Kerley, T.L. Matthews and T.C. Blanchard, 'Religiosity, Religious Participation and Negative Prison Behaviors', *Journal for the Scientific Study of Religion*, 44/4 (2005), 443–57.

This finding is in line with Rhazzali's argument about Muslims in Italian prisons.[2] Focusing on Muslims, he shows that detainees find themselves in a distinctive situation that does not simply reflect the outside world. By contrast, Beckford, Khosrokhavar and Joly in *Muslims* stress the continuity between life outside and life inside prison for Muslim inmates in France and in the UK. In order to identify possible similarities between prison and wider society with regard to religion, I propose to review some relevant observations in current discussions in sociology about religiosity in modern conditions and to apply the concepts offered to the discourses of the prisoners and ex-inmates. I thereby focus mainly on two types of phenomena: religious *bricolage*[3] (the construction of religious experience sliding into the subjective, private and individual realm – the individual is free to establish whatever relationship to religion s/he wants) and religious conversion. Conversion is particularly important here, because for secular East German inmates and ex-inmates it is the most common type of relation to religion. I shall point to the impact that institutions have on 'inventing' and constructing spirituality, and to the importance of religious knowledge, religious belonging, and religious diversity therefore. All these concepts take on a specific meaning for persons experiencing imprisonment, while in prison and at release. I seek to offer a possible reading of this meaning.

Religious *Bricolage*

The *bricolage* approach anchors religion in the individual and inscribes it in the continuum of theories of religious privatization. To anticipate the argument briefly, it may be noted that a two-step account of the contemporary religious situation is widely accepted in the sociology of religion. First, the process of appropriation or construction of religious beliefs is strongly individualized: individuals 'pick up' content or forms of beliefs wherever they find them and mix them up, thereby constructing their own spirituality or their own religious *patchwork*.[4] Second, individuals need to share or validate their beliefs with other social actors, which leads them to look for interlocutors who present alternatives to the churches or to other major institutions of religious socialization. In the context of Eastern Germany, this is rarely found in interpersonal exchanges with the family, but rather with chaplains or pastors.

---

[2]   The studies of Rhazzali, *L'Islam* and Sullivan, *Prison Religion* also highlight the particularity of the prison context with regard to religion when considered from the inmates' perspective.

[3]   In English-speaking contexts, the notion of *bricolage* is often also expressed by 'pastiche' or 'pick and mix'.

[4]   For a recent example, see Paul Heelas and Linda Woodhead, *The Spiritual Revolution: Why Religion is Giving Way to Spirituality* (Oxford: Blackwell Publishing, 2005).

Thomas Luckmann wrote that under modern conditions religious institutions no longer control religion and individuals 'pick and choose' what to believe, selecting religious practices and ethical options according to existential or aesthetic criteria.[5] This kind of religion is composed *à la carte*, with individuals not unquestioningly accepting sets of beliefs and practices, obligations and rites of the kind that the churches provide.[6] The result is a mix of elements from different sources that are more or less religious – a religious *bricolage*. For Luckmann, *bricolage* signals that the process of the individualization and deinstitutionalization of religion is accomplished; this indicates that impersonal or standard objects or ideas are personalized, and a 'personal religion' emerges. Mary Douglas reminds us in *How Institutions Think* that the notion of *bricolage* is an extension of Lévi-Strauss's image of the *bricoleur*, who is an

> amateur craftsman who turns the broken clock into a pipe rack, the broken table into an umbrella stand, the umbrella stand into a lamp, and anything into something else. The bricoleur uses everything there is to make transformations within a stock repertoire of furnishings.[7]

Interestingly, while sociologists of religion often see religious *bricolage* as typically modern since it is opposed to a traditional religiosity, for Lévi-Strauss it primarily characterizes 'primitive' thought that is present in all types of human thinking. According to Lévi-Strauss, the 'bricoleur', as opposed to the scientist or the artist, builds his construction out of signs and not concepts.[8] According to Mary Douglas's reading of him, in modern conditions, when

> technology and the division of labour have been fixed at a certain level for generations, people can let their speculative thought run wild, but it cannot move beyond the limits set by the stable technology and the pattern of work. In a form of intellectual play, what he has called the savage mind deploys the full range of witty parallels and inversions, with elaborate transformations on its stock of analogies.[9]

It is regrettable that these limits are not sufficiently taken into account by sociologists of religion who engage in the interpretative theory of religious *bricolage*. On the contrary, religious *bricolage* has often come to qualify an

---

[5]   Thomas Luckmann, *The Invisible Religion* (London: Macmillan, 1967).

[6]   Many studies have been particularly inspired by Danièle Hervieu-Léger, 'Renouveaux émotionnels contemporains. Fin de la sécularisation ou fin de la religion?', in Françoise Champion and Hervieu-Léger (eds), *De l'émotion en religion: renouveau et traditions* (Paris: Edition du Centurion, 1990), 216–48. Cf. also issue 3 of the 2005 volume of *Social Compass*.

[7]   *How Institutions Think*, 66.

[8]   *La pensée sauvage* (Paris: Plon, 1962), 34–5.

[9]   *How Institutions Think*, 66.

unlimited extra-institutional relation to religion. The underlying assumption is that those who approach religion as patchwork express their personalities and autonomy. From an alternative perspective of *bricolage* one could argue, as Mary Douglas does with regard to limiting *bricolage* to the 'primitive' mind, that the 'notion of bric-à-brac describes well the recurrent analogies and styles of thought that characterised any civilisation'.[10] We may thus identify *bricolage* in a very wide range of practices. Further, we may look at the commonalities of different sets of *bricolage* and interpret them as limitations that are set by society or by the social order and social institutions. It is plausible to interpret, in the case of prison, chaplaincy as an order-giving institution that, jointly with timetables, bureaucracy and security measures, influences the possible extent of *bricolage* so that it is seen not only as an expression of an individual's personality but also as the result of the structural environment. Such structural frameworks bear the collective forces that have an effect on inmates and ex-inmates.

We know that the impact of structures on individuals' action is mediated by social interactions. According to Hervieu-Léger in *Pèlerin*, validation is an interaction considered crucial in the individual relation to religion in modern conditions. For this author, the modern type of validation is neither the church type, which provides institutional validation, nor the sect type, which corresponds with communitarian validation – to use Troeltsch's typology, which opposes church to sect. Hervieu-Léger proposes two new types of validation: the mutual type and self-validation.[11] She argues that the most significant form of validation is now the mutual type. The more personal the construction of beliefs, the stronger the need to validate it. The reason for this lies in the decreasing legitimacy and force of institutional forms of validation and in the limits of self-validation; the latter remains internal to the person and thus cannot be externalized. One's own conviction is not sufficient for an individual to give meaning to her or his daily experience. The assurance that one's convictions are pertinent needs to come from the outside. While this used to be the role of institutional 'meaning-givers', such as churches, it has become a question of mutual validation nowadays. In this way, individuals may validate their personal universe of meaning.[12]

Hence the novelty of our time is the chaos that reigns around different forms of validation: these have been lifted out of their traditional channels, such as the church or the family, and are now free-floating. As far as religion in a hyper-

---

[10]   Ibid.

[11]   By adding new types of validation to the conceptual tools of the sociology of religion, Hervieu-Léger aims to overcome the Christian bias that has characterized the discipline for so long. While elegantly constructed, this tool is problematic because of implicit assumptions about modernity and secularization. One assumption is the idea that the prevailing conception of religion is privatized religion. Cf. also Armando Salvatore, 'D. Hervieu-Léger, "Il pellegrino e il convertito. La religione in movimento" 2003', *Rassegna Italiana di Sociologia*, 3 (Jul.–Sept. 2004), 458–60.

[12]   *Le pèlerin*, 181.

secular context such as Eastern Germany is concerned, individuals now rely mainly on personal affinities to provide inter-individual validation. Thus, if we follow this line of reasoning and study individual validation procedures, does this mean that we then just ignore the role of institutions? Émile Durkheim argued in *Les formes élémentaires de la vie religieuse*[13] that even individual beliefs appeal to social forces. After all, in his view, individual forms of religious practice and beliefs always refer to collective forces, as they are maintained through society.[14] Thus he would exhort us to be cautious and not to confound form with substance. The substance of religion, according to Durkheim, is society. Religion is merely a form of or the expression of social forces, which makes it necessary to study what precisely these social forces are and how they may be studied rather than simply presupposed. In other words, we should be attentive not only to the extent to which religious beliefs or practices are extra-institutional, non-conformist or anti-doctrinal, but also to the extent to which non-conformism conforms with the context in which people believe and are religiously active.

Prisons are particularly interesting places where the influence of a given situation on individual action may be observed; and even more so, the influence of a situation at release. Valuable insights into the way inmates – as an institutional group – deal with religion may be gained by reading the prison magazine. There was such a magazine in prison B. I was able to study the issues published between March 2001 and July 2003 (each issue containing about sixty pages), paying particular attention to the columns that had a link with religion. The monthly magazine was edited by the inmates themselves, and contained political, cultural, social and sports reports from the outside and the inside, providing information about laws and rights, opening up debates on common concerns, and so on. For the inmates, this was a major source of information. They could express their opinions and find contact details they needed to organize their release. I found that the last page of every issue provided the schedule of activities in the Catholic and Protestant chaplaincy, under the heading *Seelsorge* ('Pastoral Care'). The magazine also included announcements about any matters that concerned the chaplaincy, such as the arrival of a new chaplain, inmates complaining that there were not enough chaplains, inmates criticizing the prison administration when they did not call the chaplains in cases where inmates had attempted to commit suicide, and so on. At Easter and Christmas, greetings from the prison chaplains were published in the middle or at the beginning of the magazine. Most issues included advertisements for the local *Caritas* support centre for ex-convicts or for the Protestant organization that offers support after release. Several issues carried an advertisement by a Protestant community offering spiritual care by mail. Additionally, the Bible was often mentioned. Since May 2002, one page had been dedicated to an inmate's comment on a verse from the Bible, in a column called *Bibellese* ('Reading the Bible'). Indeed, all references to sacred

[13]   (Paris: Le Livre de Poche, 1991 [1912]).
[14]   Durkheim, *Les formes*, 709.

matters involved the Bible even when the articles had no direct religious content, such as an article on how inmates might relate to the victims of crimes, entitled 'Versöhnen – und an die Opfer denken' ('Reconciliation – and Thinking of the Victims'). Death announcements usually had a cross drawn on the page. It was not uncommon that debates or letters related to Christian topics, such as creationism, or to art displaying Christian symbols, conversions to Christianity, guilt, and so on. In 2003, the magazine started to publish texts on topics related to religions other than Christianity. In five consecutive issues, a generous amount of space was dedicated to a factual presentation of the five world religions. The purported aim of this initiative was to inform inmates about religious diversity, with each issue containing about four pages of basic knowledge about one of the religions.[15]

My observations do not provide enough indication of the precise role the newspaper played in this prison. They do, however, suggest strongly that it may be viewed as what Goffman terms a house organ, and as such a form of institutional ceremony presenting a somehow favourable, joint and unitarian image of the institution to the outside.[16] The chaplaincy appears as part of the prisoners' lives, regardless of the strength of their personal religious commitment. The chaplaincy is there to provide help and to make connections with the outside; and it offers inmates the possibility to make a fresh start. The question of religious diversity is a relatively recent concern in prisons. Regarding 'other' religions, initially one has to get to know and understand them, but at first glance they are part neither of daily life in prison nor the institution as such.

Prison populations have a distinct profile in terms of social categories, and this presents a first filter for the range of possible religious signs that individuals may pick up. We may expect that there is great variation in what religion means to inmates, depending on religious affiliation, level of education and religious socialization, and also depending on the point they have reached in their prison sentence and the particular situation they might experience at any given time, such as crisis, segregation, and so on. To consider all these factors systematically was impossible in my qualitatively oriented study. However, the conversations I had gave me an insight into the extent to which religious *bricolage* is possible for individuals. Almost half of the inmates interviewed provided answers to the question, 'What does religion mean to you?', which did not refer to religious institutions but to the notion of 'believing' or the need to believe. Here are some illustrations of this:

> *Bernd*: For me, religion means belief.

---

[15]   The title of the series is quite significant: 'Vertrauen, Glauben & Wissen. Die 5 grossen Weltreligionen vorgestellt' – 'Trust, Faith and Knowledge: An Introduction to the Five Big World Religions'. Faith is seen here as having a strong connection to trust, which is coherent with the finding that the chaplains are people who deserve to be trusted.

[16]   Goffman, *Asylums*, 91.

Wim: What I describe as religious [is] the need to believe.

In Wim's view, religion is detached from any institution, as the following comment suggests:

Wim: I think that all monotheistic religions profess the same God and we don't really need the particular forms of the different denominations. That's what church is, that has to do with power politics, with vested interests, of course also with believing and religion, but we don't have to have it to believe.

I found forms of religious *bricolage* among those who had a strongly individualized notion of religion. Lars's statement is particularly striking in the way he referred to 'pick and mix'. To qualify his relationship with religion, he spontaneously used the word 'pick':

This religion that is told and written is only one part for me, because I like to pick out what I find important. When I read the Bible or when I listen to all those stories that are written in the Bible about Jesus or God, what he said or what he wanted to transmit, all that is often not important to me. There are many things there that I don't consider important for my life. But there are, for instance, some things that are incredibly important to me and which taught me something. I try to pick out these kernels and to live according to them ... I would not consider myself a believer; to do so, I should be living like one, but I pick out a couple of things that are good for me ... In any case I believe in the story of the Bible ... but I am also ambivalent because of the scientific knowledge, because we can now look far into space.

The individual's relationship to religion is, in this interview extract, constructed against the norms given by religious institutions and authority. Scientific knowledge is used legitimately to question religious beliefs, as is typical for Eastern Germany.[17] Interestingly, for this inmate, as for all those who regularly attended the services and activities offered by the chaplains, the chaplain was crucial for validation. They identified the chaplains as an extra-institutional figure, 'a good friend', 'a teacher' or a 'father'. For religiously involved inmates, chaplains are primarily people with whom they have a positive personal contact. We have seen, for example, how much inmates appreciate the human nature of their interaction with the chaplain. In this sense, we may understand how the notion of mutual validation becomes meaningful.

On the other hand, inmates who are at a distance from the chaplaincy offer a different interpretation of the situation. Their attention focuses instead on

---

[17]   Cf. my 'Review of Karstein, Schmidt-Lux and Wohlrab-Sahr, "Forcierte Säkularität. Religiöser Wandel und Generationendynamik im Osten Deutschlands"', *European Journal of Sociology*, 51/1 (2010), 535–7.

the institutional nature of the inmates' relation to religion. Their perspective is informed by the fact that they are located outside the relation. For them, chaplains are primarily institutional figures, and in that capacity they are more visible. When I asked inmates who did not practise any religion what religion meant to them, they referred to an institution in their answers:

> *Thilo*: Well, the church. Protestant or Catholic and whatever, somehow to profess something.

For those who are religiously involved, religion is thus not the same as for those who are not involved in religion. For the former, it is very important to have an environment that provides some validation. In this respect, Hervieu-Léger's theory is perfectly pertinent. The stronger the isolation or the further the distance from an outside institution, which is the case for inmates in the high-security sectors, the more intense inmates' expectation that their beliefs are validated by their interlocutors, be they cellmates, unit-mates or chaplains. The extent to which religious *bricolage* occurs depends on various factors, such as the level of religious knowledge as a biographical variable and structural arrangements that determine the range of signs available. In prison the range of what is on offer with regard to religion is quite narrow, but, interestingly, it is still wider in many respects than in the outside world, as the last chapter will show.

Crises and Guilt: Interventionist Relations to Religion

If to pick and mix is a current practice in prison with regard to religion, the next step is to find out whether this happens according to certain logic. The experience of imprisonment is undoubtedly one of uncertainty, crisis and chaos.[18] Crisis and chaos are part of the prison culture and of the experience of release. In this respect, Martin Riesebrodt's reflections on religion may be useful. According to this author, the belief that Western modernity was in total control over nature, the human body and social order pushed religion aside. As soon as this belief started to cave in, new religious forms emerged as practices of prevention and coverage of crises.[19] Religion as a collective attempt to provide answers to questions of uncertainty and chaos has reappeared along with the awareness of the structural effects of incertitudes.[20] According to Riesebrodt, cultural milieus

---

[18]   Joachim Neubaur's book *Einschluß. Bericht aus einem Gefängnis* (Berlin: Berlin Verlag, 2001) describes how inmates experience such crises. The book is based on many conversations with inmates, and the inmates I met recognized many of the aspects described.

[19]   Riesebrodt, *Die Rückkehr der Religionen. Fundamentalismus und der Kampf der Kulturen* (München: Beck, 2000), 50.

[20]   Examples of this are the ecologically disastrous consequences of the Industrial Revolution or societies' economic dependency on uncontrollable market competition.

steer the awareness of incertitude and channel religious experiences. A cultural milieu is defined by a situation in which identity is primarily shaped not by ascribed but by constructed cultural elements, such as extra-economic, social and moral worldviews.[21] If we consider that prison produces cultural milieus, the previously discussed 'prison culture', and that chaos and crisis characterize this culture, traces of these milieus would then be found in the content of, and the motivations cited for, religious action. My analysis of the data actually identified some homogeneity in the 'inventions' or 'constructions' that the inmates had made out of the available religious elements. When I asked devout inmates how they would qualify their beliefs, they all spoke about them in terms of help and forgiveness and mercy, regardless of their particular religious affiliation. None referred, for instance, to the image of a punishing God. The following interview extracts are representative of this approach:

> *I*: Since you have a belief in God, what kind of God is that? How do you imagine God in particular with regard to punishment?
>
> *Martin*: Well, that he gives me a new chance when I am released, that I don't mess up again … that he stands on my side, that he brings me back on to the right path.

Roland, who had become a Buddhist, explained the ups and downs he went through in his search for a way to deal with his feelings of guilt due to his repeated violent crimes:

> I ended up attempting suicide several times … Then I had therapy for two years, which helped me to some extent … it helped me see that my crimes were not something separate from me, that I had to take them on like a stone, I could reconcile them with who I am, put them into my life story. After this therapy I could say, 'OK, I know the causes, I know how it came to these excesses.' And I could conceive them as part of myself, a small part, a dark part, but a part of me. I managed to do that thanks to the therapy. But the therapy could not help me deal with my guilt, only Buddhism did that to some extent, so that today I can carry my guilt without it eating me up.

While secular therapies could help him to stop his self-destructive impulses, only a Buddhist spirituality offered him the means to situate his guilt in a transcendent order. Wim, who had been in his late fifties when he was imprisoned for the first time, summarized a similar point as follows:

Riesebrodt (ibid.) elaborates on the uncertainties of modernity, but his interpretation in terms of the individualization and pluralization of lifestyles does not result in the dissolution of any notion of class. For Riesebrodt, issues of social origin are crucial.

[21]   Ibid., 72.

> Well, I don't know anybody here – and it doesn't apply to me … – who experiences God as punishing – that would be diametrically opposed to my understanding of God; it would anyway, but it certainly does in here.

The issue of guilt is closely connected to inmates' religious experience in prison. In this context, religion is seen as a support, an alleviation of pain. While historically the legitimacy for using religion in prison was based firmly on the association between the internalization of guilt and the individualization of punishment, the situation now seems to have changed. According to the inmates interviewed, punishment seems to be experienced as something dealt out by the prison institution, not something arising from religion. On the contrary, for inmates who participate in the activities offered by the chaplaincy, religion is associated with a (symbolic, relational, and so on) space of freedom. Guilt is certainly at the point where both institutions overlap. If inmates feel no guilt, the change brought about by the prison administration, or rather the discourse about rehabilitation proclaims, cannot happen.[22] Religion thus enables dealing with feelings of guilt and offers a framework for interpretation, whereas the prison experience as such only creates feelings of revenge, sadness and anger. In their accounts or storylines[23] on religion, inmates referred often to guilt. For them, religion has the potential to diminish guilt. Riesebrodt has worked out this concatenation of actions, and he proposes to study religion by asking why people act religiously. He thereby concentrates on what he calls interventionist practices within all types of religious traditions. These practices, he maintains, aim ultimately to prevent natural, personal or social crises, or to manage these once they have occurred. In other words, crises often trigger religious reactions, because crises demonstrate the limits of human beings. As Riesebrodt writes, the universality of religious systems of beliefs, practices and institutions insinuates that humans have only a limited capacity to cope with extreme types of incertitude. Through religion, social groups have articulated their trust in their capacity to handle crises. Religion's role as a resource for the prevention and handling of crises meets individual as well as collective existential needs.[24]

In the context of imprisonment and release, the notions of intervention and crises make sense. Entering prison and being released entail crises, as this means

---

[22]   The same narrative is now used with the notion of shame, which presents a more secular approach: cf. Kenneth D. Jensen and Stephen G. Gibbons, 'Shame and Religion as Factors in the Rehabilitation of Serious Offenders', in Thomas P. O'Connor and Nathaniel J. Pallone, *Religion, the Community and the Rehabilitation of Criminal Offenders* (New York: The Haworth Press, 2002), 215–30.

[23]   Borrowing from Marteen Hajer, I use the notion of the storyline as a condensed statement that summarizes complex narratives used as 'short hand' in discussions, as 'narratives on social reality through which elements from many different domains are combined and that provide actors with a set of symbolic references that suggest a common understanding' – *The Politics*, 62.

[24]   Riesebrodt, *Rückkehr*, 48.

unwanted radical change.[25] The vocabulary inmates used to express this (not only in the interviews, but also for instance in their applications addressed to the rehabilitation programme) is very close to the vocabulary people use when they speak about crises: inmates talked about having been broken, about needing help, and so on. Wim said that in prison one's metaphysical needs are unfulfilled and the only place to address such needs is the chaplaincy:

> You're broken in your metaphysical needs and here this offer [the chaplaincy] is the only possibility to take care of them.

The following account by Lars shows very clearly how personal crisis and larger political crisis can be linked in a person's life, especially in a context such as Eastern Germany:

> I always thought I had a good childhood: I went to school, I had professional training, and some years later I came into conflict with the law for the first time. That also led me to break with my parents; or rather, they broke with me. Because prison was the worst for them, for their honour and for their careers. Also the party held them to account for why I had ended up in prison and so on, so they said they no longer wanted to have anything to do with me. That was the break with my parents. And then things just carried on like that. I then ended up in prison again for a year because of a car accident, then because I tried to escape and then I got 15 years for several felonies and attempted armed robbery. I did 10 of the 15 years, but then I committed more crimes and was recalled, so I had to do the remaining five years and three more. Now, I still have two and a half years left. But during my time in prison the [Berlin] Wall came down, the GDR collapsed, and that's when I first made contact with the church or had any discussions about faith.

In spite of all the spiritual patchwork they do, inmates have a fairly similar understanding of the role of religion. Therefore, the situation of being totally caught up in the institution of prison has a significant impact on their discourse about religion. The storyline goes as follows: help is needed, and religion may provide some of the help needed. A similar line of argument characterizes also another type of religious development that the modernist point of view highlights – conversion.

---

[25]   See for the subjective experience of change and crisis in Germany the numerous studies by Mechthild Bereswill: for instance, *Gefängnis und Jugendbiographie. Qualitative Zugänge zu Jugend, Männlichkeitsentwürfen und Delinquenz*, JuST-Bericht Nr. 4. (Hannover: KFN, 1999); *Haft (er) leben, Zentrale Überlebensstrategien und biographische Selbstentwürfe männlicher Jugendlicher in Haft*, JuST-Bericht Nr. 6 (Hannover: KFN, 2001); *Doing Violence: Concepts of Masculinity, and Biographical Subjectivity – Three Case Studies*, Forschungsbericht Nr. 85 (Hannover, KFN, 2002).

Religious Conversion through Imprisonment: A Story of Change

Much has been written about prisoners' religious radicalization over the last ten years, but few of these writings are based on first-hand observation.[26] The abundance of discourses on prison by authors who had barely set foot in a prison has fed a powerful imagining about prisoners' either excessive or opportunistic religiosity. As mentioned in the first chapter, the belief that religion has an active role to play in rehabilitation in prison is rooted in the philanthropic project to transform the prison experience itself into a religious experience. This belief still attracts the attention of numerous criminologists.[27] The account of how this would happen follows a precise storyline: prison means solitary confinement, be it symbolically or physically; it means having endless time on one's hands; it means sadness, despair, deprivation – these are the conditions that encourage inmates to think about fundamental, metaphysical, transcendent questions of life and death and to address other spiritual issues.[28] At first sight, the inmates' discourses also point to such a story: Wim, for instance, insisted that in prison an inmate is 'broken by his metaphysical needs', adding that he 'didn't go to church as often [when he was] outside'. Most of the inmates interviewed who were regularly involved in religion agreed that their religious practice had increased in prison compared to what it had been before when they were outside.[29] How come, then, that in spite of all the changes that prisons have undergone this story still holds?[30] The idea that inmates' religious practice is greater in prison or that they have more intensive religious needs in prison than they do when they are outside is held by the majority of the ministers and chaplains interviewed. There are two slightly different ways of interpreting increased religious involvement in prison or

---

[26]   See, for instance, J. Carlile, 'Islamic Radicalization Feared in Europe's Jails: Treatment of Muslim Inmates Varies across EU', MSNBC News, 8 July 2006, at http://www. msnbc.msn.com/id/13733782/ns/world_news-islam_in_europe/t/islamic-radicalization-feared-europes-jails/#.T9IreNX2Z-M, accessed 8 June 2012.

[27]   Cf., for instance, O'Connor and Pallone (eds), *Religion*.

[28]   For the psychological impact of long-term imprisonment, see, for example, Stanley Cohen and Laurie Taylor, *Psychological Survival: The Experience of Long-Term Imprisonment* (Harmondsworth: Penguin Books, 1981 [1972]). Unfortunately, this passionate study, like many others on imprisonment, only touches on religion in passing.

[29]   Looking at this issue from a gender perspective shows that the usual correspondence between women and religious practice is absent in prison, although the degree of women's practice remains high: cf. Irene Becci and Mallory Schneuwly-Purdie, 'Gendered Religion in Prison? Comparing Imprisoned Men and Women's Expressed Religiosity in Switzerland', in *Women's Studies*, 41 (2012), 1–22.

[30]   The fact that in the United States the 'estimated average attendance at religious services in state prisons throughout the country is *only* 32%' – Thomas P. O'Connor and Michael Perreyclear, 'Prison Religion in Action and its Influence on Offender Rehabilitation', in O'Connor and Pallone (eds), *Religion*, 11–33, at 21, emphasis added – explains the much greater interest in this topic among social scientists.

telling the story of inmates' increased religiosity. One account stresses the novelty of religious feelings in prison, the creation of a religious need in a situation of incarceration, in particular in a situation of deprivation. Harry Dammer writes that one of the reasons for religious involvement in prison is certainly the fact that 'religion serves to mitigate the psychological and physical deprivations created by imprisonment'.[31] Deprivation is often cited by inmates who are not committed to any religion as a reason for what they observed as an increased religious activity in prison:

> *Lars*: That's caused by the loneliness in the cell, one simply thinks differently … It's because you sit such a long time in your cell … If you are with three men, at some point, you don't have anything to tell each other any longer and you start to occupy yourself or just to think a lot and so you find silence.

A closer look reveals that other inmates and some chaplains have a less romantic linear vision of religiosity in prison. For chaplains, that was precisely what made their job interesting. The increased interest that inmates seem to have for religion in prison is, they thought, connected strongly to the specific context of the institution:

> *Chaplain Anton*: They [the inmates] are not more religious, I think they are more direct, more accessible, and in some way also self-conscious in the sense that – sometimes they say to me, 'That's not true what you're saying about the good Jesus. I don't buy that.' And that's where it becomes interesting. A member of my parish would never dare ask me such a question.

The fact that one tends to be more attracted by religion while imprisoned may also be interpreted via a slightly different kind of reasoning. According to Peter Berger's perspective,[32] religious questions are ontological elements of human nature, and therefore people deal with them in different ways, depending on their relevant social circumstances. Thus increased religious involvement in prison is just the expression of a human aspect that exists anyway, not an attitude that emerges in a situation of detention. The following quote from an interview with a Catholic chaplain illustrates this point of view:

> *I*: Can we say that inmates are more religious than the people outside?

> *Chaplain Benedict*: Yes, we can say that. It's simply an emergency situation, a need. When someone is imprisoned, the basic right to freedom is taken from him and he can only rely on himself. In particular, there are the long hours spent in the cell,

---

[31] Harry R. Dammer, 'The Reasons for Religious Involvement in the Correctional Environment', in O'Connor and Pallone (eds), *Religion*, 35–58, at 56.

[32] *The Sacred Canopy: Elements of a Sociological Theory of Religion* (Garden City, NY: Doubleday, 1967).

sometimes inmates have to stay 23 hours in their cell because they don't work or do anything. And if they have few contacts outside, they are really abandoned. 'What gives meaning to my life, what keeps it going?' These are the big questions that arise and then comes the question about God, and this is why I would say that, here, the religious question is much clearer. Outside it is put aside by the workload or by TV or by drinking beer; here, it breaks through. Well, I would say the religious question can be seen very well here and some experience it as something extreme. I know at least five or six inmates who read the Bible three to four hours every day. I know two inmates who are very much involved in religion, one in the Orthodox religion, the other reads a lot of literature from the Pentecostal movement. He wants to become a preacher in a Pentecostal church one day.

Thus utilitarian reasons may first lead inmates to religion, but this does not preclude the possibility of their becoming sincere believers. Indeed, most of the religiously committed consider that the other inmates have a purely instrumental relation to the chaplaincy and that they are virtually the only sincere participants:

> *Christof*: When I think how many people here go to church, of all prisoners here
> … we are a total of 450 … there are 10, 12, 15 men in the room, but I am sure half
> of these 10, 12, 15 men are just hangers-on or they don't know why they are here.

The sincere motives to which the quote above refers correspond to Dammer's study,[33] which, on the basis of inmates' classifications, identifies hope, motivation, direction and meaning for life, peace of mind, positive self-esteem, and changes in lifestyle. According to Dammer, utilitarian motives include using the chaplaincy as protection, meeting with other inmates, having the opportunity to interact with women volunteers, and having access to prison resources. The distinction between 'utilitarian' and 'sincere' involvement is not always clear cut for the particular context of the prison, as the prison culture promotes insincerity and double discourses, which leads inmates constantly to 'wear a mask' (Johan).

Concerning degree of religious involvement, only a minority of the inmates I interviewed had not been affected by the experience of detention, while most of the believing convicts experienced an increase of their religiousness in prison. However, less than one in four inmates or ex-inmates converted to a religion while in prison, as was the case for Justus:

> I don't really have a religion; I am not baptized and was not raised with religion,
> but I think I have found the Christian faith in here.

The convert is one of the emblematic figures chosen by Danièle Hervieu-Léger in *Le pèlerin* to characterize religion in modernity. Her way of theorizing conversion ties in with important studies in considering it a process that may comprise at

---

[33]   'Reasons', 39–45.

least three different types; the usual interpretation considers the change from one religious affiliation to another. This is rarely the case in Eastern Germany, where most people have no religious affiliation to start with. Here, what is frequently observed in terms of conversion is an individual's change from no religious belonging to the adoption of a religion. While Hervieu-Léger distinguishes this type of change from the reaffirmation of one's belief and practice within a religion, I shall consider them jointly, because for the inmates and ex-inmates who had some religious affiliation before converting through prison it had no importance. The connection to religion was so loose that it had no significant impact on the life of the person concerned. For instance, Izmil affirmed his Muslim identity in prison and used this to explain perceived unfair treatment, whereas being a Muslim had held no importance for him outside prison. I shall describe the cases I observed in some detail by drawing on the accounts that inmates gave in answer to the questions I asked them in line with Riesebrodt's approach: Why do inmates convert? Is the process of conversion facilitated in prison? Their narratives of conversion run along two basic oppositions: a 'before and after', and an inside (the religious community) and outside (the context questioning the beliefs).

Roland was in the process of 'converting' to Buddhism when I interviewed him. He had made an intensive and sustained effort to search for a way to express his spirituality until he finally decided to become a Buddhist. When I met him, his head was shaved and his ears pierced. In his case, the process of conversion had been of a very rational nature and had occurred primarily through reading:

> I used … to have a very critical relation to religion. I couldn't really relate to the story of God as the creator. I used to say, 'Those who need to believe in God are' – I don't know – 'too weak to believe in themselves', or whatever, that was my attitude. Nevertheless I used to like it, the way Christians live. Also the way the chaplains here do things and what they do, they do everything, that always kind of attracted me … although I couldn't really relate to the philosophy … At some point I started to be interested in religion because I had recognized a couple of things myself that were true. First, I looked at religion in general. I compared religions and at some point I found a philosophy somewhere that was for me, the one that suited me, and that's rooted in Buddhism. I am now studying religion, have studied Buddhism for one and a half years, and soon I will make my vows as a lay member so that I count as a proper Buddhist, and in the mid-term, when I get out, I shall probably also make my vows as a monk … I have been interested in Buddhism now for three and a half years … It started with a book and then it became more intensive. I had nothing to do with religion before. I did not grow up as a Christian.

Roland's aspirations for the future are spiritual, while his past is secular. He is quite sure that if he had not been incarcerated for so many years he would not have converted to Buddhism:

> *I*: Do you think that you would have had the same experience outside prison?

Roland: I don't think so.

I: Why?

Roland: That's a good question. I used to be a rowdy, I guess.

For Justus, however, converting to Catholicism was more like an emotional journey. It had been much easier for him to access Catholicism and it was clearly his contact with the Catholic chaplain that had led him to this path. Although his religious commitment was very strong when I met him, he had very little knowledge of religion, which meant that he could hardly distinguish Catholicism from Protestantism. For him, the new religious belonging was primarily a means to stay away from a secular and material world that he was not attracted to and that he qualified as capitalistic:

> *Justus*: I'm also considering whether to continue my life in the direction of the church, maybe in the direction of becoming a priest. This is one of the ways at the moment how I imagine my life. I don't feel like working for whatever company outside, I'd rather continue with this direction. Prison chaplaincy or something like that. Whatever is available.
>
> *I*: But then you will have to decide which denomination to belong to, Catholic or Protestant.
>
> *Justus*: I think I will be a Catholic then … simply because of the name. 'Catholic' means 'all-encompassing' … and then I can make up my mind to go for that.

These two accounts tell us something about establishment. The two inmates were of a similar age and had similar levels of education yet had converted in very different ways. Roland had to invest a significant amount of energy to fulfil his desire for conversion, while Justus, who converted to an established religion, had an easier passage. As Mary Douglas suggests, when they seek to understand the processes in individual decisions, sociologists should place them within the institutional frame in which they act. In her words, this means that,

> For better or worse, individuals really do share their thoughts and they do to some extent harmonize their preferences, and they have no other way to make the big decisions except within the scope of institutions they build.[34]

For both converts, the religious community is very important. The commonality of these two cases is that the new religious belonging represented for inmates the possibility to leave previous deviant lives behind. The following quote indicates this. When I

---

[34]   Douglas, *How Institutions Think*, 128.

asked Roland whether other inmates took his new identity seriously, he answered that inmates who had converted were no longer considered potential accomplices:

> Some do take me seriously in what I do, but others, mainly my old mates who are still strongly rooted in that milieu, who are still into organized crime, they say, '[Roland] has been in prison for too long … prison has taken him, he has built himself an altar and prays to the Buddha, they got him.'

Two ex-inmates also told me about their conversions. Both had converted privately in prison and had confirmed their conversion by ritual only after they had left prison. Hans's story is a very good illustration of Diane Austin-Broos's affirmation that the convert is on a 'quest for human belonging',[35] and looking for closeness and recognition in a community. During the last seven years of his imprisonment, Hans had participated in group therapy for alcoholics; this therapy was organized by Sebastian. At that time, Hans had regular contact not only with the Catholic and Protestant chaplain, but also with Sebastian:

> I went to see them a lot because I was simply searching for something that could give me peace, because I couldn't cope with my crime [pauses] I was looking for something that would give me peace, but that [pauses] didn't give me peace either, so [pauses] I started to pray sometimes, but I didn't believe in it all that much and [pauses] they also started to look at me differently, like, 'Ah, he goes to church, he goes to see the Baptist', and the others started to tease me with, 'He and his God', and,. 'He can't help him anyway', and, 'He's crazy anyway' … even more so when we had the detox zone; then it was particularly bad because we had open cells, a kitchen, we had our own shower … I then got more and more into religion – there were ups and downs, so sometimes more, sometimes less, but I always stuck to that belief because I realized that it gave me some sort of stability … then someone from the community came who taught us the Bible – so really talks about believing and real Bible classes … from the Baptist community … so the contact was made with that community where I was later baptized in 2000 … I then attended the services regularly and then the [pauses] idea developed slowly that I wanted to be baptized. I actually wanted to be baptized during my detention because two others in our rehab group had been baptized, but [Sebastian] always told me to take my time and that we would do that outside. And he had been really taking care of me for the last ten years. And I had also been talking a lot with [Chaplain Benedict, but] I had not yet come to a final decision. Only after a while did I decide to put my life into Sebastian's hands – I mean the Baptist community –, because I wanted to make a new start with being baptized as an adult.

---

[35] 'The Anthropology of Religious Conversion: An Introduction', in Andrew S. Buckser and Stephen D. Glazier (eds), *The Anthropology of Religious Conversion* (Lanham, MD: Rowman & Littlefield, 2003), 1–11, at 2.

Hans's sentence was reviewed after the *Wende*, with the result that he was released earlier than planned, in 2000. His religious conversion coincided with his prison release but had taken a long time to prepare. Interestingly, many of the ex-inmates who completed a questionnaire I prepared for them[36] said also that they had experienced a change regarding religion while they were imprisoned. When I asked how they would describe that change, some answered that they now had 'an ordered life', thereby using the institutional vocabulary, while others confirmed that there had been 'no durable religious roots' in their lives before. Only one convert wrote, 'I have found the answers to some questions – responsibility, honesty, later baptism.' Key to understanding this specific type of religiosity might be consideration of the two types of religiosity as arranged on a continuum: one type would be the religiosity of the areligious critics or sceptics, who form the majority, while the other would consist of religious converts who remained religious once released. Close to the first pole we would find those who had formed strong ties with the prison chaplain and who kept meeting him once they were outside, but who considered him as a person and not as the representative of a religion. Only a few respondents in my field were located at the opposite pole. They had converted – or were on the way to convert – to the Baptist, Protestant Lutheran or Catholic Church or to the Salvation Army. They now prayed every day or read the Bible, but more important for them was the fact that they had

---

[36]   The questionnaire was filled in by 18 former inmates whom I met in different rehabilitation programmes in East Berlin. One of them was a woman. All except one were German citizens. One third were between 55 and 66 years old, another third between 44 and 50, and the remainder between 19 and 36. One person was married, one was engaged to be married, the others were either single or divorced/separated/widowed. Two had more than four children, nine had either two children or one child, the rest had no children. Two thirds had grown up in the former GDR, the rest in West Germany. Only one had a higher education; of the others, one half had a secondary school education, the other primary school education. Twelve had been imprisoned in Berlin, three in West Germany, and the rest in the provinces of Saxony or Saxony-Anhalt. Seven had been convicted for crimes related to property, sometimes combined with violence; three had committed crimes against people (such as assault and murder); two had not respected the authority of state officials; one had defrauded. One was in prison during the GDR period for attempting to leave the country. After their release, most were in rehabilitation programmes; only one found shelter in a parish, while five had either gone to their families or friends or had found their own accommodation. Three had no accommodation after being released from prison, and one was still homeless at the time of the interview. Some had been homeless before they were imprisoned. Two thirds thought that their drug addiction was the main reason why they had committed crimes. Other reasons they cited were having criminal friends, being poor, experiencing the end of the GDR (*Wende*), and feeling dissatisfied. In addition, they stated that violence, lack of motivation and courage, unemployment, their lack of education or their psychological state had led them to criminal acts. Only two stated that they had received a Protestant education; one said he had been brought up as a Roman Catholic; and one noted simply that he had a Christian education. Another considered his atheist education to have been religious.

chosen the religious community as a community to belong to. An example is the experience of Wolf,[37] who converted to Lutheran Protestantism. I interviewed him in a Christian Evangelical rehabilitation programme situated on the eastern outskirts of Berlin. After he had told a pastor he met in prison of his violent crime committed within a right-wing group, the pastor asked him whether he actually hated the person he had almost killed or foreigners in general. He answered with hesitation:

> 'Have you ever hated people?' – I say, 'Well, not hate, but I just kept some distance.' [pauses] 'Well,' he said, 'that's OK [pauses] It's a question of how you feel – so you didn't feel hate then' – I say, 'No' [pauses] – and so that happened and then he gave me something like a questionnaire about Christian beliefs and what I believe, and so on, and so on. [pauses] Also I was prepared for religion … slowly prepared for baptism and everything and at some point I felt and sensed something and slowly went down that path.

The religious practice of the converts I interviewed was by then not exclusive, as they participated willingly in other Christian discussion groups, but they privileged the relationship with the community to which they have converted. They were well aware that they are somewhat exceptional and that most of those who, like them, were religiously active in prison stopped practising after leaving the institution. This heightened their sense of being different.

All the inmates' accounts show also that for prisoners the process of conversion can vary greatly. It can be a strategic, an intellectual or an emotional enterprise. The religion to which most inmates convert does not seem be chosen at random, as it is often the religion that had a strong presence in prison. This review suggests that there is probably some kind of logic that conversion follows. The 'conversion' to Buddhism appears to be an exception, as inmates do not generally convert to a religion at all or they convert to one of the religions present in prison through chaplaincy.

There were only a few converts among the East German ex-convicts I met, although several were in close contact with the chaplains in prison. I knew that Ulrich had been participating in religious activities in prison. One day I asked him if he continued doing so now. His first answer was, 'No, I have not thought about it and I do not really have time for that now.' As our conversation went on, however,

---

[37]   Wolf, a strong man in his forties from Brandenburg, lived in a rehabilitation programme led by Baptists when I met him and attended their Bible groups. At the age of 4, he was put into a home and remained there until he was 14. He remembers that time as a very traumatic one. He began an apprenticeship twice, which he interrupted after half a year. He committed his first crime as an adult during the GDR, and experienced a lot of violence in prison. After repeated imprisonments, he found a job as a refuse collector during unification, lasting until 1999, when he was fired. He had multiple addictions and had converted to Protestantism after his near-death experience during a surgery. His last crime was related to his activities within a right-wing rock group.

he explained that it was not only a question of time. The situation outside prison was, he argued, completely different:

> You know, that is because it is very different here outside. I mean, those who have never been in there cannot imagine. Here it is completely different, here you do not need to sit on the seat and wait until they open the door, here you stand up and you open the door. You know, you can go out to the courtyard. Today everything is different. There, inside, you make different things; here you have to think differently.

I found that the majority of the released East German prisoners actually abandoned any kind of religious practice after release. Manfred, for instance, who had his first contact with religion during his imprisonment, did not convert and completely abandoned any practice once outside. While religious practice is encouraged in prison – most of all through chaplaincy –, the opposite is true outside. Only the few inmates who had converted remained religiously active outside prison, and they did so thanks to the religious community they had found outside that offers them 'human warmth, and dedication' (Yanna). These cases seem to fit very well within Austin-Broos's description of religious conversion as 'a form of passage, a "turning from and to" that is neither syncretism nor absolute breach'.[38] This passage, after a possible first experimental phase maybe in prison, 'becomes a deliberate change with definite direction and shape. It shows itself responsive to particular knowledge and practice. To be converted is to reidentify, to learn, reorder, and reorient'.[39] Since release makes for another change, converts may be better prepared for it. However, for the converts, entering the religious community outside means also a redefinition of their religiosity from what they had learned in prison into something that is completely new for them. Analysis of the changes in religiosity and spirituality after release from prison shows the social situatedness of these personal experiences and highlights the type of secularity existing in the context of Eastern Germany. The context of the rehabilitation programme I have observed may indeed be characterized as hyper-secular.

Historians studying Berlin's religious past stress that, as early as the first decades of the nineteenth century, large sections of its inhabitants clearly turned to a more secular life.[40] The secular character of the city was reinforced during the more than

---

[38]   Austin-Broos, 'Anthropology', 1.
[39]   Ibid., 2.
[40]   In 1874, only 20 per cent of couples had a Protestant wedding and only 62 per cent of newborns were baptized: cf. Hans-Ulrich Wehler, *Das Deutsche Kaiserreich, 1871–1918* (Göttingen: Vandenhoeck & Ruprecht, 1973), 119. See also Hugh McLeod, *Piety and Poverty: Working-class Religion in Berlin, London and New York, 1870–1914. Europe Past and Present* (London: Holmes and Meier, 1996).

forty years during which Berlin was a divided city.[41] While a capitalist model of development was dominant in the West, provoking also resistance and tensions, in the eastern part of the city – the capital of the GDR – the Socialist government built large estates in the city centre to house working-class families instead of renovating older buildings that it considered to be 'a reminder of capitalist living conditions, which were supposed to have been overcome by socialism'.[42] Large parts of the area of the housing programme are under renovation today, but this restoration does not signify the gentrification of the area, as happened in other parts of East Berlin.[43] On the contrary, this area is characterized by marginalization, in economic, cultural and political terms. There are no cinemas, no theatres. One square becomes animated when the market takes place a couple of times per week. Neither tourists nor students are attracted to the location. It is still on the way from Socialism to post-Socialism.[44] Indeed, I myself had never come to this area before spending a year as an ethnologist in the rehabilitation programme. Additionally, it is known for criminal activities: during the 1990s, the war between groups engaged in black marketeering was waged here; and even today, some of that kind of activity seems to continue. Some people do not seem to mind the rather desolate state of this urban space[45] – in fact, it seems to be the very thing that attracts them. This is, for example, the case for the ex-prisoners who were at the halfway house I observed. In my view, the location of the halfway house in the city of Berlin reflects symbolically different aspects of the social situation of ex-inmates. The ex-inmates of the programme knew very well that they were now meant to change;

---

[41]   The districts in the East and in the West have undergone very different urban transformations. See, for example, Frank Eckardt, 'In Search for Meaning: Berlin as National Capital and Global City', *Journal of Contemporary European Studies*, 13/2 (2005), 189–201.

[42]   Hartmut Häussermann, 'From the Socialist to the Capitalist City: Experiences from Germany', in Gregory Andrusz, Michael Harloe and Ivan Szelenyi (eds), *Cities after Socialism: Urban and Regional Change and Conflict in Post-Socialist Societies* (Oxford and Cambridge: Blackwell, 1996), 214–31, at 219.

[43]   See Andrej Holm, 'Urban Renewal and the End of Social Housing: The Roll Out of Neoliberalism in East Berlin's Prenzlauer Berg', *Social Justice*, 33/3 (2006), 114–28.

[44]   Since the unification of Germany, political power in this area has been in the hands of the left-wing party. The local authorities have sought to keep the Socialist past alive by naming streets and squares in the location after local Socialists who had been victims of the Nazi regime. Often they stress the continuity with the socialist past.

[45]   The distinction between place and space was proposed by Michel de Certeau in his study *The Practice of Everyday Life*. In opposition to place, which is simply the physical environment, space is the outcome of people's strategies to appropriate a place: it is 'a practiced place' (Certeau, *The Practice*, 117), the 'product of the subject's interaction with the existing environment' – B. Reynolds and J. Fitzpatric, 'The Transversality of Michel de Certeau: Foucault's Panoptic Discourse and the Cartographic Impulse', *Diacritics*, 29 (1999), 63–80. As my aim is to account for the perspective of the actors involved, I shall draw on his notion of space.

therefore, the concept of *liminality* is a good description of their experience,[46] as I shall elaborate in the next chapter. When they arrive at the halfway house, ex-inmates find themselves in a subjective state of *liminality*, no longer inside the prison and not yet really outside it, but on the way to the outside.[47] In this delicate phase, belonging to a community may be of great value for the person, but it also involves drawing boundaries between different communities and thereby defining others outside of it.

The Experience of Religious Diversity in a Hyper-secular Context

Inside prison, as I have shown, the population is religiously more diverse; this raises the question to what extent religion contributes to drawing boundaries and causing conflicts to erupt.[48] In my fieldwork I found that the inter-religious relations among prisoners do not give rise to direct confrontation. Quite the opposite, at first sight the inmates' comments suggest that religious plurality in prison is well accepted. When I asked inmates about their experience of the social environment in prison, they answered that they knew a wide range of inmates who had different religious affiliations:

Justus: Well, Christians, Muslims, Sikhs, everything.

I: Do you also know any Muslims here, for instance?

Johan: Yes.

I: Are they friends?

Johan: Yes, no problem.

---

[46]   Jonathan Ortiz in *Almost Home: Halfway Houses as Liminal Space* (Saarbrücken: Dr. Müller., 2008) also applies the concept of *liminality* to a halfway house, but focuses on techniques of control.

[47]   Drawing on one of the three phases that mark rites of passage, as Arnold van Gennep observed, the *liminal*, or 'threshold' period, which involves being between two states, Victor Turner adapted the concept to describe social processes in contemporary Western societies. See Van Gennep, *Les rites de passage; étude systématique des rites de la porte et du seuil, de l'hospitalité, de l'adoption, de la grossesse et de l'accouchement, de la naissance, de l'enfance, de la puberté, de l'initiation, de l'ordination, du couronnement des fiançialles et du mariage, des funérailles, des saisons, etc.* (Paris, É. Nourry, 1909), and Turner, *The Ritual Process: Structure and Anti-structure* (New York: Aldine De Gruyter, 1995 [1969]).

[48]   We know from a number of studies that fights, conflicts and struggles are frequent in prisons. To mention only one recent historical survey: Christian de Vito, *Camosci e Girachiavi. Storia del carcere in Italia 1943–2007* (Rome and Bari: Laterza, 2009).

> *Kai*: [The opinion about chaplaincy] certainly is very divided … some say, 'It's certainly very interesting and I would participate', and some say, 'That's not for me, I had connections with the church all my life', others say, 'I'm sorry, I am an atheist.' Yet others get drunk every night and then touch black cats because that is what makes them comfortable. Everyone has to decide for himself, it varies a lot.

Jamal also shared this view:

> *I*: Are most of the people with whom you are together … Muslims? … Or are there also other religions?
>
> *Jamal*: Yes, Christians for instance, Buddhists also, there's one [Buddhist], there's a Vietnamese guy, he believes in a snake, I don't know what religion that is, no idea.

Inmates tended to talk openly about religious diversity. To judge by the answers that inmates gave me to the question of how different religions coexisted, there is mutual respect and recognition in prison. This is particularly true for Muslim inmates, who were mentioned the most when specific arrangements were discussed. The following interview extract relates Kai's friendship with a Muslim inmate in prison:

> *Kai*: Every time I see him washing his feet, I know, for the next 20 minutes I close his cell, and he may not be bothered and I don't let anybody into the cell, anybody who wants to go in, is told, 'No, no, not now.'

Religious tolerance appears to be standard, which sometimes creates the impression that it has actually turned into religious indifference. Comments such as the following were very common:

> *Bernd*: Every religion is the same to me.
> Justus: In the end I think we believe in one God, and whatever you call him, how exactly you live by him, that's your own business.

This way to express recognition or tolerance shifted towards indifference, for instance when some inmates talked about beliefs they did not really know much about. My impression was that many saw religion almost as an aesthetic preference; and, as Adam Seligman states, if something is 'a matter of taste (aesthetics) and of no great significance, (trivial) tolerance does not effectively enter the picture'.[49] None of the inmates used exclusive terms when they talked about religious diversity:

---

[49]   Adam Seligman, 'Secularism, Liberalism and the Problem of Tolerance: The case of the USA', paper presented at the conference Migration, Religion and Secularism: A

Jamal: Everybody has his own belief and, I think, I respect everybody. There are, for instance, Christians here who go to church, have a crucifix and whatever, others believe in cows, in a cow, or in snakes and I respect everybody. Everybody has his own faith ... I respect everybody, of course. If he tells me he believes in a snake, I say, 'That's your problem, not mine.'

I: Does it happen that inmates talk about religion among themselves?

Kai: Yes, I have experienced that and there are even very lively discussions ... but for the different religions, it's more a mutual getting to know each other: 'And what do you believe or in which direction does your faith go?' Although – I have learned that somehow it's always the same. Well, the basic idea of religions is always the same.

This indifference can ultimately be seen as a consequence of the East German 'secular norm' of neither having a religious belonging nor a religious knowledge. Indeed, the experience of religious diversity forms no part of what East Germans usually acquire during their lifetimes, as a conversation I had with Bernd illustrates:

I: Have you ever met a Buddhist monk?

Bernd: No.

I: A Hindu?

Bernd: No.

I: An Imam?

Bernd: No.

I: An Orthodox priest?

Bernd: No ... I was once in a Russian Orthodox church; in [a Saxon town], there's a Russian church ... during the GDR period, when I was a little boy, that's the only thing I experienced in this regard.

Other inmates confirmed the 'norm' of not belonging to any religious tradition:

Stefan: I don't know anybody here who belongs to a religion in any way.

Comparative Approach (Europe and North America), University of Paris 1 – Sorbonne and Ecole Normale Supérieure, Paris, 17–18 June 2005).

Martin: I share my cell with two other inmates, but I don't think they belong to anything.

If we compare the responses of the religiously inactive inmates with those of the religiously involved, we may see a significant difference between the two, which is that the latter are generally ignored by the former. One interpretation of this could refer to the invisibility of religion, in Luckmann's sense: individuals may be religious or spiritually committed, but this does not manifest itself. The religiously involved inmates tend to limit their religious practice to situations deemed appropriate. For instance, they seem to talk about religion almost exclusively with other religiously active persons, as they know more people who, like them, are religiously committed. Another interpretation could refer to the lack of inmates' knowledge about religious matters. Moreover, some of the inmates' answers indicate that the question about other people's religious affiliation might be considered unwarranted, because religion is a private or a completely irrelevant matter. Two interviewees in prison A were categorical about that:

I: If you think about the people you're with most, what religion do they belong to?

Franz: No, I make a point of not being interested in that.

I: Do you know the people who go to the religious service here in [prison A]?

Thilo: No, I don't know anybody who goes to the service. None of the people … I'm with goes to the religious service. At least, I haven't seen any. I haven't asked anybody, I have to say, that's why I don't know who goes and who doesn't.

This last interview extract indicates that the inmates interviewed treat religion as an irrelevant private matter and do not necessarily include it in their conversations with other inmates. The answers I collected through my questionnaire to ex-inmates gave similar results. To my question, 'How would you define your religious attitudes today?', respondents gave the following answers: 'No', 'Quiet', 'Positive because I was educated as a Christian', 'No way – never had any', 'No religion', 'No answer', 'Pagan – atheist – was never baptized'. To obtain more elaborate answers, I decided to rephrase the question and asked whether they considered themselves to be religious and, if so, to what extent. The answers to this question were as short as those to the previous ones. One person considered him/herself to be very religious. Two others considered themselves religious rather than not religious, while eight others classified themselves as not religious at all.

Conclusion

In this chapter, we have seen how the notions of patchwork, validation, conversion and religious indifference, which are widely discussed in the current literature of the sociology of religion, are entangled in a complex web of social interactions. In situations such as imprisonment and release, believing and conversion are better understood if seen in relation to the meaning of belonging. Belonging continues to be a pertinent category to study here in order to understand the meaning and motivation of believing, also because social and religious belonging overlap. This overlap will become even clearer in the next chapter.

To sum up, existing theories of the way 'free' people (people who are not in detention) relate to religion can be used – in a slightly modified way – to analyse the conditions and difficulties faced by people living in prison. On release from prison, ex-convicts need to reorder their mind according to the outside world, where the religious frame is much looser. The experience of crisis plays an important role with regard to religion, as do the prevailing structures. This is why I have also considered the 'prison culture' in which individual actions are embedded. This does not mean that the individual is conceived as determined by the cultural or structural elements. However, such elements form the repertoire from which individual meanings and practices in the realm of religion and its boundaries emerge.

Chapter 5

New Religious Belongings:
Inside, Outside and in Liminality

Most studies that are concerned with religion in modern conditions claim that belonging and believing have never been as disconnected as they have in recent times.[1] In Hervieu-Léger's view, belonging does not refer necessarily to the idea of religious affiliation, but to a notion that provides identity. Religion still nourishes the process of identification at one or more of the following four levels: community, ethics, culture, emotion. Therefore, even the most individually composed religion has an important role to play in terms of binding people together in collectivities, either in temporal or in spatial terms.[2] However, what does this mean in a particular situation such as during and after imprisonment? My findings show that, while believing outside institutional affiliations has certainly reached an important legitimacy, the question of belonging continues to play a cardinal role in the articulation of beliefs. In fact, the answers that the interviewed inmates and ex-inmates gave to the question of religious belonging in my enquiry demonstrate the high complexity of such a notion. For many inmates, 'having a religion' does not necessarily mean belonging to a religious community. In order to belong to a community, the community has to be in some way present in one's mind, either because it is remembered or because it is physically visible. Inmates may 'belong' to communities that are visible in prison, but it is difficult for them to be part of invisible ones.

Being a prisoner dominates the definition of inmates' individual status. In their daily lives, inmates are first of all treated as inmates, then they are men or women, tall or small, Catholic, Muslim, and so on. Their status as inmates is glued to their identity, although many try various ways to be rid of it or at least to diminish its impact. The first assertion Ulrich made when I picked him up at the gates of the Brandenburg prison in the spring of 2007, together with an intern of the Berlin association for ex-inmates I was observing, was that the worst he had to face in prison was to be with criminals, to be treated as an ordinary inmate. He tried to draw a distinction by considering himself simply as a person who had made some mistakes in his life. Religion serves as a powerful means to diminish the impact of the imposed inmate identity. In my enquiry I found a substantial discrepancy

---

[1]   Grace Davie, 'Believing without Belonging: Is this the Future of Religion in Britain?', *Social Compass*, 37/4 (1990), 455–69, at 455.

[2]   As discussed in the previous chapter for Riesebrodt, too, religion may be a possible source of identification.

between the various dimensions that usually define belonging: religious rites during one's lifetime (at birth, in youth, marriage, and so on), religious socialization (what individuals have learned about religion and practised in the family), and current religious practice. In other words, convicts experience important religious changes in their lives, with most of these occurring in prison. Some examples will clarify my point. One inmate was baptized as a Catholic, but no longer considered this a criterion of belonging:

> *Martin*: I don't belong to any faith, I am not a Catholic – well, I am a Catholic because I was baptized in the Catholic Church, but that doesn't really count.

Once the category of belonging has become flexible, the vocabulary inmates use when they express this type of identification is no longer rigid. Their sense of belonging is generally expressed as a feeling rather than in relation to a religious institution:

> *Roland*: Well, I feel I belong to Buddhism.

The distinction between institutional and personal resources is well illustrated by the following quote:

> *Wim*: I used to be a Christian, now I am someone who defines himself as a believer but not as a follower of a religion.

Belonging can also be the result of *bricolage*. One inmate in particular had a modernist religious identification in that he was the main reference point for the way he put various – and sometimes opposing – types of belonging into a coherent account. When the individual is the central reference point, s/he establishes a coherence that is likely to puzzle others:

> *Johan*: I am a Protestant, but over the years I changed to Judaism. Now I am Jewish– Christian … My mother was Jewish, but she had been baptized as a Protestant because of my grandfather, he wanted that – and then I also went to Israel.

In this somewhat unusual case, where someone combines two religious affiliations, the context needs to be considered. When I asked this inmate whether he could make a distinction between belonging and identification, he misunderstood the question – which was not surprising given that the question was vaguely formulated – and provided an answer about the context. His comment offers an interesting insight into the importance of taking the embeddedness of religion into account:

> *I*: If we consider the double belonging in your case … do you feel… part of a larger community and, if so, which? What would you say? [*pauses*] It is one thing to say,

'I am a Christian or a Jew', and it's another thing to say, 'I belong to a parish or to a religious community.'

Johan: [*pauses*] Do you mean [to ask] where I belong to more? … Well, I mean here in prison, it is rather the Christian [community] simply because I think I am the only Jew here.

If individuals have a double belonging, as this quote shows, either may be used depending on what the situation requires. Such a tactic exemplifies that social actors handle their relationship with religion according to the context, with the context described here encouraging a Christian belonging. Another way of handling this relation may be irony. Although all the inmates interviewed claimed that they were not remotely ashamed of their increased religious involvement in prison, it seemed that a different attitude prevailed in their relationships with other inmates, in particular non-practising ones. One Muslim inmate, for instance, told me about a short verbal exchange that is quite revealing in this regard. Some inmates were teasing another prisoner about his religious practice just before he was released.

Jamal: We used to tease him – someone said to him, 'All this praying you do, are you going to pray outside or where are you going?' And he says …, 'The first thing I'm going to do is go to a brothel.'

In prison, as in daily life, individuals present the Self in many different situations and in many different ways.[3] If religious belonging is a source of identification, it is also possible to play with it and use belonging strategically or to associate religious belonging with non-religious aspects. One inmate remembered an exchange with a Jewish inmate on this topic:

Thilo: He had the chain with the symbol, you know.

I: The Star of David?

Thilo: Yes, but he professed it only later. Only when – how should I say – you know, we were sitting on that bus and he only, I guess, confessed it when he knew me a little better. Because we were about six in the compartment and everybody talks and you get to know each other. And he told me there for the first time that he was a Jew, that he had had this and that experience. He was one of those, he would use that to his advantage because in Germany – with Jews, there's a problem, you know. And if there's a Jew there and they don't give him something, he told me very clearly, he says openly that he is a Jew. So he usually gets the permits.

---

[3]   Cf. Erving Goffman, *The Presentation of Self in Everyday Life* (Woodstock, NY: Overlook Press, 1973 [1959]).

As inmates need constantly to refine their tactics to obtain advantages in prison, religion becomes a tool that is used for such purposes. It may be used as a source to diversify the way the Self is presented in a given situation. These observations help us to grasp the variations in the meaning that inmates attach to religious belonging.

For the converts interviewed, belonging to the community means also belonging to God or other forces experienced as religious, which one interviewee expressed as, 'I know where I belong to and who is leading me.' They all stressed how important it was for them that the members of the religious community of which they were now part knew their life story. Contrary to what they knew from the institutions where they had come from, they would find 'Wärme, Zuwendung' (warmth, affection/attention) in the religious community, as Hans and Yanna worded it. Hans found it particularly important that the members of the congregation knew his life story and separated his person from the crime he had committed: he was not simply a name there, but a person. He appreciated that, when meeting members of the congregation, 'They want to know how you are and welcome you warmly. I never experienced such a community before.' Other inmates or ex-inmates, such as Yanna, also stressed the importance of feeling welcome. What they experienced was the embodied practice of the idea of 'loving the sinner and hating the sin' that is central to many Christians. Since their 'sins' – their crimes – had been linked to their person necessarily and repeatedly throughout their entire journey through the different institutions, seeing the two elements disconnected from one another felt like a great relief, almost like a miracle, because, psychologically, this had appeared impossible to them. For them, meeting somebody who was able to make the disconnection was basically a transcendental experience.

Social isolation is one of the major concerns faced by ex-prisoners. Research confirms that the social networks and family relationships of ex-inmates tend to fade during their periods of detention and are no longer there when they leave prison.[4] Once released, they cannot simply reoccupy the place they had previously in society.[5] While people are imprisoned, their place in society usually disappears: families often split up when one of them has committed a crime, former employers do not want to be associated with a criminal, friendships and cultural connections discontinue, economic circumstances and housing often become precarious, health problems increase, and – in some cases – the right to reside in a particular country is revoked. Howard Becker's classic analysis of outsiders points out that, when 'a rule is enforced, the person who is supposed to have broken it may be seen as a special kind of person, one who cannot be trusted to live by the rules agreed on by

---

[4]   Cf. Condry, *Families* and Katarzyna Celinska, 'Volunteer Involvement in Ex-Offenders' Readjustment: Reducing the Stigma of Imprisonment', *Journal of Offender Rehabilitation*, 30/3–4 (2000), 99–116.

[5]   I offer a fuller discussion of the question of social stigma in Irene Becci, 'Trapped between In and Out: The Post-institutional Liminality of Ex-prisoners in East Berlin', *Tsantsa*, 16 (2011), 90–99.

the group. He is regarded as an outsider.'[6] In Hans's case, this was most evident, as his crime had consisted in causing the death of a family member. He told me:

> Because it happened in our family and … I have tried to re-establish contact with the family, I wanted to talk to them, I sent a pastor to see them, I have [*pauses*] sent letters, others wrote letters for me, I have written letters myself, but they were so concerned and embittered that no contact was possible. In a way, that is understandable, from a human point of view, I mean purely from the point of view of the way feelings work, but somewhere … I think they're missing a chance in a way to clear the decks because I don't want to accuse anybody or whatever, that's far from what I want, I just want to belong to the family again, so that they say, 'Listen, you did this, we cannot forgive this; that's unforgivable, but you are part of the family again.' I don't want to live with these people, or anything, I don't want that. I just would like to … be part of the family, be accepted by the family.

Hans wanted exactly what the Baptist community outside was offering: to be recognized as a human being despite his crime or, to put it differently, despite his sinful past. Belonging to a religious or spiritual community provided Hans with the kind of fundamental recognition theorized by Axel Honneth, which is the basis for not alienating social interaction.[7] As for Yanna, who considered the Salvation Army as her family, the expectations coming from the religious community are not always easy to deal with: responsibility is reformulated, and the relationship is easy at the beginning but becomes increasingly exigent. The following excerpts from an interview with Hans show that belonging and believing acquired a very different aspect once he was outside prison. In the interview, he told me:

> For me believing was formulated anew the day I entered the parish … then I had to invent everything anew for me because there are also rules when you are in the congregation … it's different from sitting in prison and hearing about it and doing stuff for myself, but as soon as you are baptized, you also have a certain responsibility towards the congregation. Community also means responsibility … and for me responsibility always used to mean, 'You have to do this or that', and if you did not do it, you were punished.

How far inmates or ex-inmates are able to follow the mode of life offered by the community depends on many factors, one of them being the continuing cultural effect of the prison experience on life after prison.

---

6   Howard Becker, *Outsiders: Studies in the Sociology of Deviance* (New York: The Free Press, 1963), 1.

7   Axel Honneth, *Kampf um Anerkennung. Zur moralischen Grammatik sozialer Konflikte* (Frankfurt am Main: Suhrkamp, 1992).

The Reproduction of Prison Culture Outside[8]

The way out of the total institution of the prison is long and ridden with obstacles. The high rates of recidivism in European countries testify to a failure due to multiple factors that I do not discuss here.[9] Rather, I shall concentrate on one powerful barrier to integration, which Byron Harrison and Robert Schehr design in the following way:

> After serving several months or years in a controlled, structured prison, the most important transition component is for ex-offenders to be able to support themselves.[10]

When a prisoner is released, the institution's control over the individual ceases and returns to society, and also, to a certain extent, to the ex-convict him/herself. One major obstacle to the readjustment of control is cultural in nature: the culture of ex-inmates is often highly 'prisonized', as sociologists put it. According to Clemmer's perspective, as discussed previously, the cultural references of prisonized persons are likely to clash with those of the outside society.[11]

When they arrive at the halfway house I observed, former prisoners go through a series of processes that may be looked at as rites of passage. They agree a plan with the social workers that usually involves undergoing therapy linked to their addiction, looking for a job, and learning to keep house and to be orderly and avoid conflict. Ex-prisoners knew only too well that entering the programme meant that they had to follow rules and make an effort because their time at the halfway house was limited. They were expelled if they did not keep the house rules, or they were transferred to other programmes if they had specific needs. After two years,

---

[8]   This section draws largely on a previous publication of mine: 'Trapped'.

[9]   There is a large body of literature on desisting from committing crimes and on recidivism. Recent studies – for instance Peggy C. Giordano, Stephen A. Cemkovich and Jennifer L. Rudolph, 'Gender, Crime, and Desistance: Toward a Theory of Cognitive Transformation', *American Journal of Sociology*, 107/4 (January 2002), 990–1064, and Peggy C. Giordano, Ryan D. Schroeder and Stephen A. Cernkovich, 'Emotions and Crime over the Life Course: A Neo-Meadian Perspective on Criminal Continuity and Change', *American Journal of Sociology*, 112/6 (May 2007), 1603–61 – have pointed to the need for approaching this area not only in terms of job stability, marital status or education, but also in terms of social interactions including emotions.

[10]   Byron Harrison and Robert Carl Schehr, 'Offender and Post-release Jobs: Variables Influencing Success and Failure', *Journal of Offender Rehabilitation*, 39/3 (2004), 35–68, at 57.

[11]   Having studied the situation of ex-convicts in more recent years, scholars still take prisonization very seriously. Cf., for instance, Celinska, *Volunteer* as well as Mechthild Bereswill, 'Inside-out: Resocialisation from Prison as a Biographical Process. A Longitudinal Approach to the Psychodynamics of Imprisonment', *Journal of Social Work Practice* 18/3 (2004), 315–36.

'clients' often wanted to live near the halfway house and kept close connections with the programme: they continued to come to the free brunches and lunches or requested the assistance of the social workers in financial or juridical matters.

The programme offered by halfway houses prolongs the rite of release because their mission is to build bridges for ex-prisoners so that they are able to reintegrate in society, but actually they create the conditions for *liminars* to continue their experience almost indefinitely. The reason why this happens is, I suggest, linked to the enduring stigma of imprisonment. Ironically, while ex-prisoners try to get rid of their past because it is perceived as a stigma, the rehabilitation programme and the area where it is located define them by this very stigma. In Goffman's vocabulary, stigma is 'an attribute that is deeply discrediting'.[12] Further, it is always relational: 'An attribute that stigmatizes one type of possessor can confirm the usualness of another, and therefore is neither creditable nor discreditable as a thing in itself.'[13] Individuals who are stigmatized thus face a dilemma. On the one hand, they seek to hide their stigma or to eliminate it in order to be seen as normal and as part of the wider society; on the other hand, they often think that they deserve a different treatment from that given to 'normal' people because of their stigma. As a consequence, their social interactions are strained by contradictory expectations and attitudes that make for unexpected consequences. The social relations ex-inmates constructed among themselves and with social workers were indeed very tense. Social workers were concerned continuously with knowing whether 'clients' had lied to them and with the question of how to handle 'wrong' information. Georg Simmel points to the most fundamental role secrets play in social relationships – 'the one who has a secret is also aware that he has a certain power to manipulate the relation to others.'[14] The risk of being manipulated was real for the staff, because they could not control everything that was going on in the house – for instance, what happened at night –, and that was the time when most of the troubles started. Social workers always double-checked the information that they received from the inhabitants. Trust in the relationship was under constant scrutiny from both sides. Often in the morning inhabitants would turn up and complain about noise or about someone having bothered them during the night. Rarely were versions relating to what had occurred concordant. The social workers asserted often that lying and hiding were the characteristics of a 'prisoner mentality' and that the inhabitants would continue cheating on each other in the outside world, just as they used to do as prisoners, 'because it does not stop when they are released', Doris would

---

[12]   *Stigma*, 3.

[13]   Ibid. Cf. also Regina Austin, '"The Shame of It All": Stigma and the Political Disenfranchisement of Formerly Convicted and Incarcerated Persons', *Columbian Human Rights Law Review*, 36 (2004), 173–92, who focuses on stigmatization processes that are linked with political disenfranchisement.

[14]   'Das Geheimnis. Eine sozialpsychologische Skizze', in Alessandro Cavalli and Volkhard Krech (eds), *Aufsätze und Abhandlungen 1901–1908* (Frankfurt am Main: Suhrkamp, 1997 [1907]), 317–23, at 319.

tell me. If an inhabitant accused another of some misbehaviour, the accused would counterattack, saying that the accuser was incapable of 'keeping his mouth shut' and that he collaborated with the social workers. Sometimes one inhabitant started to complain, with the others following him and becoming louder and louder. The social workers called this 'typical prison behaviour' that aimed to cause 'a mutiny like in prison'. Sometimes, they wondered whether there was something like a 'con spirit'.[15] The idea that ex-convicts still thought and behaved as prisoners explained quite contradictory situations: on the one hand, it was typical for ex-convicts not to say what they did not like about others, but, on the other hand, the contrary was equally typical.

Concealing information or blurring the boundaries between what is and is not legitimate is an important tactic for ex-convicts to establish new relationships. However, this appears dubious to those who are dealing with them, as the following example illustrates. As Philipp had committed a robbery while drunk, he had been convicted to serve seven years in prison but was released after four years because he agreed to a detoxification therapy at an Evangelical institution on the eastern outskirts of the city. After only a couple of days, he escaped from there and found shelter in the observed halfway house. I was very interested in Philipp's experience at the Christian detoxification centre and wanted to visit it, but it turned out that access was impossible for outsiders. One day Philipp introduced me to one of his friends, who was also a new client and looked like an alcoholic; Philipp told me that I could go to the centre with his friend and pretend that I was accompanying him, as he was looking for a detoxification programme. I explained to Philipp that I appreciated his willingness to help me, but that I could not accept. My point about sound scientific practice or my way of distinguishing between legitimate and illegitimate means seemed not to persuade him as a valid reason to refuse his offer.

On a number of days every week, the inhabitants could help prepare and eat brunch or lunch in the common living room. Often I helped out in the kitchen and was impressed by the skills the ex-convicts showed in cooking for a large number of people. Having prepared the meal, however, they would never sit down and eat with the others. Usually everyone ate in silence and left as soon as they had finished their meal, leaving the dirty dishes on the table. Evidently, eating together was not considered a pleasant occupation; to inhabitants, such moments tended to recall the experience of constraint, as for years they had been obliged to eat in the prison community. The social workers stressed often how important it was to create the conditions that allowed the inhabitants to acquire a sense of what was 'nice' (*schön*), in the aesthetic and moral sense of the word. 'Nice' flowers were put on the table, for instance, but only a few inhabitants seemed to notice. Frequently Doris stressed that the task of the social workers was to set an example of what was a 'nice life'. She thought that prisonized people needed to regain their aesthetic sense and their

---

[15]   In German, 'Knacki Seele'. This was the case when the social workers were upset. There were also situations when they supported individuals' attempts to hide the stigma of imprisonment, mostly with clients they considered harmless to society.

ability to take care of not only their material environment but also themselves and their relationships. The ex-convicts did not respond very much to such remarks. They were constantly at risk of relapsing and they knew that their relationships with the social workers were crucial in this respect. The stigma of imprisonment was thus reasserted in daily relations, also by those who were supposed to work for the former inmates' social reintegration after their release.

If we compare the way inmates perceive and relate to chaplains with their attitude towards social workers, we notice that the latter do not enjoy the same acceptance. The chaplains' motivations for their action, also being religious, appeared much more credible to inmates, while the inhabitants of the halfway house did not consider the social workers' life as 'normal'. In their view, 'normal' people would have better-paid jobs and, most of all, avoid any contact with ex-prisoners. Therefore, the oddest rumours circulated about why Doris and myself were working and spending time on the programme. The ex-inmates thus seemed caught in the 'trap of low self-esteem': as they were no longer used to other people showing them respect, consideration and support, they suspected that any interest taken in them was a means to some end.

The Difficulty of Reconnecting to Free Space

The cheap second-hand furniture and the high turnover made it quite difficult for the inhabitants to keep their flats really tidy. Ulrich, who cleaned his flat meticulously and often called me to show me how clean it was, was a rare exception. The majority of the inhabitants, however, allowed their flats to become rather filthy. Frequently it took inhabitants months to realize that they were in charge of their flats. Ex-convicts, especially when they had the experience of long-term imprisonment, had to get used to having their own keys to open and close their doors or deciding whether to have the heating on or off. The social workers' low level of intervention was meant to establish responsible relationships between people who were on an equal footing. However, as the social distance remained at a high level, the lack of intervention encouraged the normalization of deviant behaviour. The social workers accepted that much of the ex-inmates' deviant behaviour would never really change, but they thought it was important to continue with the discourse of change: they encouraged 'clients' to start therapies, apply for jobs, and so on.

A space that turned out to be particularly interesting was the courtyard between the front and the side of the house. This was where the inhabitants spent most of their time outside, as it was protected from the outside world. Whenever the weather was fine, they would be in the courtyard smoking or chatting with one another, with some looking down from their windows. An inhabitant who had been homeless for a number of years before he had joined the programme gradually became responsible for cleaning up the courtyard, a task that he took very seriously. The ex-inmates also liked going to the parks in the area or sitting on the benches situated in front of warehouses, but they felt ill at ease when they were outside the location. None of my proposals to visit other areas of Berlin was taken up, nor were suggestions, made by staff, to go to the zoo or the cinema. The 'clients' preferred to watch a film at home, because, as they would say, 'at home I have peace'. This negative response could be interpreted in terms of former inmates' low 'cultural capital' limiting their curiosity for exploration, but Goffman offers a more interactive understanding of this attachment to the area:

> To the extent that the individual is a discredited person, one looks for the routine cycle of restrictions he faces regarding social acceptance; to the extent that he is discreditable, for the contingencies he faces in managing information about himself. For example, an individual with a facial deformity can expect ... to cease gradually to be a shocking surprise to those in his own neighbourhood, and there he can obtain a small measure of acceptance; at the same time, articles of dress worn to conceal part of his deformity will have less effect here than they will in parts of the city where he is unknown and otherwise treated less well.[16]

The ex-convicts therefore spent most of their time in their flats, the yard or the immediate environment. In the next section, I shall explore some important features of this urban environment by foregrounding the way in which it frames religious involvement or desistance.

The Challenge of Embedding Religion in the Urban Post-Socialist Space

The area surrounding the halfway house could be characterized by Michel Foucault's concept of 'heterotopia',[17] which is 'another type of place', reserved for a particular part of the population (the unemployed, ex-inmates, right-wing extremists, the homeless, residents without permits) or for 'odd' activities ('hanging out', trafficking). In media reports, the area was associated regularly with violent events linked to right-wing groups or gangs.[18] The local inhabitants are clearly frustrated about this situation. Their reaction is to downplay the importance of right-wing activities and violence in general, while political authorities generously finance local programmes that promote anti-racism.[19] The ex-prisoners at the observed halfway house knew

---

[16]   *Stigma*, 91–2.

[17]   Michel Foucault, 'Des espaces autres', in *Dits et écrits II, 1979–1988* (Paris: Gallimard, 2001 [1984]), 1571–81.

[18]   Cf., for instance, 'World Cup Guide Highlights Germany's Racist Hotspots', *Deutsche Welle*, 3 May 2006, at http://www.dw-world.de/dw/article/0,2144,1991934,00. html, accessed 1 May 2011, or Tim Zülch, 'Rechte Ecken in Berlin', *Tageszeitung*, 23 May 2008, at http://www.taz.de/!17653/, accessed 2 July 2012.

[19]   A good recent example is Martin Schwarzbeck's short article 'Mein Kiez' in Berlin's cultural youth magazine *Zitty*, 14.–27.7.2011, 26–8. Norbert Elias and J.L. Scotson point to

that they would find a high degree of anonymity in this area. Apart from one exception, none of the ex-inmates of the housing programme had come from the area where the halfway house was located. While, to quote the urban sociologist Häussermann, one key characteristic of Socialist cities was the 'non-existence of local self-government',[20] locality is now crucial for issues of governance. Therefore in 2006 one of the district mayors launched a forum,[21] a movement promoting civil society by coordinating and encouraging social and cultural activities in the *Kiez*.[22] The forum's aim is to improve the quality of life in this urban space. Its members – individual citizens and associations – meet five times per year to discuss local problems, which are linked mostly to the manifest – in acoustic and aesthetic terms – presence of right-wing extremists in the area.[23] Additionally, having at its disposal some funding from local government, the forum regularly invites applications for funding cultural initiatives. Although only about a quarter of the inhabitants in the area belong to a religious community at all, a rather high number of religious groups are based there,[24] one being the Baptist community of which Hans is a member. I shall concentrate on the way this Baptist congregation tackles major social problems in the area and thereby also offers a community to converted ex-convicts. I suggest

---

the difficulty that socially disadvantaged areas have in controlling their public image: *The Established and the Outsiders: A Sociological Enquiry into Community Problems* (London: Frank Cass & Co Ltd., 1965).

20   'From the Socialist', 222.

21   I participated at the forum's meetings in 2007 as a member of the rehabilitation programme for ex-convicts.

22   In northern Germany, the word 'Kiez' refers, in an evocative way, to a small part of a city, as it is demarcated by local residents who usually name it after a main street. Dwellers then live there in the spirit of an urban village: they know each other well and meet in the squares, cafés or shops.

23   At the time of my fieldwork, neither Vietnamese nor Turkish people participated in the forum.

24   Ex-convicts and other persons in need find also support in the Lutheran church of the area, but this support is limited to a weekly meal. The Lutheran Church was one of the few churches the GDR government allowed in 1978 to reconstruct its damaged buildings in East Berlin. There was, however, a restrictive condition: there was to be no tower so that nobody would recognize such buildings as churches. A crucifix now stands in front of the Lutheran church, but it remains a modest building. By contrast, the government allowed the New Apostolic community to build their church at a corner of the main street, after its previous chapel had been destroyed to allow the construction of new buildings for the Stasi: see Christian Halbrock, *Stasi-Stadt – Die MfS-Zentrale in Berlin-Lichtenberg. Ein historischer Rundgang um das ehemalige Hauptquartier des DDR* (Berlin: Christoph Links, 2009). The government wanted to disarm the critics who had spoken out about the demolition of the sacral building by offering this small religious community a disproportionately big building: see Nils Grübel and Stefan Rademacher (eds), *Religion in Berlin. Ein Handbuch* (Berlin: Weißensee Verlag, 2003). The Apostolic church is the most visible in this urban space, but it does not convey the same openness as the other two churches do, as it is very much oriented towards the members of its own community, most of whom live outside the area.

that this religious community embodies and transmits community-oriented values that are particularly important in German post-Socialist secularity.

The Baptist community in the area is very small, with fewer than 200 members. In 2008, the *Evangelisch Freikirchliche Gemeinde* (Evangelical Free Church), as Baptists have been labelled since Nazism, made a big point of celebrating its seventy-fifth anniversary in the area, thereby emphasizing that it had been part of the area since pre-Socialist times. In fact, shortly after the political change in 1989, a number of Western evangelical groups came to Eastern Germany to Christianize this new field, but their efforts proved quite unsuccessful. In order to set itself apart from other evangelical groups, the Baptist congregation in the area stresses that it shares the experience of the GDR with the other residents. During the Socialist regime, the German Baptist community was split into two and the government hindered communication between Baptists in West and East Germany. The Baptists in the eastern part of Germany slowly developed their own organizational structures and orientation, which were different in some respects from those of their Western counterpart, such as decision-making processes within the community.[25] The reunification of Germany did not erase these dissimilarities: on the contrary, the Eastern German Baptists started to stand up for themselves and take responsibility for the differences from the West.

The Baptist church, built in 2001 and replacing a much smaller chapel, is a large modern building with a big crucifix at the entrance gate. According to the pastor, the congregation's identification with the area is very strong.[26] Members try to reach out to the space around the church in various ways: for example, they organize religious services in the railway station, 'just next to McDonald's', as the pastor posted on their website. A tactic that the Baptists often used is to link their presence to other main attractions in the area. For example, a large choir consisting of 30 people sang the Gospel, with over 150 people attending the service. For the organizers it was very important to be placed next to McDonald's, so that a lot of people, 'who were only on their way to get some fast food', could stop and maybe 'enter a church for the first time in their lives', as the pastor told me during a conversation in March 2007.

Indeed, going to church to attend an ordinary religious service requires a proactive attitude towards religion that is absent in the area. Therefore, once weekly, the Baptists open the church to host cultural activities and playtime for all the local children, or they distribute posters in the nearby women's prison, offering inmates the opportunity to make Christmas presents for their children. Ever since the forum was constituted, the Baptist pastor has taken an active part in it. The Baptist congregation was the only religious group to be a member of the

---

[25]   Cf. Birgit Marchlowitz, *Freikirchlicher Gemeindeaufbau. Geschichtliche und empirische Untersuchung baptistischen Gemeindeverständnisses* (Berlin: De Gruyter, 1995).

[26]   The pastor I interviewed in March 2007 is a West German who wanted to come to the '*Neue Bundesländer*', as he described them, to grasp the challenge of working in a very secular environment. He had been the pastor of this parish for six years.

Figure 5.1   The altar and the seats for the religious service to be held in the hall of the railway station in Halle/S. © Irene Becci, July 2006

forum; some Lutherans from the main established church participated as individual citizens. The Baptists' collective involvement arose from the congregation's attitude towards the *Kiez*, as the pastor affirmed:

> As a parish, we want to be, in a very conscious way, a *local* parish (*als Gemeinde auch Kiezgemeinde sein*) … this means, and my predecessors did this, too, that we try to be on good terms with the local urban administration and with the other congregations and the Christian churches in this *Kiez*.

Being part of this urban space is even interpreted as part of a divine plan: 'We are not here by coincidence, not in this street nor in this *Kiez*. On the contrary, we want to find out what we can offer to the district here and to the people of this district.' During the meetings the pastor often stood up to express his opinion – he was obviously an experienced preacher – and to introduce the Baptist community to those present. As he told me, it was much easier for him to discuss religion with East Germans, because they did not know who the Baptists were and therefore had no preconceptions, unlike the West Germans, who were usually prejudiced against any religion other than the Roman Catholic or Lutheran Church. After some meetings the pastor was elected as one of the speakers of the forum and he offered the church hall for the forum's meetings, arguing that it was larger than the rooms of a local agency. Surprisingly, this offer was well received, making the Baptist community one of the most visible groups participating in the forum. The Baptist congregation regularly organizes lunches, concerts and activities for children and young people in the urban space, which is always supported by the forum. Additionally, another member of the Baptist community was personally involved and very committed in a relationship with an ex-inmate who once attended one of the congregation's celebrations. In contrast to other political initiatives, the Baptists offered to mediate between the local people and the right-wing extremists. They had a lot of faith in their capacity to influence people, while the other participants of the forum were sceptical and thought them rather naïve. Others, including the Lutherans, instead proposed initiatives that would help locals to protect themselves or to prevent violence. The Baptists, however, wanted to make contact with the right-wing extremists and hoped that their faith would facilitate change. Sebastian has daily contact with right-wing extremists in prison and explained his motivation as follows:

> I see everybody as a child loved by God, with a way of life and a view of life that can be changed, and I really love the guys here and I have literally learned here what it means, that God loves the sinner but not the sin.[27]

He and other members of the congregation were convinced that the Christian faith is capable of bridging the psychological paradox of 'hating the sin without hating the sinner'.[28] They approached people with a discourse of change – possibly conversion – and community. Hans's choice – now a member of this congregation – is a very good illustration of what is needed to keep a religious involvement at release. Although he could have joined other Baptist congregations in East Berlin, he chose to be part of this particular congregation, 'because', he said, 'here, the people are okay for me', and they had become a kind of 'replacement' for his family.

After they have been released, ex-inmates usually look first for a place where they can live in anonymity, and cities are, as I have argued, most appropriate for this. However, within a city, ex-inmates search for communities that may help them to reorient their aspirations and become emancipated from the stigma. The religious or spiritual community allows those who were in a process of conversion to feel recognized as persons. This stands in contrast to what several Protestant prison chaplains and pastors told me about their parish, which they considered very bourgeois and where all the initiatives taken to encourage the parish to welcome

---

[27]   On the radio station Antenne Brandenburg, *Apropos* show, broadcast 1 July 2008: *Frei von Sucht, frei von Gewalt*, 'Away from addiction, away from violence.'

[28]   I refer here to George Herbert Mead's idea, which he developed in his essay on punitive justice: human beings tend impulsively to associate an offence with the person who committed it and '[it] is quite impossible psychologically to hate the sin and love the sinner' – 'The Psychology of Punitive Justice', *American Journal of Sociology*, 23 (1918), 577–602, at 592.

ex-inmates had failed. When talking about Hans, the Baptist pastor insisted that in his congregation there was

> no prejudice because somebody had been in prison or so, not at all. We say it openly and he wanted us to tell the congregation that he was coming to our services at the end of his imprisonment. We told him that week, 'You will be released, may God bless you, and we know that you have been in prison for more than fifteen years [*sic*]' – he also wanted us to say it openly; the congregation has no problems at all with that – not at all.

The pastor had a sound theological explanation for this, which was based on a fundamental distinction between the church's morality and biblical morality. According to him, within the church,

> the notion of guilt has a moral component, from a biblical point of view that's not the case … The Bible sees guilt as a question of lifestyle: am I able to manage my life myself or do I refer to the One who has created me? That's why I don't want to talk to these people in a different way from the way I talk to other people: where do I feel safe, who knows me the way I am, who loves me the way I am and who understands me … the Bible says that we need to be responsible for what we do, but also that God can liberate us. The Bible is much less moral than we humans are and the Church also contributes to moralizing religion in a way that I find very uncomfortable. It is not my way of preaching … I am not the judge who says you were wrong or you need to do it differently. I really want people to live in a way that makes them responsible for themselves and realize that life is much more than moral laws or moral categories.

Among Baptists, conversion means that one's prison past is no longer a stigma, and this is why a community is vital for change. In the religious community they belong to, ex-inmates experience a sharp contrast to the aggressive relationships in everyday urban life where they are often caught up in fights, disputes or assaults. Depending on what a person is striving for, belonging to a community can offer him/her a range of sources of personal empowerment. Hans's account shows that, for him, being part of the Baptist community fulfils his quest for the recognition of his identity and offers him a place within society, a substitute family, the possibility to take personal responsibility, a sense of collective boundaries, norms, and, finally, hope in life. He said:

> When I became a member of the congregation … through baptism … The first time I introduced myself, that was in 2000 … I had mixed feelings: will the congregation accept me the way I am or will they say, 'No, we don't want to have anything to do with you, this guy should go to another congregation', or whatever. And I was lucky – in the congregation, from the infants to the elderly, everybody is represented there; we are a very well-structured congregation from

the point of view of age – there are also young people, adults, elderly people and therefore the congregation is also quite lively ... through faith we are a big community (*Gemeinschaft*); everyone has his talents and abilities and they can be put to use in the congregation ... I found it great that they accepted me and they – many of them know my story ... not all of them, but the majority with whom I talked, they know my story, that is, also my crime and how I came to the faith ... I now have a substitute family (*Ersatzfamilie*) in the congregation. I was in the process of learning to stand up for what I believe.

Outside prison, Hans had to learn to face a certain secular hostility:

I hear a lot about 'your God does not exist', or I experience some kind of hostility ... I don't know either what will come afterwards, well, the Bible says that everything will be better. Okay ... that's what it says. But whether it will really be like that, I don't know either. I will see it when the time comes, but I can stand up for it and say, 'Okay, that's what the Bible says and that's how it will be.' I don't know if it will be like that, I still have my doubts, but I have the hope, I would say that it will be better after – after this whole tale of woe (*Leidensgeschichte*) of mine, from my childhood until my imprisonment and also during my imprisonment, that at some point something will come ... After my release when I got to know this congregation, I practically started my life again, also through the congregation, there are people who like me, people I trust ... I have a completely different life from the one I used to have, I am not used by others any longer ... or by my own parents, as it used to be ... that is all different now and through this faith one somehow hopes that it will be better at some point, that – let me say it like this – one will receive reparation for something.

In his a posteriori reconstructed narrative, his interest in Christianity had been a constant presence in his life, which had been hindered first by Socialism, then by the prison institution, but was finally revived by meeting committed Baptists. Socialist scepticism towards non-scientific beliefs still remains but is now combined with a personal stance. Not surprisingly, these two major life events, together with the sudden entry into a post-Socialist urban context, brought out in Hans the need for clarification and mental reorganization. As a member of the studied congregation, Hans tried to connect his experience in prison to his religious life and took friends from prison to the church services. One of them, the pastor told me,

now comes to the services regularly ... He just came out of prison, after more than 15 years, I did not really ask what he did, one can imagine if it got him 15 years. We helped him, just after he had come out of prison, to put furniture in his flat, we gave him housewares and furniture, and food [*pauses*] that's his [Hans's] way of integrating people into the church.

Being so closely integrated in and giving so much importance to the community may also have a reverse side, as an older member of the Baptist congregation told me when he talked about his experience of assisting an imprisoned Baptist who had been excluded from the congregation for his sexual crimes:

> When the first Baptist congregation was formed in Berlin in 1837, they did some work with alcoholics, they had recognized the social needs in Berlin … but once these people had stopped drinking and become members of the community and then became recidivists, they were dropped … and one would say, if someone has become a Christian, he has to behave himself.

So as long as ex-inmates do not relapse into criminality, such a religious community may be a powerful help and in a way replace the missing chaplaincy outside prison. Recidivism, however, is as severely sanctioned in religious as in secular contexts.

Conclusion

This section has offered an analysis of the social boundaries that prevent people who have experienced long-term imprisonment from re-entering society as full citizens. The total institution of the prison leaves deep moral and physical traces in the *habitus* of ex-inmates, a *habitus* that does not help in preventing stigmatization. The combination of the stigmatization that operates outside the prison and the prisonized *habitus* that ex-inmates bring with them when they leave prison makes it difficult for both ex-inmates and those supporting them to consider the halfway house as more than a *liminal* experience. Belonging to a religious community is here a powerful resource to frame the *liminality*.

Eliminating stigma is a *sine qua non* for ex-convicts to leave their *liminal* state. Many seem to find it hard to achieve this, either because they find it impossible to remove the stigma or because their *liminal* state is a prolonged experience that leads at best to marginality. While my findings cannot be said to apply to all the released prisoners, they point to the potential – and sadly ironic – unintended consequences of such programmes as halfway houses, which cannot achieve their aim if conditions inside prisons do not change. What is clearly missing outside prison compared to inside is a chaplaincy – that is, a structured frame of religious experience. For converts, religious communities take up such functions; for the others, pragmatic and vital everyday needs and crises are managed in the dominant secular way.

Conclusion in a Comparative Perspective

This study sought to offer insights into the way prison and religion are embedded and transformed in a post-socialist context during imprisonment and at release, both at an institutional and at a personal level. Certainly, real existing Socialism had its own way of conceiving and managing both religion and punishment. The hostility of the GDR state towards religion and the churches has certainly 'forced' the secularization of punishment and rehabilitation. The link between the state and the churches was weakened, but the state instrumentalized the link at times, also using religious actors to increase social control. Above all, the period of the GDR led many inhabitants to form a strong mistrust towards the government, especially those who had experience of the GDR's total institutions, be they prisons or youth working houses. This lack of trust was not swept away completely by the changes that occurred in 1990 and thus continues to have an impact on the way chaplains, and also social workers, for instance, organize their work with prisoners and former prisoners. Inmates who experienced imprisonment during the GDR still relate to the chaplaincy in a particular way, seeing it either as very much in line with or, contrarily, as an ally in the resistance against an all-invading government.

During the reunification process, the main Christian churches were re-established, thereby obtaining a number of legal privileges and assuming a number of obligations in prisons as well as in the wider realm of social care. While at first the state essentially took over and attacked the churches' legacy, re-establishment served to redress the balance of power between them. However, tensions regarding control persist between the two institutions: this situation is reflected in the prison chaplaincy and, albeit less clearly, in the society outside prison, as the case of the rehabilitation programmes for ex-convicts has shown. Today, in Eastern Germany, the situation is such that those integrated in society see themselves as necessarily secularized. Being 'normal' here means not having a religious affiliation and demonstrating a rather 'fluid spirituality'.[1] Indeed, Eastern Germany is known for its secular culture, but identification with the Lutheran Church has remained important also. Protestantism has a historical link with the Prussian government, which in turn played a leading role in shaping the modern German state during the process of Germany's unification.

---

[1]   For this concept, cf. Dorothea Lüddeckens and Rafael Walthert, *Fluide Religion. Neue religiöse Bewegungen im Wandel: theoretische und empirische Systematisierungen* (Bielefeld: Transcript, 2010).

I shall now place the considerations made in this book in a comparative perspective, based on my work in Italy and Switzerland.[2] This will allow me to return to the discussions I proposed earlier about the implications of religious establishment generally and of the meaning of religious communities and spiritual care for prisoners and ex-prisoners in particular.

Comparative Thoughts concerning the Notions of Pastoral and Spiritual Care

Historically, spiritual care in prison was an element that contributed to controlling the prison population and allowed or facilitated self-control, either in a humanistic and philanthropic way or by using repressive methods. The presence of the established religions in prison was first justified with reference to territorial aspects – as the expression *cuius regio, eius religio* suggests –, then, in the twentieth century, with reference to demographic aspects. It was only after the Second World War that the prison chaplaincy developed as a means of guaranteeing religious freedom. In other words, religious freedom in prison was one of the achievements of the postwar period, reflecting a change in attitude towards religion. With regard to spiritual care in prison, one may observe that during that period the individual subject became a central concern. The term 'pastoral care' was replaced with the term 'spiritual care'. Contrary to what legal approaches or Weberian interpretations suggest, one cannot simply consider pastoral care as a religious presence in the organized modernity and spiritual care as a postmodern (or post-secular) approach. This interpretation would mean that chaplains' work offers only individual support, but I hope to have demonstrated that this is not the case. Today, institutional support provides a combination of these modalities for prisoners and ex-prisoners. Still, the distinction allows us to locate arrangements in different European countries on a spectrum. The studies that have examined spiritual care in prison, including those in England and Wales,[3] Norway and Denmark,[4] France[5] and Italy,[6] show that it is too simplistic to reduce the distinction to denominational issues. Spiritual care differs to various degrees both within the same denominational tradition and in relation to the degree of establishment – that is, organizational structure and self-understanding are defined in terms of pastoral rather than spiritual care (as in France and Italy). Having worked on the

---

[2]   The Swiss research comprised teamwork in the context of the 58th National Research Program of the Swiss National Science Foundation. Cf. www.pnr58.ch, accessed 14 June 2012. The study of the Italian case was part of my doctoral dissertation. Parts of this conclusion are based on my article 'Multiple Locations'.

[3]   Hunt, 'Testing'.

[4]   Lene Kühle and Inger Furseth, 'Prison Chaplaincy from a Scandinavian Perspective', *Archives de sciences sociales des religions*, 153/1 (2011), 145–58.

[5]   Sarg and Lamine, 'La religion en prison'.

[6]   Cf. Becci, *Religion and Prison*, and Rhazzali, *L'Islam*.

situations in Italy and Switzerland in addition to the East German case, I would like to offer some reflections on the organization and perception of spiritual care in a comparative perspective. Such a comparison is particularly interesting because it foregrounds different denominational and linguistic regions. The most noteworthy differences between these cases may be found in the religious composition, the level of religious practice, and the social significance of the churches, while the structural – meaning juridical and political – position of prison chaplains does not vary very greatly. Therefore, there are a number of commonalities in Swiss and Italian prisons that are reflected also in the ways the chaplains and the chaplaincy are perceived. This indicates that the structural impact of political and juridical regulations is significant in the religious field. Certainly, the type of prison, its internal regulations, its size, its territorial location (urban or rural), and the penal functions it fulfils (whether pre-trial, catering for female or male inmates, open or high security, and so on) make each prison a specific case.[7] They may vary within a given country, but consideration of legal-institutional regulations will enable me to offer some reflections across the different countries.

In **Italy**, the constitution formulated after the Second World War introduced new principles in the penitentiary realm that remain valid today. Article 27 put in place the new pillars of the prison system: prisoners should not receive any treatment that is considered to be against human dignity and they should be re-educated. As far as religion is concerned, the attendance of religious services was redefined: attendance continues to be compulsory, as it had been during the war, but close observance of religious doctrine is not. The obstacles preventing individuals from abandoning the Catholic faith or from converting to another religion were removed. As in Germany, the state sees the church as an indispensable partner in accomplishing the task of rehabilitating inmates. After the war, prison chaplains regained some of the autonomy they had lost during the years of fascism, but in 1963 the state decided unilaterally to institute a chaplains' inspector, who is answerable to the Ministry of Justice and has the duty of overseeing the standard of religious care. As to religious freedom more generally, it was not until 1975 that important steps were taken, as part of the encompassing reform of the penal law: the obligation for inmates to attend religious services was abolished and freedom of religion was recognized. Article 1 of the new law states that the treatment of prisoners must be absolutely impartial: no one should be discriminated against for his/her religious beliefs. A further notable element was the change from considering religious behaviour as a criterion for judging whether a prisoner was behaving 'well' to considering it as a right of all citizens. Also, Article 26 of the new law states that, in every prison, one or more chapels should be put in place and there should be at least one priest. However, similar provisions were not made for non-Catholic religious communities, although their imprisoned members are allowed to request spiritual assistance by a representative of their respective communities.

---

[7]   See, for example, Becci and Schneuwly-Purdie, 'Gendered'.

As a reaction to the fear of terrorist violence in the 1970s, the Italian state reinforced its police force and made it more aware of the potential for preventing such violence within the prison population. One major reform affected prison law in 1986, with the introduction of the *legge Gozzini*, whose name derives from an independent left-wing senator who promoted its content.[8] It proposed to soften conditions in prison to some extent. The promise of early release hoped to encourage inmates to collaborate with juridical authorities. This provision favoured convicts who decided to cut their links with terrorist organizations or organized criminality. The prison population could be better controlled because the whole prison staff – including chaplains and nuns – were transformed into observation points. The conditions that inmates had to meet in order to benefit from the various measures the reform had introduced were mostly disciplinary in nature. It appears that this change in the overall prison system allowed the chaplains to regain the controlling and observing functions they had lost. The increase in the number of inmates applying for alternative measures created a huge workload for the prison staff, resulting in a number of staff suffering from 'burnout'. Therefore, it was not a surprise that the spirit of the law – which had envisaged improving inmates' social, physical, material and mental conditions – soon disappeared. Instead, the new legislation led slowly to a 'carrots and sticks' system and increased the level of social control over inmates.

In parallel to these developments, the Vatican and the Italian government started to revise the Lateran Pacts in 1976.[9] Although it was recognized that the Lateran Pacts presented a major problem for the Italian state because they formed a treaty, the text that replaces them uses the same vocabulary. Expressions such as 'new agreements' and 'suitable consultations to be made in order to solve different possible cases in the future' indicate that the concordat was designed to be open-ended and perpetually changing without ever disappearing. At the centre of the debates was the question of freedom of religion – this time understood as the freedom to practise one's religion, rather than as the freedom of the church in a

---

[8]   This is law no. 663, which was approved in 1986. Mario Gozzini was a so-called 'Catho-Communist'. He had been studying and teaching the history of religions. For inmates, the name 'Gozzini' has become synonymous with benefits allowing them to maintain positive family and work relationships: cf. *I pugni nel muro. Linguaggio e frammenti di vita dei detenuti del carcere di San Vittore*, 'Terre di mezzo' 85 (Piacenza: Editrice Berti, 2001), 66.

[9]   The process of rewriting the pacts took several years: cf. Francesco Margiotta-Broglio, 'Il negoziato per la riforma del concordato tra governo e parlamento', in Silvio Ferrari (ed.), *Concordato e Costituzione. Gli accordi del 1984 tra Italia e Santa Sede* (Bologna: Il Mulino, 1985), 6–18; Federico Del Giudice, *Il nuovo Concordato. Analisi storica, politica e giuridica del nuovo testo: commento e raffronti con la legislazione precedente* (Napoli: Simone, 1984); Silvio Ferrari, *Concordato e Costituzione. Gli accordi del 1984 tra Italia e Santa Sede* (Bologna: Il Mulino, 1985); Mario Alighiero Manacorda, Marcello Vigli and Gianni Long, *Stato e Chiese. Il potere clericale in Italia dopo il 'nuovo concordato' del 1984 tra Craxi e Wojtyla* (Viterbo: Nuovi equilibri, Stampa alternativa, 1995).

given territory, as the previous text had stated.[10] The church obtained the right both to communicate its moral principles within the state's territory and to create all the necessary structures for Catholics to practise fully what their affiliation involves, in any situation. The church's presence is thus guaranteed in all public institutions, including prisons. The state is made responsible for providing the means that the church needs to respond to the religious demands of Catholics, who make up the large majority of the population. Two major changes affected religious care in prison: the status of the chaplain passed from being simply aggregated to the prison to being part of personnel, as in charge of spiritual care, and the notion of pastoral care was replaced by that of spiritual care.[11] This change indicates a tendency to individualization in the approach to religion, which is similar to the approach taken by the chaplaincy in Eastern Germany. It denotes a shift from a top-down principle (pastoral care), in which an asymmetrical, hierarchical relationship between a religious organization and a passive, receptive individual prevails, towards a bottom-up model (spiritual care), with a dialogical relationship in which the individual is autonomous and asks for assistance, requesting of the state to have spiritual care provided by his/her chosen religious community. Spiritual care is now considered an inmate's right that is protected by the state, not an obligation imposed upon prisoners by the joint action of state and church. Prison chaplains have exhorted each other not to miss this change in atmosphere and to concentrate on the spiritual aspects of their role: 'We need to stop being the chaplain who "does everything" … We need to have, clearly in front of us, the prominent task of evangelization.'[12] Only a couple of years earlier, the idea of pastoral care had been dominant: 'the true mission of the chaplain consists in the work of rehabilitation and of moral reconstruction of the persons the Lord has brought to his care.'[13] Pastoral care was implicitly and explicitly dominant in the second half of the last

---

[10]   One of the biggest achievements of the revision was 'the new tax system devised by the government to fund not only the Catholic Church … but also other churches recognised by the government' – Michael W. Homer, 'New Religions in the Republic of Italy', in James Richardson (ed.), *Regulating Religion: Case Studies from around the Globe* (New York: Kluwer Academic/Plenum Publishers, 2004), 203–12, at 208. Significant modifications concerned marriage, state schools, and financial aspects. An important novelty – the state's refusal to consider the Roman Catholic Apostolic religion as the sole religion of the state – is mentioned only in the additional protocol.

[11]   This change made the chaplain's position less precarious from a juridical point of view, but it kept it under the surveillance of the Ministry through the inspector. The nomination of the inspector was no longer dependent on a mutual agreement between church and state, but the church had the authority to designate someone who then had to be confirmed by the state authority: cf. Andrea Drigani, *L'assistenza spirituale negli ospedali e nelle carceri* (Rome: LAS, 1988).

[12]   Quoted in Elvio Damoli, Antonio Lovati and Luciano Baronio, *Ero in carcere e mi avete visitato* (Bologna: Dehoniane, 1988), 45.

[13]   Nicola Pelle, *Esperienze di un parroco e cappellano delle carceri* (Milan: Nuovi Autori, 1986), 87.

century, but we may observe a move towards a more individually oriented spiritual care accompanied by resisting tendencies as well.

The logic of pastoral care continues to exist in parallel to that of spiritual care in the contexts considered here. As in Germany, there is now the permanent presence of at least one Catholic chaplain in all Italian prisons, who must be present for at least three hours per day. Chaplains are now excluded from most of the formal disciplinary functions, but they are the only religious actors represented in the committee that establishes the rules of inmates' treatment. The chaplains' main tasks are to celebrate religious services and to teach the Catholic doctrine, to arrange private meetings with inmates at the latter's request, and to provide inmates with social and material care. Chaplains have access to practically all parts of the prison, including the prison cells. They are allowed to distribute the Catholic magazine, usually one copy for each cell.[14] They are paid by the state, enjoying all the state benefits, but as state employees they are subject to state control.[15] These arrangements make the Catholic faith an integral part of daily life in Italian prisons, which is not exactly the case in Eastern Germany where the moral or community dimension of religion is as prominent. Since 2000, various adjustments have been made in order to guarantee equality for non-Catholics: some concern diet, so that the prison administration has ensured that inmates who want to follow particular religious dietary rules receive the appropriate food.[16] Representatives of other religions are allowed to visit inmates on request, but the permanently employed chaplains remain the main dispensers of spiritual care in the prisons. This is crucial considering that the proportion of non-Italian inmates has increased significantly, having reached around 36.5 per cent in 2007.[17]

In **Switzerland**, the legal framework varies, as the constitution of 1848 regulates the relations between the churches and the state at canton level. Therefore, there are as many differences in church–state relations as there are cantons. At the federal level, there is only a basic recognition of religious freedom. The differences between cantons also affect state institutions. Some cantons have only general regulations concerning spiritual care in prison and leave the details to the individual institutions, while others have elaborated meticulous rules. Some regulations are written in neutral terms – thus including all kinds of

---

[14]   *Famiglia Cristiana*, the most important national Catholic magazine, dedicates a column to prison matters or publishes letters from and to prisoners.

[15]   A chaplain's wage is very low in Italy. The full-time chaplain of a Florentine prison told me that he earned just over 500 euros per month.

[16]   For details about religious minorities, cf. Massimo Introvigne, 'Religious Minorities in Italy: Legal and Political Problems', *Religion-Staat-Gesellschaft*, 1 (2001), 127–40; Vittorio Parlato, *Le intese con le confessioni acattoliche* (Turin: G. Giappichelli, 1996); Aires, 'Germany's Islamic Minority'.

[17]   Marcelo Aebi and Natalia Delgrande, *Council of Europe Annual Penal Statistics: Survey 2007* (Lausanne: University of Lausanne, 2009).

religions –, while others refer clearly to Catholicism or Protestantism.[18] In the prisons, the position of the chaplain varies: he may be highly integrated with the rest of the prison regime or an independent actor within the institution. Differences between cantons also exist with regard to both the amount of time for which the chaplain is employed and the chaplaincy's institutional position: sometimes the chaplain's position depends on the respective churches, because it is financed by them, whereas sometimes it has a more direct link with the prison authority. Despite all these differences, there is, however, a significant consensus between the two main denominations in Switzerland,[19] and this accounts for a gap in the recognition of the two established religious traditions (Roman Catholicism and Protestantism) on the one hand, and all the other religious communities on the other hand. Therefore, every prison in Switzerland has a Catholic and Protestant chaplaincy and chapels or churches of the two denominations, regardless of the religious composition of the detained population. Contrary to Eastern Germany, the majority of inmates in Switzerland are Catholic or Protestant, although they no longer constitute the majority. During the last decades, religious affiliation has become increasingly plural as a consequence of the high proportion of foreign inmates (69.7 per cent according to the 2007 Annual Penal Statistics of the Council of Europe). In recent decades, prisons have come to offer specialization in their different services, so that there has been an increase in the number of doctors, social workers, psychologists, psychiatrists, tutors, and so on who are employed. This process of professionalization is a phenomenon that cuts across cantons and has prompted chaplains to redefine their role and functions in prison. For the last two decades, chaplains have pointed increasingly to the importance of inter-religious competences and interdisciplinary profiles. They do not consider their professional task in prison to be the defence of Christianity as the only truth to which inmates have to convert in order to obtain redemption. The Christian faith is now more like a common language enabling dialogue and bridging gaps between inmates, staff, and the outside world. Individual spiritual care is now the chaplains' most important activity. Further, the prison authorities officially expect such a commitment. That the chaplains' work is of a confidential nature is guaranteed, as it is in Italy and (Eastern) Germany.

Despite the range of historical, institutional, political and denominational differences, the three cases seem to have at least three things in common, as far as the official location of religion is concerned: first, the established religion is considered to contribute to the process of rehabilitation and integration, which is, second, thanks to the fact that established religion has lost its overt disciplinary functions; third, in all three cases inmates belong increasingly to religions other

---

[18] Cf. Joelle Vuille and André Kuhn, 'L'exercice de la liberté de conscience et de croyance dans les établissements de privation de liberté en Suisse', *JusNewsletter*, 12 April 2010; online review at http://jusletter.weblaw.ch/, accessed 19 July 2011.

[19] Irene Becci and Claude Bovay, 'Les représentations sociales autour de la pluralisation religieuse en Suisse', *Social Compass*, 2 (2007), 145–59.

than those of the traditional chaplains. However, an important difference may be observed in the definition of the chaplains' main activity. While in Italy material support is still considered important in addition to moral guidance, in Germany prison chaplaincy comprises both pastoral and spiritual care, but the latter is clearly privileged. In the Swiss case, spiritual care is viewed as the dominant element of their work by prison chaplains themselves.

Inmates' Perceptions of Pastoral Care in the Three Countries

If the structural – mostly juridical and material – definitions of the chaplains' roles resemble each other that much, one might expect inmates to have similar experiences and perceptions of chaplaincy. The differences mentioned above with regard to the distinction between pastoral and spiritual care should also be observed. Thus the aim of this section is to assess, through analysis of the answers to one of my questions about how inmates found out when they arrived in prison that there was a chaplain, whether the inmates' perception of and relationship with the chaplains reflect this situation. The answers were similar to those I received in Germany. Everybody in prison knows the chaplain and knows how to make contact with him or her.[20] Inmates acquire this knowledge mainly through other inmates, posters and advertisements, the prison newspaper, or staff. An inmate tends to recognize the chaplain immediately even if he has never met him before, not least because of his outward appearance: the chaplain has no uniform and carries no weapons, but he carries a lot of keys and may be met in almost any section of the prison. Information about the chaplaincy is distributed by the inmates themselves and is part of the knowledge necessary for prison life. Some prisoners told me that they had read about the chaplaincy in the inmates' paper. In Switzerland, too, a number of inmates mentioned the chaplains' visibility.

Another question addressed what the chaplain meant to inmates and how their relationship with him could be described. In general, the feelings expressed by inmates about chaplains were positive. None of them, regardless of their own religious involvement, wanted to do without the prison chaplain. A chaplain is usually considered 'a teacher', 'a good friend', or 'a person you can trust' – all terms that one may interpret in terms of spiritual care, the consequence of individual support.

The inclusive nature of the chaplain's job, especially concerning material support, was stressed most of all in Italy and was almost absent in Switzerland. Juridically, the chaplain is considered part of the prison staff, but he still has particular privileges compared to other staff. What these privileges entail may differ according to context: while in Italy the privileges imply also greater freedom in providing items that inmates need, for instance, in the other cases the privileges relate to spatial or relational issues. In both Germany and Switzerland,

---

[20]   The large majority of the chaplains in the three countries are men.

inmates appreciated greatly the chaplains' level of cultural education, which allowed for more intense discussions. The relationship with the chaplain is free from any disciplinary aims – inmates were very grateful for this and trusted him more than other staff. For inmates, the chaplain's neutrality was an established fact. My question, on which side – that of staff or inmates – does the chaplain stand, received straightforward answers, but they differed most between Italy and Germany. In Italy, the dominant idea was that the chaplain was on good terms with everybody – staff and inmates.

In all three countries, the institutional regulations have a visible impact, but the way this impact is reflected in the socially constructed understandings and meanings of religion varies. In Italy an understanding of religion in terms of pastoral care is still very much present, while in Switzerland and Eastern Germany the notion of spiritual care prevails. Over half of the Italian inmates I interviewed were regularly involved in religious activities. They clearly stated that their level of religious practice had increased in prison, and they gave a wide range of reasons why this was so. Interestingly, most of them were affiliated with an established religion. In a Tuscan prison, I interviewed Wu, for instance, a young Chinese man,[21] and Nouri, an Iranian inmate who was about 40 years old; both had converted to Catholicism. When Wu was imprisoned, he did not speak any Italian at all. It was only by chance that he started to participate in the religious services offered by the Catholic chaplain: he had just followed the prison officers out of curiosity when they opened his cell door. Wu was particularly fascinated by the emotions that arose in him when he took part in the religious service. His religious apprenticeship was well supported by the activities of the chaplaincy. Conversely, what attracted Nouri to Catholicism was an idea of modernity. He had experienced Khomeini's Islamic revolution, and therefore associated Islam with repression, social conflicts, Arab domination, and religious intolerance. For him, Christianity was a commitment to peace, dialogue and freedom. In both cases, the inmates made contact with Christianity through the chaplaincy at a time when they were imprisoned and isolated in a foreign context. Their religious conversion involved a combination of social and political questions. Many Christian inmates I interviewed related that they had experienced a religious turning point while in prison: at some point they interpreted a strange feeling, an emotional explosion or an impressive meeting with someone as a divine intervention or sign that changed their lives in a significant way.[22] Interestingly, their accounts bear similar traits: the religious experience is told as something that came to them – as the chaplains

---

[21]   When I asked him whether he had received a religious education, he answered: 'A little, only my father [was] a little bit Buddhist. But he had no religious beliefs.' 'And you don't know a lot about Buddhism?' I enquired. 'I, a little, I don't know anything about Buddhism', he replied.

[22]   Sentences such as the following are typical: 'I was praying, looked at the crucifix and had the impression that Jesus was watching me in a special way as if he wanted to tell me something.'

had previously –, not the other way round. According to Paolo, an ex-inmate I interviewed in Italy in 2003, it is actually when they are released that ex-prisoners get more involved in religious communities:

> Actually, the context you find, those who help you outside are 90 per cent organized around the parish, the church, the nun, the priest and this favours some sort of involvement ... also Catholic voluntary associations.

While Paolo was very active in left-wing political networks, he knew a number of ex-inmates who became committed Catholics and were very involved in Catholic organizations. He could not find a definite answer to the question whether they had, as he said, 'made a serious religious commitment' or 'simply liked the new environment that welcomed them, unlike other environments.' The previous discussions of the German case suggest that the two options go together but also that in Italy, contrary to Eastern Germany, the religious frame in the outside society is much more organized, allowing for some continuity at release.

I have documented how inmates perceive chaplains as in-between figures, in particular when compared to other staff. In the eyes of the inmates, chaplains do not really belong to the prison system and the activities they organize connect them to the world outside prison. The chaplaincy seems to be the only place where inmates receive recognition as human beings rather than as prisoners who need to be diagnosed. For the inmates who take part in chaplaincy activities, the chaplaincy represents a space of freedom within the boundedness of the prison. However, as the chaplain is an employee of the prison, he has to contribute to the prison's explicit task of rehabilitation, which places him in a position of complicity with regard to the other prison functions, such as controlling and punishing inmates.

One of the interesting discoveries I made is that inmates' perception of the chaplains varies according to their relation to the prison administration and to their own religious involvement. This is the reason why taking part in the activities offered by the chaplaincy is helpful to some inmates in terms of 'rehabilitation' but not to others. For inmates who are affiliated with established religions, intensive religious participation in prison is a positive resource. Their increasing religious involvement is considered to reflect an ability to change and adapt to the nation-state's model of citizenship.

As indicated earlier, the storyline linking isolation and high religious commitment dwelt at the heart of the penitentiary regime that the Quakers in New England had invented. Whereas the prison system has been completely re-theorized and restructured in modernity, this storyline still accompanies and partly legitimizes imprisonment, despite the secularization processes. A further finding is that, while inmates' religious practice is often higher in prison than outside it, this is not necessarily the result of isolation or prison itself. Instead, this change should be interpreted as the outcome of a mixture of different factors in a person's life course. First of all, as described previously, some social groups in the prison population are over-represented compared to the social composition outside prison

– for instance, foreign nationals, members of particular religious minorities, drug addicts, and people with low levels of education. The experience of imprisonment makes for affective, intellectual and spiritual isolation, but constitutes also a harsh physical impact. Simultaneously the institution frames individuals' relation to religion and provokes their resistance against this framing. The study of ex-inmates' perspectives shows that prisoners do not just take over the institutional script of religious conversion as linked to rehabilitation:[23] without doubt they are influenced, but they also appropriate their stories.

Religion provides a powerful repertoire for dealing with questions of death, illness, and crises. In prison, religious involvement offers a plausible framework for such issues because it positions the experience of crises in a larger context. Contrary to a widely assumed point of view, religious experience is not linked directly to issues of guilt. Of course, religious commitment allows some prisoners to find a way of dealing with the feeling of guilt that is linked to the crime for which they are imprisoned – which is why, for them, religious freedom is crucial –, but most religiously committed inmates tend to see religion as a means that will help them organize their lives after having been punished. They draw a clear distinction between the secular authority, on the one hand, against which the crime was committed and which never really forgives them for it, and a sacred, transcendent authority, on the other hand, that is merciful and forgiving. Religion might be controlling or encouraging of self-control, but it does not punish.

I have shown also that religious commitment needs to be interpreted in terms of belonging. Belonging to a religious community creates a link that reaches out to life outside prison and offers a way of escaping from the all-defining category of 'prisoner' or 'ex-prisoner'. Further, we have seen that some religious conversion takes place in prison and some conversions turn into actual religious commitment once the convert is released. At that point, he will be baptized and get to know a concrete religious community.

Additionally, the way prisoners relate to religion shows to some extent that for them prison has failed in its role to rehabilitate: this becomes clear when we observe their attempts to rehabilitate at the point of their release. The experience of long-term imprisonment continues to have an impact after release when ex-convicts often slip into a liminal existence. Inside prison, many religiously committed inmates perceive religion as a way to escape prison; when they are outside prison, religion is a way to connect with a protective community. In the case of Eastern Germany, a number of ex-inmates found a very different society when they were released, where the structural settings for religion, such as the state–church relationship, were inverted, although society remained strongly secularized. Through religious communities ex-convicts will try to connect with

---

[23] On the notion of institutional script, see Irene Kühnlein, 'Spuren einer stationären Psychotherapie in den Biographiekonstruktionen und den Handlungsorientierungen der Betroffenen', in Erika Hoerning and Michael Corsten (eds), *Institutionen und Biographie. Die Ordnung des Lebens* (Pfaffenweiler: Centaurus, 1995), 193–205.

the freedom wider society affords, while retaining a liminal status. The barrier between the two perspectives – from inside and from outside prison – appears clearly as insurmountable. Paolo's words cautioned me, and sounded very similar to those of Ulrich or Manfred:

> Inside, inside it is a completely different world. The person who is inside will never be you. If you talk to someone inside and you meet her one month after her release, she will be another person. A completely different person.

Nevertheless, and this was the challenge of this study, one may gain unique insights by analysing both viewpoints jointly through the lens of religion. The outside sheds light on the inside, and vice versa. Both are, finally, as embedded in society as much as religion.

References

Aebi, Marcelo and Natalia Delgrande, *Council of Europe Annual Penal Statistics: Survey 2007* (Lausanne: University of Lausanne, 2009).

Aires, Wolf, 'Germany's Islamic Minority: Some Remarks on Historical and Legal Developments', in James Richardson (ed.), *Regulating Religion: Case studies from around the Globe* (New York: Kluwer Academic/Plenum Publishers, 2004), 103–12.

Amnesty International, *Amnesty International und die DDR. Die Arbeit für die Menschenrechte in der DDR von 1961–1989. Katalog zur Wanderausstellung* (Bonn: Amnesty International, 2003 [2002]).

Anheier, Helmut K. and Eckhard Priller, 'The Non-Profit Sector in East Germany: Before and After Unification', *Voluntas: International Journal of Voluntary and Non-profit Organizations*, 2/1 (1991), 78–94.

Anheier, Helmut K., Eckhard Priller and Annette Zimmer, 'Civil Society in Transition: The East German Third Sector Ten Years after Unification', *East European Politics and Societies*, 15/1 (2000), 139–56.

Arnold, Jörg, 'Corrections in the German Democratic Republic: A Field for Research', *British Journal of Criminology*, 35/1 (1995), 81–94.

Asad, Talal, *Genealogies of Religion: Discipline and Reasons of Power in Christianity and Islam* (Baltimore, MD, and London: The John Hopkins University Press, 1993).

Asad, Talal, 'Reading a Modern Classic: W. C. Smith's "The Meaning and End of Religion"', in Hent de Vries and Samuel Weber (eds), *Religion and Media* (Stanford, CA: Stanford University Press, 2001), 131–47.

Asad, Talal, 'Religion, Nation-State, Secularism', in Peter Van der Veer and Hartmut Lehman (eds), *Nation and Religion: Perspectives on Europe and Asia* (Princeton, NJ: Princeton University Press, 1999), 178–96.

Assmann, Jan, *Herrschaft und Heil. Politische Theologie in Altägypten, Israel und Europa* (Frankfurt am Main: Fischer, 2002).

Augé, Marc, *Le Sens des Autres. Actualité de l'anthropologie* (Paris: Fayard, 1994).

Austin, Regina, '"The Shame of It All": Stigma and the Political Disenfranchisement of Formerly Convicted and Incarcerated Persons', *Columbian Human Rights Law Review*, 36 (2004), 173–92.

Austin-Broos, Diane, 'The Anthropology of Religious Conversion: An Introduction', in Andrew S. Buckser and Stephen D. Glazier (eds), *The Anthropology of Religious Conversion* (Lanham, MD: Rowman & Littlefield, 2003), 1–11.

Bäcker, Gerhard, Reinhard Bispinck, Klaus Hofemann and Gerhard Naegele, *Sozialpolitik und soziale Lage in Deutschland*, vol. 2 (Wiesbaden: VS Verlag, 2000).

Baubérot, Jean, *La morale laïque contre l'ordre moral* (Paris: Seuil, 1997).

Baum, Gregory, *The Church for Others: Protestant Theology in Communist East Germany* (Grand Rapids, MI: William B. Eerdmans Publishing Company, 1996).

Beaumont, Gustave de and Alexis de Tocqueville, *On the Penitentiary System in the United States, and its Application in France; with an Appendix on Penal Colonies, and also Statistical Notes*, trans. Francis Lieber (Philadelphia, PA: Carey, Lea and Blanchard, 1833).

Becci, Irene, 'Collapse and Creation: The Rise and Fall of Religion in East German Offender Rehabilitation Programmes', Working Paper no. 109 (Max Planck Institute for Social Anthropology, Halle/Saale, 2008).

Becci, Irene, 'Entre pluralisation et régulation du champ religieux. Premiers pas vers une approche en termes de médiations pour la Suisse', *Social Compass*, 48/1 (2001), 21–36.

Becci, Irene, 'Penser le pouvoir pastoral dans les prisons actuelles', in M. Cicchini and M. Porret (eds), *Les sphères du pénal avec Michel Foucault* (Lausanne: Antipodes, 2007), 237–50.

Becci, Irene, *Religion and Prison in Modernity: Tensions between Religious Establishment and Religious Diversity – Italy and Germany* (Florence: European University Institute, 2006).

Becci, Irene, 'Religion im Aufbau der Haftentlassenenhilfe in Ostdeutschland', in Gert Pickel and Kornelia Sammet (eds), *Religion und Religiosität im vereinigten Deutschland. Zwanzig Jahre nach dem Umbruch* (Wiesbaden: VS Verlag, 2011), 279–90.

Becci, Irene, 'Religion's Multiple Locations in Prison: Germany, Italy, Switzerland', *Archives de sciences sociales des religions*, 153/1 (2011), 65–84.

Becci, Irene, 'Review of Monika Wohlrab-Sahr, Uta Karstein and Thomas Schmidt-Lux, "Forcierte Säkularität. Religiöser Wandel und Generationendynamik im Osten Deutschlands"', *European Journal of Sociology*, 51/1 (2010), 535–7.

Becci, Irene, 'Tactiques religieuses dans les espaces carcéraux d'Allemagne de l'Est', *Revue d'histoire des sciences humaines*, 23 (2010), 141–56.

Becci, Irene, 'The Curious Attraction of Religion in East German Prisons', in Courtney Bender and Pamela Klassen (eds), *After Pluralism: Reimagining Religious Engagement* (New York: Columbia University Press, 2010), 296–316.

Becci, Irene, 'The Rehabilitation of Ex-offenders in Eastern Germany: A Religious–Secular Configuration', in Malgorzata Rajtar and Esther Peperkamp (eds), *Religion and the Secular in Eastern Germany: 1945 to the Present* (Leiden and Boston: Brill, 2010), 167–87.

Becci, Irene, 'Trapped between In and Out: The Post-institutional Liminality of Ex-prisoners in East Berlin', *Tsantsa*, 16 (2011), 90–99.

Becci, Irene and Claude Bovay, 'Les représentations sociales autour de la pluralisation religieuse en Suisse', *Social Compass*, 54/2 (2007), 145–59.

Becci, Irene and Mallory Schneuwly-Purdie, 'Gendered Religion in Prison? Comparing Imprisoned Men and Women's Expressed Religiosity in Switzerland', *Women's Studies*, 41 (2012), 1–22.

Becci, Irene and Joachim Willems, 'Gefängnisseelsorge in der sich wandelnden ostdeutschen Gesellschaft. Eine Analyse der kulturellen, theologischen und sozialen Spannungen', *International Journal of Practical Theology*, 13 (2009), 90–120.

Becker, Howard, *Outsiders: Studies in the Sociology of Deviance* (New York: The Free Press, 1963).

Beckford, James A., *Social Theory and Religion* (Cambridge: Cambridge University Press, 2003).

Beckford, James A., '"Start Together and Finish Together": Shifts in the Premises and Paradigms Underlying the Scientific Study of Religion', *Journal for the Scientific Study of Religion*, 39/4 (2000), 481–95.

Beckford, James A. and Sophie Gilliat, *Religion in Prison: Equal Rites in a Multi-faith Society* (Cambridge: Cambridge University Press, 1998).

Beckford, James A., Danièle Joly and Farhad Khosrokhavar, *Muslims in Prison: Challenge and Change in Britain and France* (New York: Palgrave Macmillan, 2005).

Beckley, Robert E., H. Paul Chalfant and D. Paul Johnson, 'Germany's Reconstruction: The Role of the Eastern German Evangelical Church before and after Reunification', in William H. Swatos (ed.), *Politics and Religion in Central and Eastern Europe* (Westport, CT: Greenwood, 1994), 163–77.

Bellah, Robert Neelly, *Beyond Belief: Essays on Religion in a Post-traditional World* (New York: Harper & Row, 1970).

Berdahl, Daphne, *Where the World Ended: Re-unification and Identity in the German Borderland* (Berkeley, CA: University of California Press, 1999).

Bereswill, Mechthild, *Doing Violence, Concepts of Masculinity, and Biographical Subjectivity: Three Case Studies*, Forschungsbericht Nr. 85 (Hannover: KFN, 2002).

Bereswill, Mechthild, *Gefängnis und Jugendbiographie. Qualitative Zugänge zu Jugend, Männlichkeitsentwürfen und Delinquenz*, JuST-Bericht Nr. 4 (Hannover: KFN, 1999).

Bereswill, Mechthild (ed.), *Haft (er) leben, Zentrale Überlebensstrategien und biographische Selbstentwürfe männlicher Jugendlicher in Haft*, JuST-Bericht Nr. 6 (Hannover: KFN, 2001).

Bereswill, Mechthild, 'Inside-out: Resocialisation from Prison as a Biographical Process. A Longitudinal Approach to the Psychodynamics of Imprisonment', *Journal of Social Work Practice*, 18/3 (2004), 315–36.

Bereswill, Mechthild and Werner Greve (eds), *Forschungsthema Strafvollzug* (Baden-Baden: Nomos, 1995).

Berger, Peter, *The Sacred Canopy: Elements of a Sociological Theory of Religion* (Garden City, NY: Doubleday, 1967).

Bergmann, Jörg, 'Das Subsidiaritätsprinzip – zwischen Sozialstaat und Lebenswelt', in Adalbert Evers (ed.), *Sozialstaat* (Gießen: Ferber, 1998), 240–63.

Besier, Gerhard, *Der SED-Staat und die Kirche 1969–1990. Die Vision vom 'Dritten Weg'* (Berlin: Propyläen, 1995).

Besier, Gerhard, *Der SED-Staat und die Kirche 1983–1991* (Berlin: Propyläen, 1995).

Besier, Gerhard and Stephan Wolf (eds), *'Pfarrer, Christen und Katholiken'. Das Ministerium für Staatssicherheit der ehemaligen DDR und die Kirche* (Neukirchen-Vluyn: Neukirchener Verlag, 1991).

Böhm, Alexander, 'Zum 75-jährigen Bestehen der Evangelischen Konferenz für Gefängnisseelsorge in Deutschland', *Reader Gefängnisseelsorge*, 11 (1995), 39–49.

Bottéro, Jean, *Naissance de Dieu. La Bible et l'historien* (Paris: Gallimard, 1992).

Bourdieu, Pierre, 'Genèse et structure du champ religieux', *Revue française de Sociologie*, XII (1971), 295–334.

Bourdieu, Pierre, *Le sens pratique* (Paris: Ed. de Minuit, 1980).

Bourdieu, Pierre, *Pascalian Meditations* (Paris: Seuil, 1997).

Bui, Pipo, *Envisioning Vietnamese Migrants in Germany* (Berlin, Hamburg and Münster: Lit, 2003).

Carlile, J., 'Islamic Radicalization Feared in Europe's Jails: Treatment of Muslim Inmates Varies across EU', MS NBC News, 8 July 2006, at http://www.msnbc.msn.com/id/13733782/ns/world_news-islam_in_europe/t/islamic-radicalization-feared-europes-jails/#.T9IreNX2Z-M, accessed 8 June 2012.

Casanova, José, *Public Religions in the Modern World* (Chicago, IL: University of Chicago Press, 1994).

Celinska, Katarzyna, 'Volunteer Involvement in Ex-Offenders' Readjustment: Reducing the Stigma of Imprisonment', *Journal of Offender Rehabilitation*, 30/3–4 (2000), 99–116.

Certeau, Michel de, *The Practice of Everyday Life* (Berkeley, CA: University of California Press, 1984), 36–7.

Champion, Françoise, 'Des rapports Eglise(s)-Etat dans l'Europe communautaire', *Le Débat* (nov.–dec. 1993), 46–72.

Champion, Françoise, 'Les rapports Eglise–Etat dans les pays européens de tradition protestante et de tradition catholique: essai d'analyse', *Social Compass*, 40/4 (1993), 589–609.

Clear, T.R., P.L. Hardyman, B. Stout, K. Lucken and H.R. Dammer, 'The Value of Religion in Prison', *Journal of Contemporary Criminal Justice*, 16/1 (2000), 53–74.

Clemmer, Donald, *The Prison Community* (New York: Holt. Rhineheart [1940] 1958).

Cohen, Stanley and Laurie Taylor, *Psychological Survival: The Experience of Long-term Imprisonment* (Harmondsworth: Penguin, 1981 [1972]).

Combessie, Philippe, *Sociologie de la prison* (Paris: La Découverte, 2001).

Condry, Rachel, *Families Shamed: The Consequences of Crime for Relatives of Serious Offenders* (Cullompton: Willan Publishing, 2007).

Côté, Pauline, 'Culture séculière, culture religieuse, ethos civique et administration publique du sumbole', *Social Compass*, 46/1 (1999), 57–74.

Crozier, Michel and Erhard Friedberg, *L'acteur et le système. Les contraintes de l'action collective* (Paris: Éditions du Seuil, 1977).

Dähn, Horst, *Konfrontation oder Kooperation? Das Verhältnis von Staat und Kirche in der SBZ/DDR 1945–1980* (Opladen: Westdeutscher Verlag, 1982).

Dammer, Harry R., 'The Reasons for Religious Involvement in the Correctional Environment', in Thomas P. O'Connor and Nathaniel J. Pallone (eds), *Religion, the Community and the Rehabilitation of Criminal Offenders* (New York: The Haworth Press, 2002), 35–58.

Damoli, Elvio, Antonio Lovati and Luciano Baronio, *Ero in carcere e mi avete visitato* (Bologna: Dehoniane, 1988).

Davie, Grace, 'Believing without Belonging: Is This the Future of Religion in Britain?', *Social Compass*, 37/4 (1990), 455–69.

Davies, Christie, 'Goffman's Concept of the Total Institution: Criticisms and Revisions', *Human Studies*, 12/1 (1989), 77–95.

De Vito, Christian, *Camosci e Girachiavi. Storia del carcere in Italia 1943–2007* (Rome and Bari: Laterza, 2009).

Décarpes, Pascal, 'Der DDR-Strafvollzug vor und nach der Wende. Die Umgestaltung des Gefängnislebens zwischen Herrschaft, Rechtsstaat und Willkür', in Sandrine Kott and Emmanuel Droit (eds), *Die ostdeutsche Gesellschaft. Eine transnationale Perspektive* (Berlin: Ch. Links Verlag, 2006), 88–103.

Del Giudice, Federico, *Il nuovo Concordato. Analisi storica, politica e giuridica del nuovo testo: commento e raffronti con la legislazione precedente* (Naples: Simone, 1984).

Denzin, Norman K., 'Strategies of Multiple Triangulation', in Denzin (ed.), *The Research Act in Sociology: A Theoretical Introduction to Sociological Method* (New York: McGraw-Hill, 1970), 297–313.

DeWalt, Kathleen Musante and Billie R. DeWalt, 'Participant Observation', in H.R. Bernard (ed.), *Handbook of Methods in Cultural Anthropology* (Walnut Creek, CA: AltaMira Press, 1998), 259–99.

Douglas, Mary, *How Institutions Think* (New York: Syracuse University Press, 1986).

Douglas, Mary, *Leviticus as Literature* (Oxford and New York: Oxford University Press, 1999).

Drigani, Andrea, *L'assistenza spirituale negli ospedali e nelle carceri* (Rome: LAS, 1988).

Durkheim, Émile, *Les formes élémentaires de la vie religieuse* (Paris: Le Livre de Poche, 1991 [1912]).

Eckardt, Frank, 'In Search for Meaning: Berlin as National Capital and Global City', *Journal of Contemporary European Studies*, 13/2 (2005), 189–201.

Eick-Wildgans, Susanne, *Anstaltseelsorge. Möglichkeiten und Grenzen des Zusammenwirkens von Staat und Kirche im Strafvollzug* (Berlin: Druncker & Humboldt, 1993).

Elias, Norbert and J.L. Scotson, *The Established and the Outsiders: A Sociological Enquiry into Community Problems* (London: Frank Cass & Co Ltd., 1965).

Engler, Wolfgang, *Die Ostdeutschen als Avant-Garde* (Berlin: Aufbau Verlag, 2002).

Ferrari, Silvio, *Concordato e Costituzione. Gli accordi del 1984 tra Italia e Santa Sede* (Bologna: Il Mulino, 1985).

Flick, Uwe, *Triangulation. Methodologie und Anwendung. Qualitative Sozialforschung*, Bd. 12 (Opladen: Leske+Budrich, 2002).

Förster, Thomas, 'Beratung Straffälliger unter spezifischen Bedingungen in den neuen Bundesländern', in Raimund Hompesch, Gabriele Kawamura and Richard Reindl (eds), *Verarmung – Abweichung – Kriminalität. Straffälligenhilfe vor dem Hintergrund gesellschaftlicher Polarisierung* (Bonn: Forum Verlag Godesberg, 1996), 112–23.

Foucault, Michel, 'Des espaces autres', in *Dits et écrits II, 1979–1988* (Paris: Gallimard, 2001 [1984]), 1571–81.

Foucault, Michel, '"Omnes et singulatim": Towards a Critique of Political Reason', in James D. Faubion (ed.), *Power. Vol. 3 Essential Works of Foucault, 1954–1984* (New York: New Press, 2000), 298–325.

Foucault, Michel, 'Pourquoi étudier le pouvoir. La question du sujet', in Hubert L. Dreyfuss and Paul Rabinow (eds), *Michel Foucault. Un parcours philosophique au-delà de l'objectivité et de la subjectivité* (Paris: Gallimard, 1992 [1988]), 298–308.

Foucault, Michel, *Security, Territory, Population: Lectures at the Collège de France, 1977–1978*, ed. Michel Senellart (London: Palgrave Macmillan, 2007).

Foucault, Michel, *Surveiller et Punir. Naissance de la prison* (Paris: Gallimard, 1975).

Foucault, Michel, 'The Subject and Power', in Hubert L. Dreyfuss and Paul Rabinow (eds), *Michel Foucault: Beyond Structuralism and Hermeneutics* (Chicago, IL: Chicago University Press, 1983), 208–28.

Förster, Thomas, 'Beratung Straffälliger unter spezifischen Bedingungen in den neuen Bundesländern', in Raimund Hompesch, Gabriele Kawamura and Richard Reindl (eds), *Verarmung – Abweichung – Kriminalität. Straffälligenhilfe vor dem Hintergrund gesellschaftlicher Polarisierung* (Bonn: Forum Verlag Godesberg, 1996), 112–23.

Freie Hilfe Berlin e.V., *10 Jahre Freie Straffälligenhilfe in Berlin. Festzeitung zum 10 jährigen Jubiläum des Freie Hilfe Berlin e.V.* (Berlin, 29–31 March 2000).

Friedrich-Ebert-Stiftung and Forum Berlin (eds), *Gemeinnützige Arbeit statt Knast* (Berlin: Friedrich-Ebert-Stiftung, Forum Berlin, 2002).

Furseth, Inger, *Muslims in Norwegian Prisons and the Defence* (Trondheim: Tapir Akademisk Forlag, 2001).

Gabriel, Karl, 'Déchristianisation et sécularisation: aspects sociologiques et statistiques', in Paul Colonge and Rudolf Lill (eds), *Histoire religieuse de l'Allemagne* (Paris: Cerf, 2000), 333–48.

Gallinat, Anselma, '"Menacing Buildings": Former Political Prisons and Prisoners in Eastern Germany', *Anthropology Today*, 22/2 (2006), 19–20.

Garland, David, *Punishment and Modern Society* (Oxford: Clarendon Press, 1990).

Giallombardo, Rose, 'SOcial Roles in a Prison for Women', *Social Problems*, 13/3 (1966), 268–88.

Gibbs, John J., 'The First Cut is the Deepest: Psychological Breakdown and Survival in the Detention Setting', in Robert Johnson and Hans Toch (eds), *The Pains of Imprisonment* (Beverly Hills, CA: Sage Publications, 1982), 97–114.

Giebeler, Eckart, *Hinter verschlossenen Türen. Vierzig Jahre als Gefägnisseelsorger in der DDR* (Wuppertal and Zürich: Scm R. Brockhaus, 1992).

Giordano, Peggy C., Stephen A. Cernkovich and Jennifer L. Rudolph, 'Gender, Crime, and Desistance: Toward a Theory of Cognitive Transformation', *American Journal of Sociology*, 107/4 (January 2002), 990–1064.

Giordano, Peggy C., Ryan D. Schroeder and Stephen A. Cernkovich, 'Emotions and Crime over the Life Course: A Neo-Meadian Perspective on Criminal Continuity and Change', *American Journal of Sociology*, 112/6 (May 2007), 1603–61.

Glaser, Barney G. and Anselm L. Strauss, *The Discovery of Grounded Theory: Strategies for Qualitative Research* (Chicago, IL: Aldine Publishing Company, 1967).

Goeckel, Robert F., 'The Catholic Church in East Germany', in Pedro Ramet (ed.), *Catholicism and Politics in Communist Societies* (Durham, NC, and London: Duke University Press, 1990), 93–116.

Goffman, Erving, *Asylums: Essays on the Social Situation of Mental Patients and other Inmates* (Harmondsworth: Penguin, 1991 [1961]).

Goffman, Erving, *Frame Analysis: An Essay on the Organization of Experience* (New York: Harper and Row, 1974).

Goffman, Erving, *Stigma: Notes on the Management of Spoiled Identity* (Englewood Cliffs, NJ: Penguin, 1990 [1963]).

Goffman, Erving, *The Presentation of Self in Everyday Life* (Woodstock, NY: Overlook Press, 1973 [1959]).

Gorski, Philip S., 'Historicizing the Secularization Debate: Church, State, and Society in Late Medieval and Early Modern Europe, ca. 1300 to 1700', *American Sociological Review*, 65/1 (February 2000), 138–67.

Gorski, Philip S. and Ates Altinordu, 'After Secularization?', *Annual Review of Sociology*, 34 (August 2008), 55–77.

Grübel, Nils and Stefan Rademacher (eds), *Religion in Berlin. Ein Handbuch* (Berlin: Weißensee Verlag, 2003).

Günther, Ralf, *Seelsorge auf der Schwelle. Eine linguistische Analyse von Seelsorgegesprächen im Gefängnis* (Göttingen: Vandenhoeck & Ruprecht, 2005).

Haenell, Carl Wilhelm, *System der Gefängniskunde* (Göttingen: Vandenhoeck & Ruprecht, 1866).

Hajer, Marteen, *The Politics of Environmental Discourse* (Oxford: Oxford University Press, 1995).

Halbrock, Christian, *Stasi-Stadt – Die MfS-Zentrale in Berlin-Lichtenberg. Ein historischer Rundgang um das ehemalige Hauptquartier des DDR* (Berlin: Christoph Links, 2009).

Harrison, Byron and Robert Carl Schehr, 'Offender and Post-Release Jobs: Variables Influencing Success and Failure', *Journal of Offender Rehabilitation*, 39/3 (2004), 35–68.

Häussermann, Hartmut, 'From the Socialist to the Capitalist City: Experiences from Germany', in Gregory Andrusz, Michael Harloe and Ivan Szelenyi (eds), *Cities After Socialism: Urban and Regional Change and Conflict in Post-Socialist Societies* (Oxford and Cambridge: Blackwell, 1996), 214–31.

Heelas, Paul and Linda Woodhead, *The Spiritual Revolution: Why Religion is Giving Way to Spirituality* (Oxford: Blackwell Publishing, 2005).

Heinecke, Herbert, *Konfession und Politik in der DDR. Das Wechselverhältnis von Kirche und Staat im Vergleich zwischen evangelischer und katholischer Kirche* (Leipzig: Evangelische Verlagsanstalt, 2002).

Heritage, John, 'Conversation Analysis and Institutional Talk: Analyzing Data', in David Silverman (ed.), *Qualitative Research: Theory, Method and Practice* (London: Sage, 1997), 161–82.

Hervieu-Léger, Danièle, *Le pélerin et le converti. La religion en mouvement* (Paris: Flammarion, 1987).

Hervieu-Léger, Danièle, 'Renouveaux émotionnels contemporains. Fin de la sécularisation ou fin de la religion?', in Françoise Champion and Danièle Hervieu-Léger (eds), *De l'émotion en religion. Renouveau et traditions* (Paris: Edition du Centurion, 1990), 216–48.

Hervieu-Léger, Danièle, *Vers un nouveau Christianisme?* (Paris: Cerf, 1986).

Hildemann, Klaus D. (ed.), *Die Freie Wohlfahrtspflege. Ihre Entwicklung zwischen Auftrag und Markt* (Leipzig: Evangelische Verlangsanstalt, 2004).

Hillerich, Imma, 'Bildungspolitik und Religion. Die Diskussion um das Schulfach LER in Brandenburg', in Manfred Brocker, Hartmut Behr and Mathias Hildebrandt (eds), *Religion – Staat – Politik. Zur Rolle der Religion in der nationalen und internationalen Politik* (Wiesbaden: Westdeutscher Verlag, 2003), 199–222.

Holm, Andrej, 'Urban Renewal and the End of Social Housing: The Roll Out of Neoliberalism in East Berlin's Prenzlauer Berg', *Social Justice*, 33/3 (2006), 114–28.

Homer, Michael W., 'New Religions in the Republic of Italy', in James Richardson (ed.), *Regulating Religion: Case Studies from Around the Globe* (New York: Kluwer Academic/Plenum Publishers, 2004).

Honneth, Axel, *Kampf um Anerkennung. Zur moralischen Grammatik sozialer Konflikte* (Frankfurt am Main: Suhrkamp, 1992).

Hunt, Stephen, 'Testing Chaplaincy Reforms in England and Wales', *Archives de sciences sociales des religions*, 153/1 (2011), 43–64.

I pugni nel muro. Linguaggio e frammenti di vita dei detenuti del carcere di San Vittore, 'Terre di mezzo' 85 (Piacenza: Editrice Berti, 2001).

Iannacone, Laurence R., 'Voodoo Economics? Reviewing the Rational Choice Approach to Religion', *Journal for the Scientific Study of Religion*, 34/1 (1995), 76–89.

Introvigne, Massimo, 'Religious Minorities in Italy: Legal and Political Problems', *Religion – Staat – Gesellschaft*, 1 (2001), 127–40.

Jahn, Sarah, 'Gefängnisseelsorge in der Bundesrepublik Deutschland', in Michael Klöcker and Udo Tworuschka (eds), *Handbuch der Religionen* (Landsberg and Munich: Olzog Verlag, 2011 [1997]), 1–22.

Jaschke, Hans-Gerd, *Rechtsextremismus und Fremdenfeindlichkeit. Begriffe – Positionen – Praxisfelder*, 2nd edn (Opladen: Westdeutscher Verlag, 2001).

Jensen, Kenneth D. and Stephen G. Gibbons, 'Shame and Religion as Factors in the Rehabilitation of Serious Offenders', in Thomas P. O'Connor and Nathaniel J. Pallone (eds), *Religion, the Community and the Rehabilitation of Criminal Offenders* (New York: The Haworth Press, 2002), 215–30.

Johnson, B.R., 'Religious Programs and Recidivism among Former Inmates in Prison Fellowship Programs: A Long-term Follow-up Study', *Justice Quarterly*, 21/2 (2004), 329–54.

Johnston, Normann, Kenneth Finkel and Jeffrey A. Cohen, *Eastern State Penitentiary: Crucible of Good Intentions* (Philadelphia, PA: Philadelphia Museum of Art, 2000).

Jordan, Hermann, *Luthers Staatsauffassung. Ein Beitrag zu der Frage des Verhältnisses von Religion und Politik* (Darmstadt: Wissenschaftliche Buchgesellschaft, 1968).

Karstein, Uta, Thomas Schmidt-Lux and Monika Wohlrab-Sahr, *Forcierte Säkularität. Religiöser Wandel und Generationendynamik im Osten Deutschlands* (Frankfurt am Main: Campus, 2009).

Kemper, Franz-Josef, 'Restructuring of Housing and Ethnic Segregation: Recent Developments in Berlin', *Urban Studies*, 35/10 (1998), 1765–89.

Kerley, K.R., Matthews, T.L., Blanchard T.C., 'Religiosity, Religious Participation and Negative Prison Behaviors', *Journal for the Scientific Study of Religion*, 44/4 (2005), 443–57.

Khosrokhavar, Fahrad, *L'islam dans les prisons* (Paris: Balland, 2004).

Klippenstein, Lawrence, 'Conscientious Objectors in Eastern Europe: The Quest for Free Choice and Alternative Service', in Sabrina P. Ramet (ed.), *Protestantism and Politics in Eastern Europe and Russia: The Communist and Postcommunist Eras* (Durham, NC, and London: Duke University Press, 1992), 276–309.

Knoblauch, Hubert, 'Europe and Invisible Religion', *Social Compass*, 50/3 (2003), 267–74.

Knoblauch, Hubert, *Populäre Religion. Auf dem Weg in eine spirituelle Gesellschaft* (Frankfurt am Main: Campus Verlag, 2009).

Kollmorgen, Raj, *Ostdeutschland. Beobachtungen einer Übergangs- und Teilgesellschaft* (Wiesbaden: VS-Verlag für Sozialwissenschaften, 2005).

Kollmorgen, Raj, 'Ostdeutschlandforschung. Status quo und Entwicklungschancen', *Soziologie*, 38/2 (2009), 9–39.

Kösters, Christoph (ed.), *Caritas in der SBZ/DDR 1945–1989. Erinnerungen, Berichte, Forschungen* (Paderborn: Ferdinand Schoeningh, 2001).

Kühle, Lene and Inger Furseth, 'Prison Chaplaincy from a Scandinavian Perspective', *Archives de sciences sociales des religions*, 153/1 (2011), 145–58.

Kühnlein, Irene, 'Spuren einer stationären Psychotherapie in den Biographiekonstruktionen und den Handlungsorientierungen der Betroffenen', in Erika Hoerning and Michael Corsten (eds), *Institutionen und Biographie. Die Ordnung des Lebens* (Pfaffenweiler: Centaurus, 1995), 193–205.

LeCaisne, Léonore, *Prison. Une Ethnologue en Centrale* (Paris: Editions Odile Jacob, 2000).

Leistner, Alexander, '"Kirche muss Probiergemeinschaft sein". Typen des Verhältnisses von Religion und Politik in den Biographien von Friedensaktivisten', in Gert Pickel and Kornelia Sammet (eds), *Religion und Religiosität im vereinigten Deutschland. Zwanzig Jahre nach dem Umbruch* (Wiesbaden: VS Verlag, 2011), 325–41.

Lévi-Strauss, Claude, *La pensée sauvage* (Paris: Plon, 1962).

Liebling, Alison and Helen Arnold, *Prisons and their Moral Performance: A Study of Values, Quality, and Prison Life* (Oxford: Oxford University Press, 2004).

Luckmann, Thomas, *The Invisible Religion* (London: Macmillan, 1967).

Lüddeckens, Dorothea and Rafael Walthert, *Fluide Religion. Neue religiöse Bewegungen im Wandel: theoretische und empirische Systematisierungen* (Bielefeld: Transcript, 2010).

Luzar, Claudia, *Rechtsextremismus in der Weitlingstraße 'Mythos oder Realität?' Problemaufriss im Berliner Bezirk Lichtenberg* (Berlin: ZDK Gesellschaft Demokratische Kultur, 2006).

Maeder, Christoph, 'Alltagsroutine, Sozialstruktur und soziologische Theorie. Gefängnisforschung mit ethnographischer Semantik', *Forum Qualitative Sozialforschung*, 3/1 (2002), at http://www.ssoar.info/ssoar/View?resid=9596&lang=en, accessed 31 May 2012.

Maeder, Christoph, 'Narrative Zivilisierung im Strafvollzug: die Macht der Versetzung', in Hubert Knoblauch (ed.), *Kommunikative Lebenswelten.*

Beiträge zur Ethnographie einer geschwätzigen Gesellschaft (Konstanz: Universitätsverlag Konstanz, 1996), 125–43.

Manacorda, Mario Alighiero, Marcello Vigli and Gianni Long, *Stato e Chiese. Il potere clericale in Italia dopo il 'nuovo concordato' del 1984 tra Craxi e Wojtyla* (Viterbo: Nuovi equilibri, Stampa alternativa, 1995).

Mangoldt, Hans von, *Die Verfassungen der neuen Bundesländer. Einführung und synoptische Darstellung. Sachsen, Brandenburg, Sachsen-Anhalt, Mecklenburg-Vorpommern, Thüringen* (Berlin: Duncker & Humblot GmbH, 1997).

Marchlowitz, Birgit, *Freikirchlicher Gemeindeaufbau. Geschichtliche und empirische Untersuchung baptistischen Gemeindeverständnisses* (Berlin: de Gruyter, 1995).

Margiotta-Broglio, Francesco, 'Il negoziato per la riforma del concordato tra governo e parlamento', in Silvio Ferrari (ed.), *Concordato e Costituzione. Gli accordi del 1984 tra Italia e Santa Sede* (Bologna: Il Mulino, 1985), 6–18.

Masuzawa, Tomoko, *The Invention of World Religions, or, How European Universalism was Preserved in the Language of Pluralism* (Chicago, IL: Chicago University Press, 2005).

McCutcheon, Russell, 'The Category "Religion" in Recent Publications: A Critical Survey', *Numen*, 42/3 (October 1995), 284–309.

McDaniel, C., D.H. Davis and S.A. Neff, 'Charitable Choice and Prison Ministries: Constitutional and Institutional Challenges to Rehabilitating the American Penal System', *Criminal Justice Policy Review*, 16 (2005), 164–89.

McEwen, C.A., 'Continuities in the Study of Total and Nontotal Institutions', *Annual Review of Sociology*, 6/1 (1980), 143–85.

McLeod, Hugh, *Piety and Poverty: Working-class Religion in Berlin, London and New York, 1870–1914. Europe Past and Present* (London: Holmes and Meier, 1996).

Mead, George Herbert, 'The Psychology of Punitive Justice', *American Journal of Sociology*, 23 (1918), 577–602.

Melossi, Dario, *The State of Social Control: A Sociological Study of Concepts of State and Social Control in the Making of Democracy* (Cambridge: Polity Press, 1990).

Metzler, Gabriele, *Der deutsche Sozialstaat. Vom Bismarckschen Erfolgsmodell zum Pflegefall* (Stuttgart and Munich: DVA, 2003).

Müller, Birgit (ed.), *Anthropologie der Wende. Kontroversen im Alltag der deutschen Vereinigung* (Berlin: Centre Marc Bloch, 1997).

Müller, Olaf and Detlef Pollack, 'Die religiöse Entwicklung in Ostdeutschland nach 1989', in Gert Pickel and Kornelia Sammet (eds), *Religion und Religiosität im vereinigten Deutschland. Zwanzig Jahre nach dem Umbruch* (Wiesbaden: VS Verlag, 2011), 125–44.

Nadai, Eva and Christoph Maeder, 'Contours of the Field(s): Multi-sited Ethnography as a Theory-driven Research Strategy for Sociology', in Mark-

Anthony Falzon (ed.), *Multi-sited Ethnography: Theory, Practice and Locality in Contemporary Research* (Farnham and Burlington, VT: Ashgate, 2009), 233–50.

Neubaur, Joachim, *Einschluß. Bericht aus einem Gefängnis* (Berlin: Berlin Verlag, 2001).

Neubert, Ehrhart, *Geschichte der Opposition in der DDR 1949–1989* (Berlin: Bundeszentrale für politische Bildung, 2000).

Neumann, Johannes, 'Die Kirchen und ihr Charakter als Körperschaften des öffentlichen Rechts', *Religion – Staat – Gesellschaft*, 2/1 (2001), 11–46.

Nicholls, David, *Deity and Domination* (London and New York: Routledge, 1989).

O'Connor, Thomas P. and Nathaniel J. Pallone (eds), *Religion, the Community and the Rehabilitation of Criminal Offenders* (New York: The Haworth Press, 2002).

O'Connor, Thomas P. and Michael Perreyclear, 'Prison Religion in Action and its Influence on Offender Rehabilitation', in O'Connor and Nathaniel J. Pallone (eds), *Religion, the Community and the Rehabilitation of Criminal Offenders* (New York: The Haworth Press, 2002), 11–33.

Olson, Mancur, *The Logic of Collective Action: Public Goods and Theory of Groups* (Cambridge, MA: Harvard University Press, 1971).

Ortiz, Jonathan, *Almost Home: Halfway Houses as Liminal Space* (Saarbrücken: Dr. Müller, 2008).

Parlato, Vittorio, *Le intese con le confessioni acattoliche* (Turin: G. Giappichelli, 1996).

Parsons, Talcott and Neil Smelser, *Economy and Society: A Study in the Integration of Economic and Social Theory* (Glencoe: Free Press, 1956).

Pelle, Nicola, *Esperienze di un parroco e cappellano delle carceri* (Milan: Nuovi Autori, 1986).

Pickel, Gert, 'Ostdeutschland im europäischen Vergleich – Immer noch ein Sonderfall oder ein Sonderweg?', in Pickel and Kornelia Sammet (eds), *Religion und Religiosität im vereinigten Deutschland. Zwanzig Jahre nach dem Umbruch* (Wiesbaden: VS Verlag, 2011), 165–90.

Pickel, Gert and Kornelia Sammet (eds), *Religion und Religiosität im vereinigten Deutschland. Zwanzig Jahre nach dem Umbruch* (Wiesbaden: VS Verlag, 2011).

Pilvousek, Josef, 'Caritas in SBZ/DDR und Neuen Bundesländern', in Karl Gabriel, Josef Pilvousek, Miklós Tomka, Andrea Wilke and Andreas Wollbold (eds), *Religion und Kirchen in Ost (Mittel) Europa: Deutschland-Ost* (Ostfildern: Schwabenverlag, 2003), 50–62.

Pirson, Dietrich, 'Subsidiaritätsprinzip', in Wolfgang Stammler, Adalbert Erler and Ekkehard Kaufmann (eds), *Handwörterbuch zur deutschen Rechtsgeschichte*, vol. 5 (Berlin: Erich Schmidt Verlag, 1998), 70–72.

Poggi, Gianfranco, *The State: Its Nature, Development and Prospects* (Cambridge: Basil Blackwell, 1990).

Pollack, Detlef, *Säkularisierung – ein moderner Mythos?* (Tübingen: Mohr Siebeck, 2003).

Pollack, Detlef and Gert Pickel, *Religiöser und kirchlicher Wandel in Ostdeutschland 1989–1999* (Opladen: Leske & Budrich, 2000).

Pollack, Detlef, Hagen Findeis and Manuel Schilling, *Die Entzauberung des Politischen – was ist aus den politisch alternativen Gruppen der DDR geworden? Interviews mit ehemals führenden Vertretern* (Leipzig: Evangelische Verlagsanstalt; Berlin: Berliner Debatte, 1994).

Rajtar, Matzorzata and Ester Peperkamp (eds), Religion and the Secular in Eastern Germany 1945 to the present (Leiden and Boston: Brill, 2010).

Ramet, Sabrina P., *Nihil obstat: Religion, Politics, and Social Change in East-Central Europe and Russia* (Durham, NC, and London: Duke University Press, 1998).

Renzema, Marc, 'The Stress Comes Later', in Robert Johnson and Hans Toch (eds), *The Pains of Imprisonment* (Beverly Hills, CA: Sage Publications, 1982), 147–62.

Reynolds, B. and J. Fitzpatric, 'The Transversality of Michel de Certeau: Foucault's Panoptic Discourse and the Cartographic Impulse', *Diacritics*, 29 (1999), 63–80.

Rhazzali, Mohammed Khalid, *L'Islam in carcere. L'esperienza dei giovani musulmani nelle prigioni italiane* (Milan: Franco Angeli, 2010).

Rhodes, Lorna A., 'Towards an Anthropology of Prisons', *Annual Revue of Anthropology*, 30 (2001), 65–83.

Riesebrodt, Martin, *Die Rückkehr der Religionen. Fundamentalismus und der Kampf der Kulturen* (München: Beck, 2000).

Röhling, Jens, 'Harald Poelchau', in *Reader Gefängnisseelsorge* (Berlin: EKD, 1999 [1995]), 35–8.

Rose, Nikolas, *Governing the Soul: The Shaping of the Private Self* (London: Routledge, 1989).

Rüddenklau, Wolfgang, *Störenfried. DDR-Opposition 1986–1989* (Berlin: BasisDruck, 1992).

Salvatore, Armando, 'The Euro-Islamic Roots of Secularity: A Difficult Equation', *Asian Journal of Social Science*, 33/3 (2005), 412–37.

Salvatore, Armando, 'D. Hervieu-Léger, "Il pellegrino e il convertito. La religione in movimento" 2003', *Rassegna Italiana di Sociologia*, 3 (Jul.–Sept. 2004), 458–60.

Sarg, Rachel and Anne-Sophie Lamine, 'La religion en prison. Norme structurante, réhabilitation de soi ou stratégie de résistance', *Archives de sciences sociales des religions*, 153/1 (2011), 85–104.

Schäfer, Bernd, 'State and Catholic Church in Eastern Germany, 1945–1989', *German Studies Review*, 22/3 (October 1999), 447–61.

Scharff Smith, Peter, 'A Religious Technology of the Self: Rationality and Religion in the Rise of the Modern Penitentiary', *Punishment and Society*, 6/2 (2004), 195–220.

'Schießerei unter Vietnamesen' (Gunfight among Vietnamese), *Berliner Zeitung*, 6 June 1997, at http://www.berliner-zeitung.de/archiv/schiesserei-unter-vietnamesen,10810590,9286610.html, accessed 2 July 2012.

Schmitt, Carl, *Politische Theologie. Vier Kapitel zur Lehre von der Souveränität* (Berlin: Duncker & Humblot, 2004).

Seelsorge in Gerichtsgefängnissen (Provinz Sachsen and Leitender Ausschuss der Gefängnisgesellschaft zu Halle a. S., 1888).

Seligman, Adam, 'Secularism, Liberalism and the Problem of Tolerance: The Case of the USA', paper presented at the conference Migration, Religion and Secularism: A Comparative Approach (Europe and North America) (University of Paris 1 – Sorbonne and Ecole Normale Supérieure, Paris, 17–18 June, 2005).

Shoshan, Nitzan, ,Placing in the Extremes: Cityscape, Ethnic „Others" and Young Right Extremists in East Berlin', *Journal of Contemporary European Studies*, 16/3 (2008), 377–91.

Silomon, Anke and Ulrich Bayer, *Synode und SED-Staat. Die Synode des Bundes der Evangelischen Kirche in der DDR in Görlitz vom 18. bis 22. September 1987* (Göttingen: Vandenhoeck & Ruprecht, 1997).

Simmel, Georg, 'Das Geheimnis. Eine sozialpsychologische Skizze', in Alessandro Cavalli and Volkhard Krech (eds), *Aufsätze und Abhandlungen 1901–1908* (Frankfurt am Main: Suhrkamp, 1997 [1907]), 317–23.

Smith, Wilfred Cantwell, *The Meaning and End of Religion* (San Francisco, CA: Harper & Row, 1978 [1962]).

Stark, Rodney, 'Research Note: Europe's Receptivity to New Religious Movements: Round Two', *Journal for the Scientific Study of Religion*, 32/4 (1993), 389–97.

Stark, Rodney and Laurence R. Iannacone, 'A Supply-side Reinterpretation of the "Secularization" of Europe', *Journal for the Scientific Study of Religion*, 33/3 (1994), 230–52.

Stark, Rodney and Laurence R. Iannacone, 'Response to Lechner: Recent Religious Declines in Quebec, Poland, and the Netherlands: A Theory Vindicated?', *Journal for the Scientific Study of Religion*, 35/3 (1996), 265–71.

Stark, Rodney and William Sims Bainbridge, *The Future of Religion: Secularization, Revival and Cult Formation* (Berkeley, CA: University of California Press, 1985).

Stark, Rodney and Roger Finke, *Acts of Faith: Explaining the Human Side of Religion* (Berkeley, CA: University of California Press, 2000).

Stolz, Fritz, *Grundzüge der Religionswissenschaft* (Göttingen: Vandenhoeck & Ruprecht, 1988).

Stöss, Richard, 'Rechtsextremismus', in Oskar Niedermayer (ed.), *Intermediäre Strukturen in Ostdeutschland* (Opladen: Leske+Budrich, 1996), 193–213.

Sullivan, Winnifred Fallers, *Prison Religion: Faith-based Reform and the Constitution* (Princeton, NJ: Princeton University Press, 2009).

Sykes, Gresham M., *The Society of Captives: A Study of a Maximum Security Prison* (Princeton, NJ: Princeton University Press, 1971 [1958]).

Tawney, Richard Henry, *Religion and the Rise of Capitalism: A Historical Study* (Harmondsworth: Penguin, 1938 [1969]).

Thériault, Barbara, *'Conservative Revolutionaries': Protestant and Catholic Churches in Germany after Radical Political Change in the 1990s* (New York and Oxford: Berghahn Books, 2004).

Thunser, Wolfgang, *Kirche im Sozialismus* (Tübingen: Mohr Siebeck, 1996).

TOPOS Stadtforschung, *Sozialuntersuchung Sanierungsgebiete Weitlingstraße* (Berlin: TOPOS Stadtforschung, 2007).

Turina, Isacco, 'Éthique et engagement dans un groupe antispéciste', *L'Année sociologique*, 60/1 (2010), 63–91.

Turner, Victor, *The Ritual Process: Structure and Anti-structure* (New York: Aldine De Gruyter, 1995 [1969]).

Van Gennep, Arnold, *Les rites de passage; étude systématique des rites de la porte et du seuil, de l'hospitalité, de l'adoption, de la grossesse et de l'accouchement, de la naissance, de l'enfance, de la puberté, de l'initiation, de l'ordination, du couronnement des fiançailles et du mariage, des funérailles, des saisons, etc.* (Paris: É. Nourry, 1909).

Viehöfer, Erich, 'Zur Entwicklung des Strafvollzugs in Sachsen im 18. Jahrhundert', in *Hinter Gittern. Drei Jahrhunderte Strafvollzug in Sachsen*, ed. Staatsministerium der Justiz (Leipzig: Staatsministerium der Justiz, 1998), at http://www.justiz.sachsen.de/content/683.htm, accessed 29 June 2012.

Vögele, Wolfgang, *Zivilreligion in der Bundesrepublik Deutschland* (Gütersloh: Chr. Kaiser/Gütersloh Verlagshaus, 1994).

Voyé, Liliane, *Figures des Dieux, rites et mouvements religieux* (Paris and Brussels: De Boeck & Lercier, 1996).

Vuille, Joelle and André Kuhn, 'L'exercice de la liberté de conscience et de croyance dans les établissements de privation de liberté en Suisse', *JusNewsletter*, 12 April 2010; online review at http://jusletter.weblaw.ch/, accessed 19 July 2011.

Vukov, Nikolai, 'Secular Rituals and Political Commemorations in Eastern Germany, 1945–1956', in Malgorzata Rajtar and Esther Peperkamp (eds), *Religion and the Secular in Eastern Germany: 1945 to the Present* (Leiden and Boston: Brill, 2010), 41–60.

Wachsmann, Nikolaus, *Hitler's Prisons: Legal Terror in Nazi Germany* (New Haven, CT, and London: Yale University Press, 2004).

Wacquant, Loïc, '"Suitable Enemies": Foreigners and Immigrants in the Prisons of Europe', *Punishment and Society*, 1/2 (1999), 215–22.

Wagner, Peter, Theorising Modernity: Inescapability and Attainability in Social Theory *(London: Sage, 2001), 4.*

Walmsley, Roy, *World Female Imprisonment List* (King's College London: International Centre for Prison Studies, June 2006).

Wanzura, Werner (ed.), *Moslems im Strafvollzug* (Altenberge: Verlag für Christl.– Islam. Schrifttum, 1982).

Wappler, Kristin, *Klassenzimmer ohne Gott. Schulen im katholischen Eichsfeld und protestantischen Erzgebirge unter SED-Herrschaft* (Duderstadt: Mecke, 2007).

Weber, Max, *Wirtschaft und Gesellschaft. Grundriss der verstehenden Soziologie. 1. Vol.* (Köln and Berlin: Kiepenheuer und Witsch, 1964).

Wehler, Hans-Ulrich, *Das Deutsche Kaiserreich, 1871–1918* (Göttingen: Vandenhoeck & Ruprecht, 1973).

Westendorff, Elke, 'Das war schon exklusiv', *Horch und Guck. Historisch-literarische Zeitschrift des Bürgerkomitees '15. Januar' e.V.*, 57/1 (2007), 17–19.

Woodhead, Linda, 'Five Concepts of Religion', *International Review of Sociology*, 21/1 (2011), 121–43.

Ziemer, Jürgen, *Seelsorgerlehre. Eine Einführung für Studium und Praxis* (Göttingen: Vandenhoeck & Ruprecht, 2000).

Zülch, Tim, 'Rechte Ecken in Berlin', *Tageszeitung*, 23 May 2008, at http://www.taz.de/!17653/, accessed 2 July 2012.

Zylberberg, Jacques, 'La régulation étatique de la religion. Monisme et pluralisme', *Social Compass*, 37/1 (1990), 87–96.

Zylberberg, Jacques and Pauline Côté, 'Les balises étatiques de la religion au Canada', *Social Compass*, 40/4 (1993), 529–53.

Zylstra, Sape A., 'Protestantism: Theology and Politics', in Sabrina Petra Ramet (ed.), *Protestantism and Politics in Eastern Europe and Russia: The Communist and Postcommunist Eras* (Durham, NC, and London: Duke University Press, 1992), 11–39.

Index

alcohol/alcoholic/alcoholics 29, 31, 32, 55, 67, 77, 81, 90, 119, 139, 156, 165
Amnesty International 51
Apostolic 31, 48, 171
    New Apostolic 63, 159
Assmann, Jan 11
atheist / atheistic 32, 39, 40, 43, 59, 61, 67, 80, 140, 145, 147
Austin-Broos, Diane 139, 142
authorities,
    civic authorities 10
    state / government authorities 13, 36, 49, 50
    prison authorities 47, 173
    GDR authorities 48
    local authorities 143
    political authorities 158
    juridical authorities 170
autonomy 4, 7, 9, 13, 14, 17, 62, 84, 117, 126, 169

baptism 10, 84, 140, 141, 163
Baptist 28, 29, 63, 77, 139–43, 159–65
Beckford, James A. 3, 6, 8, 13, 20, 66, 79, 80, 124
belief (personal, religious, spiritual) 3, 5, 6, 7, 9, 14, 21, 50, 59, 62, 112, 123–34, 137, 139, 141, 145, 146, 149, 164, 169, 175
    believer 6, 44, 65, 110, 113, 129, 136, 150
belong / Belonging 6, 19, 23, 26, 28, 31, 34, 42, 44, 46, 49, 58, 59, 64, 68, 88, 89, 119, 124, 137–41, 144, 146–65, 173, 176, 177
Berlin 23, 24, 29, 30, 31, 32, 39, 42, 43, 47, 52, 54, 63, 68, 70, 71, 73–7, 83, 107, 133, 140, 141, 142, 143, 149, 158, 159, 162, 165, 165

Bible 9, 11, 32, 35, 46, 38, 50, 51, 77, 99, 113, 127–36, 139–41, 163, 164
Bourdieu, Pierre 14, 58, 85
Brandenburg 23, 24, 27–32, 57, 60–61, 67, 75ff, 81, 91, 93, 105, 141, 149, 162
bricolage (religious) 21, 124–30, 150
Buddhism / Buddhist 4, 28, 63, 131, 137, 141, 145, 146, 150, 175

Caritas 16, 44, 67, 69–77, 93, 127
Casanova, José 7, 12, 13
Catholic Church 31, 40, 41, 43ff, 48, 57, 62, 63, 68, 71, 76, 105, 140, 150, 171
    Catholicism 28, 44, 58, 138, 173, 175
de Certeau, Michel 46, 82, 143
chaplaincy → prison chaplaincy 9, 36, 38, 45, 47, 49, 54, 55, 63, 65, 99, 106, 108, 110, 112, 126, 138, 167, 168, 174
charitable services, charity 37, 41, 62, 71, 75, 123
Christianity 5, 10, 12, 33, 39, 61, 68, 76, 88, 110, 110, 111, 128, 164, 173, 175
Clemmer, Donald 92, 94, 95, 154
community (religious or spiritual community) 9, 12, 15, 40, 44, 45, 59, 60, 61, 62, 63, 64, 66, 71, 77, 88, 96, 105, 108, 127, 137–44, 149–56, 159–68, 169, 171
conflict 74, 77–8, 95, 95, 95, 99, 133, 144, 154, 175
control (social control) 3, 5, 14, 40, 45ff, 50, 80, 118, 120, 154, 167, 170,
    self-control 36, 91, 115, 120, 168, 177
conversion (spiritual, religious) 21, 53, 82, 84, 89, 124, 128, 133, 134, 136ff, 142, 148, 162, 163, 175, 177
Côté, Pauline 14, 16, 17

culture, prison culture, subculture 91, 92, 95, 118, 130, 131, 136, 148–9, 154, 167

Dammer, Harry R. 123, 135–6
death 16, 30, 33, 42, 89, 90, 128, 134, 141, 153, 177
God 9, 35, 62, 110, 111, 113, 120, 129, 131, 132, 136, 137, 139, 145, 152, 162ff
dependency 84, 87
deprivation 79, 82, 134, 135
detoxication 29, 31, 32, 139, 156
discipline (disciplinary action or power) 14, 20, 34–5, 37–8, 47, 49–50, 53, 80, 94–95, 97, 108, 119–20, 126, 170, 172–3, 175
discourse 3, 4, 8, 11, 18–19, 21–3, 29, 52–3, 65, 78–80, 82, 97, 109, 110, 124, 132-134, 136, 143, 157, 162, 176
diversity (religious diversity) 1, 22–3, 78, 95, 123, 124, 128, 144–6
Douglas, Mary 11, 19, 20, 125, 126, 138
drug 28, 29, 31, 66, 71, 73, 77, 81, 90, 140, 176
Durkheim, Émile 27, 127

Eick-Wildgans, Susanne 60, 64
emotion 18, 20, 89, 99, 138, 141, 149, 154, 175
equality (inequality) 1, 66, 172
Establishment / established religions 1, 12–14, 17–23, 48, 53, 57, 60–66, 70, 78, 108–11, 119–21, 123–4, 138, 150, 153, 156–7, 161, 167–8, 172–3, 175–6
ethics 8, 10, 17–18, 59, 61, 125, 149
ethnomethodology 2, 20
evangelical 32, 35–6, 57, 77, 156, 160, 181
exclusion (social exclusion) 8, 10
existential 2, 8, 11, 82, 125, 132

family 8, 17, 29, 31–2, 44, 47, 51, 58, 64, 67, 71, 73–4, 77, 81, 90, 96, 97, 103, 106, 113, 120, 124, 126, 140, 143, 150, 152–3, 162–4, 170

feelings 16, 44, 73, 82, 87, 89, 101, 104, 106, 110, 114, 120, 131–2, 135, 140, 150, 152-153, 163, 174–5, 177
female prisoner 24, 81, 92, 169
Finke, Roger 13, 34
Foucault, Michel 3, 15–18, 34, 80, 117, 143, 158
freedom of religion 10, 22, 23, 40, 49, 53, 60–61, 63, 64, 66, 79–80, 85, 121, 168, 169, 170, 172, 177

gender 31, 42, 91, 134, 134, 154, 169
Giebeler, Eckart 45, 47
Gilliat, Sophie 1, 66, 80
Goffman, Erving 19, 34, 79, 82, 83, 90, 92, 94–6, 28, 151, 155, 158
guilt 36, 37, 100, 113, 128, 130–32, 163, 177

habitus 58, 59, 165
halfway house 24, 29, 30–32, 88, 143–4, 154–9, 165
Hebrew/ Jewish 11, 26, 35, 62, 110, 150–51
Hervieu-Léger, Danièle 6, 21, 125–6, 130, 136–7, 149
high-security / maximu security 27, 95, 108, 114, 130, 169
Hindu /Hinduism 88, 110, 146
homeless 31–2, 44,140, 157, 158
homosexual 31, 42
housing 24, 29–30, 50, 67, 73–4, 76, 91, 143, 152, 159
human rights 29, 42, 48, 60, 79

Iannacone, Laurence R. 13
identity 3, 4, 32, 34, 57, 59, 63, 82, 90, 96, 131, 137–8, 149–50, 163
individualization 79, 125, 131–2, 171
integration / re-integration 7–8, 17, 50, 64, 66, 73, 154, 157, 173
Islam /Muslim 1, 5, 8, 26–7, 58, 63, 66, 71, 80, 85, 112, 124, 134, 137, 144–5, 149, 151, 168, 172, 175, 179, 182
isolation 33, 35, 45, 95, 104, 108, 130, 152, 176
Italy / Italian 1, 23, 124, 126, 168–76

Jesus 48, 88, 99, 129, 135, 175
justice / juridical 11, 13, 18, 34, 61, 63–4, 67–8, 76, 80, 110, 123, 143, 155, 169, 170, 171, 174

Karstein, Uta 41, 57–9, 129
Khosrokhavar, Fahrad 1, 124
Knoblauch, Hubert 7, 97
Kollmorgen, Raj 57, 60

Lamine, Anne-Sophie 120, 123, 168
Lévi-Strauss, Claude 125
Liebling, Alison 10–11
liminal / liminality 144, 149, 151–3, 155–6, 159, 161, 163, 165, 177
Luckmann, Thomas 7, 125, 147
Luther, Martin (Lutheran Church) 9, 27, 29, 39, 41–2, 44, 140–41, 159, 161–2, 166

Mead, George Herbert 154, 162
Melossi, Dario 3, 18
Mennonites 48
migrant / migration 1, 16, 30, 73, 80–81, 145
military 24, 35, 38, 42, 45
minorities (religious) 48, 63, 64, 121, 172, 176
modernity (modernist) 3–5, 15, 23, 126, 130–31, 133, 136, 150 168, 175–6
morality /moral 16ff, 23, 31, 33, 36–7, 39, 41, 59, 69, 77, 90, 112, 131, 153, 156, 163, 165, 171–2, 174

nation-state / nationalism 10, 12, 17, 35
Nazi / Nazism 27, 34, 38, 45, 143, 160
non-governmental organizations/ associations 18, 70, 71, 73

officer 28, 47, 51, 52, 65, 86, 90, 92, 96, 100, 102, 104–7, 114, 116–20, 175
Orthodox (church) 63, 71, 110–11, 136, 146

pastoral care 17, 18, 33, 35–8, 45, 50, 63, 79, 99, 110, 127, 168, 171–2, 174–5
    pastoral power 15–16, 79, 121

patchwork (religious/spiritual) 124, 126, 133, 148
penitentiary 33–4, 80, 95, 169, 176
Pentecostal (mouvement/church) 136
philanthropy 33–4, 36, 64, 134, 168
pluralization 12, 18, 131, 173
pluralism 5, 11, 13–14, 29, 82
plurality (religious) 5, 14, 22, 64, 69, 144
Poelchau, Harald 45
Poggi, Gianfranco 12
politics 6, 10, 11, 22, 39, 42–4, 57, 60, 62–3, 69, 119, 129, 132
Pollack, Detlef 7, 43, 49, 58–9, 62
post-socialism 24, 30, 143
pray 24, 27, 36, 54–5, 66, 71, 77, 85, 97, 111, 139–40, 151, 175
prison staff 26, 46, 52, 64, 74, 102-103, 106, 110, 113, 116, 120, 170, 174
prison visitor 46, 49, 50, 96
prison warden 18, 22, 48ff, 54, 71–2, 76, 86, 92
prisonization 94, 154, 156, 165
privatization / privatize (religion) 14, 124, 126
Protestantism 10, 40, 42, 75, 138, 141, 167, 173
    protestant church 10, 35, 39ff, 58, 73, 75
    protestant theology 9, 39, 42, 113
Prussia 10, 35, 167
punish / punishment / Punitive 3, 10, 25, 33ff, 38, 79ff, 95, 116, 131–2, 153, 167, 176–7

Quaker 33-34, 48

racism 29, 158
radicalization 134
ramadan 26–7, 66
Ramet, Sabrina Petra 10, 39, 40, 44, 47–8, 58
recidivism/ recidivist 26–7, 31–2, 94, 119, 123, 154, 165, 187
recognition (institutional) 13, 18–9, 48, 55, 68, 120, 139, 145, 172
Reformation (Protestant) 9, 10,

rehabilitation programme 23–4, 28, 32,
    66–7, 71, 73–5, 91, 111, 133,
    140–43, 155, 159, 167
relation, social relationship 3, 82–3, 91,
    99, 155
religiosity 59, 77, 123–5 134–5, 140, 142
resistance 13, 34, 38, 41, 45, 49, 80, 108,
    117, 119–20, 123, 143, 167, 172,
    177
responsibility 1, 71, 74, 84, 120, 140, 153,
    160, 163
revival (religious) 13, 38, 58
Rhazzali, Khalid 1, 124, 168
Riesebrodt, Martin 130–32, 137, 149
right-wing extremism 29–30, 31, 60,
    158–9, 162
ritual 3, 34, 41, 59, 75, 90, 111, 139, 144,
    155
Russia 60

sacrament 10, 35–6, 63, 64
salvation 15–17, 35, 88
Salvatore, Armando 8, 126
Sarg, Rachel 120, 123, 168
Saxony 23–4, 27, 33, 36, 52, 57, 60–61,
    74, 77, 81, 83, 89–90, 140
Saxony-Anhalt 23–4, 57, 71, 74, 111–13,
    140
Schmidt-Lux, Thomas 41, 58–9, 129
sect 8, 12, 126
secularism 4, 145
secularity 8, 31, 58–60, 101, 142, 160
secularization 4, 6–13, 38, 39, 41, 58, 79,
    80, 126, 167, 178
SED – Unity Party 39–40, 44–5
self-esteem 136, 157
Seligman, Adam 145
sexuality 47, 94–5
Smith, Cantwell 3–5
social worker 21, 26, 30–31, 37, 39, 65,
    72, 75–7, 96, 112, 114, 116, 119,
    154–7, 167, 173
socialization 3, 16, 26, 44, 81, 124, 128,
    150
resocialization 16, 50, 53, 154
socialism / socialist 9, 32, 38, 39, 41–5, 47,
    49, 50, 57, 68–9, 72, 75–7, 107,
    143, 159, 160, 164, 167

Soviet 27, 38–9, 43
space 2, 14, 24, 27, 30, 46, 48, 50, 52,
    67, 82–5, 97–103, 105, 112–15,
    119, 120, 123, 128–9, 132, 143–4,
    157–62, 176
spirituality 8, 21, 59, 81, 124, 131, 137,
    142, 167
Stark, Rodney 13, 100
StaSi 45, 47, 159
stigma 95–6, 152, 155
storyline 132–4, 176
subjectivity 6, 133
subsidiarity 68, 69
suicide 47, 89, 114, 120, 127, 131
Sullivan, Winnifred 10–11, 124
Switzerland 107, 134, 168–9, 172–5
Sykes, Gresham M. 92, 95
symbolic system, symbol (religious) 6, 7,
    11, 16, 82, 89, 89, 128, 132, 151

tactic 15, 17, 45–6, 49, 53, 54, 82, 87, 103,
    151–2, 156, 160
tattoo 89–90
tax (church taxes, tax system) 36, 40, 61–3,
    171
teacher 18, 35, 37, 39, 96, 106, 139, 174
territoriality 108–9
theology 5, 9, 62–3,
    catholic theology 28,
    protestant theology 9–10, 27, 29, 39,
        42, 44, 98, 113
therapy/ therapist 26–7, 32, 104, 123, 131,
    139, 154, 156–7, 177
Thuringia 28, 57, 113
tobacco 52, 97, 101–2, 118
Tocqueville, Alexis de 33–4
tolerance 19, 145, 175
total institution 12, 79, 82, 96, 106, 112,
    115, 123, 133, 154, 165
triangulation 22

unemployment 30, 44, 60, 87–8, 90, 140,
    158
unification 37, 55, 57–61, 63, 68–72, 75–8,
    85, 141, 143, 160, 167
universality 110, 132
urban space/context 22–4, 30, 70, 143,
    158, 159, 161, 164, 169

validation 22, 126–7, 129, 130, 148
value 3, 6, 8, 11, 17, 19, 29, 43, 50, 57,
    61, 64, 69, 73–6, 84, 95, 111, 123,
    144, 160
Vatican 44, 170
Vietnam / Vietnamese 26, 28, 30, 60, 81,
    95, 110, 145, 159
violence 9, 28, 30–31, 74, 115, 133, 140,
    141, 158, 162, 170
volunteer 28–9, 31, 36, 76, 77, 96, 99, 109,
    117, 136, 152, 154

Wachsmann, Nikolaus 27, 34–5, 37–8
Wacquant , Loïc 81
Wagner, Peter 4

Weber, Max 17–18, 168
welfare 16, 36–7, 68–74
Wende 43, 52, 60, 66–71, 73–8, 107, 140
Wohlrab-Sahr, Monika 41, 58–9, 129
women 65, 71, 73, 91, 92, 96, 113, 134,
    136, 149, 160
Woodhead, Linda 3, 124
worldview (religious) 8, 17, 19, 35, 40–41,
    112, 131

young inmate 52, 59, 65, 81, 87, 89, 175
youth consecration (*Jugendweihe*) 41–2, 75

Zylberberg, Jacques 14, 16–17